MAKING IT PERSONAL

Individualising activation services in the EU

Edited by Rik van Berkel and Ben Valkenburg

First published in Great Britain in 2007 by

The Policy Press
University of Bristol
Fourth Floor
Beacon House
Queen's Road
Bristol BS8 1QU
UK

Tel +44 (0)117 331 4054
Fax +44 (0)117 331 4093
e-mail tpp-info@bristol.ac.uk
www.policypress.org.uk

British Library Cataloguing in Publication Data
A catalogue record for this book is available from the British Library.

Library of Congress Cataloging-in-Publication Data
A catalog record for this book has been requested.

ISBN 978 1 86134 797 8 hardcover

Cover design by Qube Design Associates, Bristol.
Printed and bound in Great Britain by MPG Books, Bodmin.

Contents

List of figures and tables

Figures

Tables

Acknowledgements

In 2004, a group of researchers participating in the *Active Social Policies European Network* (ASPEN, a 'virtual' network of European social scientists interested in activation policies) took the initiative to start a discussion on the increasing emphasis on the 'individualised' or 'personalised' provision of activation programmes. This initiative resulted in a series of papers that analysed the development of individualised activation from theoretical and empirical points of view. The papers were discussed during a seminar that took place in December 2004 at the Växjö University in Sweden, and were published in the Dutch journal *Tijdschrift voor Arbeid en Participatie* as well as the Italian journal *La Rivista delle Politiche Sociali*. During the seminar it was decided that the papers would be reworked into an edited volume that would elaborate the individualised provision of activation services from various theoretical points of view, as well as analyse and compare policies and practices of individualised activation services in various European welfare states.

This book is the result of this enterprise. First of all, we would like to thank Växjö University for financing and hosting the seminar. Our special thanks go to Tapio Salonen and Iver Hornemann Møller of the Department of Health Sciences and Social Work of this university. They did a great job in organising the seminar. On top of that, they were excellent hosts, during the formal as well as informal moments of the seminar. Second, we would like to thank the anonymous referees of the book proposal and the final typescript, whose comments helped us improve the coherence of this book. Last but, as usual, not least we would like to thank The Policy Press, specifically Emily Watt and Philip de Bary, for the – again, as usual – professional, flexible and supportive way in which they guided and helped us throughout the process of editing and producing this volume.

Rik van Berkel and Ben Valkenburg
Utrecht University
July 2006

Notes on contributors

Jean-Michel Bonvin (Jean-Michel.Bonvin@socio.unige.ch), PhD in Sociology at the University Paris IV-Sorbonne, is Professor at the Department of Sociology, University of Geneva, Switzerland. His main fields of interest are comparative social policy, employment and social protection, sociology of justice and social theory. Among his books are *L'Organisation internationale du travail, Etude sur une agence productive de normes* (Paris: PUF, 1998), and *Gemeinwohl, Ein kritisches Plädoyer* (Fribourg:Academia Press Fribourg, 2004, with G. Kohler and B. Sitter-Liver). He also published extensively in leading international reviews on social and labour market policies in a comparative perspective.

Vando Borghi (borghi@spbo.unibo.it) is Professor at the Department of Sociology, University of Bologna, Italy. He works at the Faculty of Political Sciences, where he teaches sociology of organisation and sociology of development. His main research interests are sociology of work and economic and organisational processes. In this perspective, he delivers research about metamorphoses of work quality and organisation, activation policies, social vulnerability, institutional and administrative transformations, and so on. An article about 'New modes of governance in Italy and the Netherlands: the case of activation policies', written with Rik van Berkel, is forthcoming in *Public Administration*.

Eduardo Crespo Suárez (ecrespo@cps.ucm.es) is Professor of Social Psychology at the Complutense University of Madrid, Spain. His main research interests are in the field of psychosociological theory (*La constitución social de la subjetividad*, Madrid: Los Libros de La Catarata, 2001) and discourses about work (*The EU's concept of activation for young people: Toward a new social contract?*, Brussels, ETUI, 2004, with A. Serrano).

Nicolas Farvaque (farvaque@idhe.ens-cachan.fr) is a researcher in economics at ORSEU (Office européen de conseil, recherche et formation en relations sociales), Lille, and at IDHE, École Normale Supérieure de Cachan, Paris, France. His doctoral dissertation (2005) discussed the relevance of the capability approach to assessing social and employment policies. In collaboration with J.-M. Bonvin, he published 'What informational basis for assessing job-seekers? Capabilities vs. preferences', *Review of Social Economy* (vol 63, no 2, pp 269-89, 2005); 'Promoting capability for work: the role of local actors' (in S. Deneulin, M. Nebel and N. Sagorsky, eds, *Transforming unjust structures: The capability approach*, Dordrecht: Springer, 2006).

Matti Heikkilä (Matti.Heikkila@stakes.fi), PhD and Professor, acts currently as the Deputy Director General of STAKES (the National Research and Development Centre for Welfare and Health), Helsinki, Finland. His main research interests are related to various welfare state issues, especially poverty, social exclusion and minimum income. He is a member of the Research Council of Humanities and Social Sciences of the Academy of Finland, a member of the COST Individuals, Societies, Cultures and Health Domain Committee and a member of the Board of the European Centre for Social Welfare Policy and Research, Vienna, Austria.

Dirk Jacobi (djacobi@gwdg.de), political scientist and sociologist, is a PhD student at the University of Goettingen, Germany. In his dissertation he is analysing discourses on employment structure and employment trends and their impact on labour market reforms. His areas of research are social policy, labour market policy, sociology of labour and discourse analysis. He wrote 'Rot-Grüne Grundsicherungspolitik und die Herausforderungen des Grundeinkommens für den deutschen Sozialstaat', in M. Füllsack, ed, *Globale Soziale Sicherheit? Grundeinkommen – weltweit?* (Berlin: Avinus Verlag, 2006).

Håkan Johansson (hakan.johansson@vxu.se) works as a researcher and lecturer in social work at the School of Health Sciences and Social Work, Växjö University, Sweden. His interests include citizenship theory, European Union social policy, and information and communication technology in public sector reform. Together with Nordic colleagues, he has directed an interdisciplinary research project on the turn to more active forms of citizenship, comparing the Nordic countries with France, Germany and the UK. He is currently editing a volume on active citizenship and welfare state change in the Nordic welfare states to be published by Routledge in January 2007.

Ilse Julkunen (ilse.julkunen@stakes.fi) is Research Manager at FinSoc, the Evaluation Unit of Social Services at STAKES (the National Research and Development Centre for Welfare and Health), Helsinki, Finland. She is also Professor in Social Work, particularly practice research and evaluation, at the Department of Social Policy and Social

Work, Helsinki University. Her main research interests are related to user perspectives, comparative welfare policies, unemployment and poverty.

Karen Kellard (Karen.Kellard@bmgresearch.co.uk) was, until November 2005, Assistant Director and Senior Research Fellow at the Centre for Research in Social Policy (CRSP), Loughborough University, UK. She is now an Account Director at BMG Research, Birmingham. Her research interests relate to labour market policy, social inclusion and lifestyles and living standards. Her recent research has involved evaluations of the New Deal for Disabled People, the New Deal for Communities, Sure Start and job retention programmes. Publications include 'Wired-up welfare', in J. Millar, ed, *Understanding social security: Issues for policy and practice* (Bristol: The Policy Press, 2003) and 'Job retention and advancement, a developing agenda?' (2002) *Benefits* vol 10, no 2, pp 93-90.

Elsa Keskitalo (elsa.keskitalo@stadia.fi) is a social scientist. She has been working as a researcher at the National Research and Development Centre for Welfare and Health (STAKES), and is currently working as a lecturer at the Helsinki Polytechnic Stadia, Finland. Her research interests are comparative welfare state analysis, minimum income and activation policies. Her publications include *Social assistance in Europe* (Helsinki: STAKES, 2001, with M. Heikkilä) and *Työttömien aktivointi: Kuntoutava työtoiminta – lain sisältö ja vaikuttavuus* (*Activating the unemployed: Rehabilitative work experience – the content and effectiveness of the Act*) (Helsinki: STAKES, 2004, Research Report 141, with M. Ala-Kauhaluoma, T. Lindqvist and A. Parpo).

Katrin Mohr (katrin.mohr@linksfraktion.de), sociologist, has recently finished her PhD on changes in labour market policy in Britain and Germany at the University of Goettingen, Germany. She now works as a social policy consultant in the German Parliament. Her areas of research and interest are theories of the welfare state, comparative social policy analysis, social structure and inequality. Her publications include 'Pfadabhängige Restrukturierung oder Konvergenz? Reformen der Arbeitslosensicherung und Sozialhilfe in Großbritannien und Deutschland', *Zeitschrift für Sozialreform*, vol 50, no 3, pp 283-312, 2004, and *Soziale Exklusion im Wohlfahrtsstaat: Arbeitslosensicherung und Sozialhilfe in Großbritannien und Deutschland* (PhD thesis to be published at the end of 2006).

Amparo Serrano Pascual (amparoserrano@telefonica.net) is researcher and lecturer at the Faculty of Political Sciences and Sociology, Complutense University, Madrid. Her main research interests are comparative employment, social and activation policies; gender policies; and the deconstruction of EU discourses. Some of her most recent publications are: *Reshaping welfare states and activation regimes* (Brussels: Peter Lang, forthcoming, ed) and *Unwrapping the European social model* (Bristol: The Policy Press, 2006, with M. Jepsen, eds).

Tomáš Sirovátka (sirovatk@fss.muni.cz) is Professor of Social Policy and Social Work at the Faculty of Social Studies, Masaryk University, Brno, Czech Republic. His research focuses on social and labour market policies, social exclusion and social inclusion. He has contributed to journals such as *Czech Sociological Review*, *Prague Economic Papers*, *Polish Sociological Review*, *Social Policy and Administration*, and *Journal of Marriage and the Family*. He has also edited several books in Czech on Czech social and labour market policy and contributed to several books in English (for example, P. Townsend and D. Gordon, eds, *New policies to defeat an old enemy*, Bristol: The Policy Press, 2002).

Bruce Stafford (Bruce.Stafford@nottingham.ac.uk) is Professor of Public Policy and Director of the Nottingham Policy Centre, School of Sociology and Social Policy, University of Nottingham, UK. He was formerly Director of the Centre for Research in Social Policy at Loughborough University and has over 25 years' experience of applied social research. He specialises in policy evaluation as well as research on social security, notably on the delivery of services, disability issues and welfare-to-work policies.

Ben Valkenburg (b.valkenburg@fss.uu.nl) is Lecturer of Labour Studies at the Faculty of Social Sciences, Utrecht University, the Netherlands. He has been involved in several research projects on Dutch labour market and activation policies, with a specific focus on groups with a large distance to the regular labour market.

Rik van Berkel (r.vanberkel@fss.uu.nl) is researcher and lecturer at the Department of Interdisciplinary Social Science, Utrecht University, the Netherlands. His research interests include unemployment, (comparative) social and activation policies and public governance. His publications include *Active social policies in the EU: Inclusion through participation?* (Bristol, The Policy Press, 2002, with I. Hornemann Møller, eds), 'The marketisation of activation services: a modern panacea?', *Journal of European Social Policy*, vol 15, no 4, pp 329-44, 2005 (with P. van der Aa).

Introduction

ONE

The individualisation of activation services in context

Rik van Berkel and Ben Valkenburg

This book explores a phenomenon that is increasingly turning into a core feature of the provision of social services: individualisation. Put in very general terms, individualisation of social service provision means that services should be adjusted to individual circumstances in order to increase their effectiveness. It is an attempt to put 'one-size-fits-all' approaches in the provision of social services in the past, and to promote tailor-made or personalised services – concepts that are usually treated as synonyms of individualised services. Of course, this 'definition' remains rather vague and imprecise. It says little about what individualised social interventions and services look like, about the process of deciding on the aims and nature of these interventions, about the autonomy of professionals and clients in this process, about power relationships between professionals and clients, and so on. That is what this book intends to do: to explore what the notion of 'individualised social services' stands for in various national contexts, not only at the level of policy formation, but also at the level of the actual implementation and delivery of services.

The individualisation of the provision of services takes place in a variety of social service areas. As several contributors to this book argue (see, for example, Chapters Two to Six), it is not simply a pragmatic, fashionable instrument to increase the effectiveness and efficiency of services, but part of reform strategies aimed at 'modernising' welfare states and modes of governing the social and the individual against the background of broader social, economic, cultural and political changes in society. Debates about individualised service provision mirror the controversies and struggles that characterise the transformation of welfare states that, as the reader will notice, resound throughout this book.

Our focus in the book will be on one particular kind of social services: activation services, that is, social services aimed at promoting the employability and labour market participation of unemployed people. A quick 'tour d'horizon' along some key policy documents reveals the increasing importance attached to individualised activation services, in European Union (EU) countries as well as in other industrialised countries. For example, the Organisation for Economic Co-operation and Development's (OECD's) *Employment outlook 2005*, which contains a full chapter on the effects of activation programmes and strategies, states in its editorial that '[p]roviding the right individualised services for displaced workers is part of the general challenge of designing effective employment services.' (OECD, 2005, p 13), and identifies individual case management as one of the activation strategies with the largest impact. At the EU level, the evaluation of the first five-year period of the European Employment Strategy (EES) pointed to the need for better-tailored active and preventive measures (EC, 2002a). One of the evaluation background papers claimed that the EES has had a positive impact on the introduction of individualised approaches of activation in many EU-15 countries (EC, 2002b). The importance attached to individualised approaches is echoed in more recent EES documents as well: for example, the employment guidelines for the period 2005-08 recommend in guideline 19 'active and preventive labour market measures including early identification of needs, job search assistance, guiding and training as part of personalised action plans.' (Council of the European Union, 2005, p 25). And many of the National Action Plans in the context of the EES (nowadays called National Reform Programmes) also include references to the importance of individualised activation services.

As was mentioned earlier, the individualisation trend takes place in other types of social services as well, such as health and care services. From that point of view, we may argue that our exploration of the individualisation of activation services is relevant for similar developments in other policy areas as well. For the process of individualising service provision raises some issues that are important irrespective of the precise nature of the service, such as:

- issues regarding what individualised social service provision exactly means;
- issues related to the position and role of clients in individualised service provision; to the relations between clients, professionals and the state more generally; to the individual responsibility of clients; to the 'governance' of services and the management of service providers; and to tensions between individual choice and voice in service provision and the collective nature of social services;

- issues related to the role of the competences and knowledge of service users in the provision of adequate and effective social interventions and support.

At the same time, one of the central arguments of this book is that contextual factors are crucial in understanding similarities and differences in the ways in which individualisation shapes and changes processes of service delivery and provision. Evidently, national contexts matter – which will become clear when we discuss and analyse national case studies in Chapters Seven to Eleven, and compare them in Chapter Twelve. But our argument about the contextuality of the process of individualisation goes beyond this. The social policy context in which this process develops is important as well. Obviously, this is one of the reasons why national contexts should be observed in the first place, as countries have different social policy traditions and welfare state regimes. But apart from differences *between* countries, social policy contexts may also account for differences that can be observed *within* countries. These differences in the nature of individualised service provision may become clear when we analyse various domains of social policy; but also when we compare various activation schemes and programmes within the same country. In other words, the general issues related to individualised service provision mentioned before, may be dealt with differently in different (sub-)areas of social policy.

A second contextual factor that should be taken into account when studying the rise of individualised social services concerns the introduction and development of new forms of governance. These new forms of governance are often legitimated, although not always necessarily motivated (see Clarke and Newman, 1997), by pointing to the need to improve the accessibility, responsiveness and quality of social services on the one hand, and to reconsider the role of citizens-as-service-users in the provision of services and their position vis-à-vis service providers on the other. The introduction of new modes of governance leaves its own marks on the individualisation of service provision, at least at a rhetorical level. Thus, the development of individualised social services in general, and of activation services in particular, takes place at the intersection of social policy and governance reforms and transformations.

As was mentioned earlier, this book intends to analyse the development of individualised activation services not only at the level of 'official' policies, but also at the level of service delivery. Ideally, studying individualised social services should include the process of (supranational, national, regional, local) policy formation, the management of the (networks of) organisations and institutions involved in service delivery, and the primary process, that is, the interactions between professionals (social workers or case managers) and the service users. As the national case studies in this book will show, what happens in the practical administration, implementation and delivery of services may deviate considerably from what was intended by policy makers. In other words, policy documents do not necessarily tell the same story as policy practices do. This may sound obvious, and it has been emphasised many times by researchers of implementation processes (see, for example, Hill and Hupe, 2002). Nevertheless, social policy research is still predominantly focused on official policies rather than on their implementation and delivery.

We can summarise the above as shown in Figure 1.1.

With Figure 1.1 we do not want to suggest that causal forces work in a top-down direction only. On the contrary, as the national case studies in this book will show, they also work bottom-up. For example, the aim to make services more individualised has contributed to a process of decentralisation in the area of activation services, devolving policy-making powers to municipalities in order to enable them to adjust policies to local circumstances. In a similar way, social policy programmes have been affected by the desire to individualise activation services: they have been made more flexible, for example, in order to avoid situations in which specific activation programmes can only be targeted at nationally defined, strictly specified client groups.

In addition, it is evident that Figure 1.1 does not give a full account of all contextual issues relevant where the rise of individualised activation services is concerned. Transformations of welfare states and modes of governance in general, and of modes of service provision in particular, need to be analysed against the background of broader societal processes. Several theoretical perspectives may be helpful in

Figure 1.1: Individualised activation services in context

Transformations of social policy ('the active welfare state') •	Transformations of governance ('new governance') •
(Conditions of) the implementation, administration and delivery process •	
Individualised activation services	

this context, each of which focuses on specific aspects of these processes, and identifies specific risks and opportunities. Jessop (2002), for example, has argued that the rise of activation (or, rather, workfare) reflects a broader transformation of socioeconomic regulation regimes from the Keynesian welfare national state to the Schumpeterian workfare postnational regime. Part of this is a 'neo-liberal turn' in policies aimed at promoting employment: activation policies are often mainly supply-side policies, and are increasingly replacing demand-side oriented policies (job creation programmes, redistribution of employment, shorter working hours, and so on; see Chapters Two, Three, Four and Six). A second theoretical perspective is provided by authors such as Anthony Giddens and Ulrich Beck, who write about the rise of the 'risk society' and pay specific attention to the process of individualisation and its ambiguous nature: on the one hand, it is a process from which individual citizens cannot escape and which confronts them with new social risks and the necessity to 'manage their own lives'; on the other hand, it opens new opportunities for the development of individual identities and life projects (Chapters Two, Three and Four). Third, there are post-Foucauldian perspectives that analyse new forms of governing the social and the individual in terms of modern techniques of discipline and control (Chapters Four and Six). Rather than taking one of these theoretical perspectives as our starting point, the book tries to show that each of them may contribute to our understanding of, and to clarifying tensions in, processes of individualising the provision of activation services.

In the following sections, we will briefly elaborate on the context elements presented in Figure 1.1.

Transformation processes and the individualisation of social services

Transformations of social policies: towards 'active' welfare states

The reforms of the social policies of the countries of the EU have been documented extensively (see, for example, Lødemel and Trickey, 2001; Clasen, 2002; Goul Andersen and Jensen, 2002; Goul Andersen et al, 2002; Saraceno, 2002; Van Berkel and Hornemann Møller, 2002). Most scholars recognise that these reforms have affected the very fundamentals on which welfare state regimes are erected: even in countries where benefit levels have not been reduced or benefit entitlement periods shortened considerably, the status of the benefit claimant has changed. Partly depending on how these reforms are being evaluated, a variety of concepts has been introduced to distinguish the 'old' from the 'new': from passive to active welfare states, from welfare states to enabling states (Gilbert, 2002), from welfare states to social investment states (Giddens, 1994), from the Keynesian welfare national state to the Schumpeterian workfare postnational regime (Jessop, 2002) (see Clarke, 2004, p 14, for a critical account of this 'process of telling history as a unilinear shift from one thing to another'). A first characteristic of these reforms is a shift in the main objectives of social policies from income protection to the promotion of labour market participation or, rather, employability (see Chapter Three) of people dependent on benefits and social assistance. The introduction of activation policies and programmes is directly related to this, of course, as in the EU these policies and programmes are considered to be one of the most important instruments to realise this shift of objectives. In the 'new' welfare states, employment instead of income protection is considered to be the best remedy against poverty and social exclusion. Second, we witness a reinterpretation of social risks as manufactured rather than external risks (Giddens, 1994, 2000). In social policy reforms, this has been 'translated' in terms of increasing the individual responsibilities of risk 'bearers' and risk 'producers'. According to Handler (2004), social citizenship has been transformed from a status into a contract, which emphasises the quid pro quo nature of income support. Gilbert (2002) writes about the shift from citizenship to membership: the Marshallian notion of rights-based ('conventional') solidarity is on the wane and is gradually being replaced by a Durkheimian form of 'conditional' solidarity. The integration of income protection and activation schemes whereby entitlements to income protection are made conditional upon fulfilling one's obligations in terms of activation, is a clear example of this trend. Standing (2002, p 168) summarises the position of the main proponents of workfare as follows: 'there should be no social rights without social responsibilities. Their view is that you cannot expect the state – your fellow citizens – to pay their taxes to support you in times of need unless you meet your social responsibilities. This position has been given the name of the *reciprocity principle* [italics in original; note omitted]. This is the heart of Third Wayism, and the New Paternalism that guided it'.

Of course, these trends and developments are not without contradictions and tensions: between the activating and protection-from-poverty functions of social benefits and social assistance, between the emphasis on individual responsibilities in strengthening employability and realising self-sufficiency through work and the actual labour market situation, and so on. Furthermore, despite trends of convergence (Gilbert, 2002), national reform strategies differ and national contexts still matter: in the nature and interpretation of problems of unemployment and social exclusion; in countries' sensitivity to normative and ethical issues that are part and parcel of the welfare state transformation processes; in their financial, administrative and institutional capacity to implement activation programmes and to service large groups of people, and so on. Because of this, we may not only observe differences in the ways specific countries give shape to the general trend towards activation, but we may also witness differences within countries in the 'activation philosophy' underlying various activation programmes. For example, the objectives of activation may be oriented exclusively at labour market participation or may involve broader notions of social inclusion (Levitas, 1998). Activation programmes may be aimed at 'as soon as possible' job placements, or may be directed at the enhancement of skills and qualifications and at realising sustainable participation in the labour market: in the words of Jessop (2002, p 156), 'activation policies can be placed on a continuum running from *flexploitation* to *flexicurity*' (emphasis in original). Activation processes may be more or less punitive. Income protection entitlements may be more or less strictly linked to programme participation. In short, even though the general transformation trends mentioned earlier can be observed in most countries, various approaches to activation, various strategies in making welfare states more 'active' and various concepts of 'active citizenship' should be distinguished (see, among others, Lødemel and Trickey, 2001; Van Berkel and Hornemann Møller, 2002; Barbier, 2004; Johansson and Hvinden, 2005; also see Chapters Two to Four in this volume). Evidently, these approaches and strategies of activation contribute to shaping the context in which the process of individualising activation services is being pursued.

Transformations of governance: towards 'new governance'

The second transformation process that may help to explain the rise of individualised social services concerns the introduction of new modes of governance. As Clarke and Newman (1997) have argued, the crisis of the welfare state did not only involve the social settlement – the social assumptions or fundamentals on which post-war welfare state arrangements were built – but also the organisational settlement, which used to be characterised by two modes of coordination: bureaucratic administration and professionalism. Again, social scientists have introduced various concepts to name the 'new' organisational settlement: the entrepreneurial state (Osborne and Gaebler, 1993), the managerial state (Clarke and Newman, 1997), and the New Public Management (Pollitt and Bouckaert, 2000). The last of the three has been characterised as a form of public management:

(1) whose proponents affirm that private sector management models and techniques can be applied in the public sector;

(2) that is associated with a commitment to plural models of the provision of public services by a mixture of business, the non-profit sector and government actors, emphasizing the importance of cost, choice and quality in the precise mix of service providers;

(3) that is associated with a revised role for government in the provision of public services, characterised as 'steering not rowing';

(4) that expresses a strong belief in the role of the market and quasi-market mechanisms in coordinating the supply and demand for public services and the use of contractual mechanisms for the governance of provision;

(5) 'that attempts a separation of the political decision-making processes from the management of public services' (Carroll and Steane, 2002, p 196).

The new modes of governance have had far-reaching implications for the way in which social services are being delivered and provided. The 'steering not rowing' principle has changed relationships between the (national, regional, local) state on the one hand, and the market and civil society (the family/household, local communities, the third sector) on the other (see Mingione et al, 2002), as well as the relationships between various levels of the state. Traditional state responsibilities and authority have been shifted outward and downward (Meyers, 1998). Actors from the market and civil society have become involved in the provision of social services, and the state has adopted the role of deciding on overall policy frameworks and of acting as a general director of the service provision process. In doing so, it has put increasing emphasis on steering, on output and outcome and on performance, sometimes introducing market mechanisms in service provision as this is expected to increase efficacy, efficiency and quality of services. In terms of the relationships between various levels of the state, processes of decentralisation and devolving autonomy and responsibilities are widespread, increasing the discretion of regional and local authorities, not only regarding the implementation and organisation of service provision but often also in policy formation as such.

The new governance and New Public Management rhetoric has been adopted across the EU, but has had different implications in different countries (see Pollitt and Bouckaert, 2003). For example, the involvement of civil society institutions in the provision of social services may be a relatively new phenomenon in some countries, it certainly is not in others. In addition, decentralisation and devolution presume a historically strong role of the national state in the provision of social services. Where this is not the case – as, for example, in Southern European countries – redefining the relationships between various levels of the state may take place, but these reforms cannot be grasped simply in terms of decentralisation and devolution.

In recent years, social scientists have shown increasing interest in documenting and analysing reforms of governance in the areas of social security and activation, enhancing the integration of social policy and public administration research in studying welfare state reforms. Research has focused on topics such as the marketisation and privatisation in the provision of activation services, the introduction of competition within the public sector, the involvement of third sector organisations and private non-profit or for-profit companies in service provision, and so on (Bredgaard and Larsen, 2005; Struyven and Steurs, 2005; Van Berkel and Van der Aa, 2005); the contractualisation of the relationships between purchasers and providers of services, and between providers and users (Sol and Westerveld, 2005); and decentralisation of service provision (Finn, 2000; OECD, 2003; Van Berkel, 2006). These studies clearly show that the institutional arena of the administration of social security and the provision of social and activation services is undergoing a process of radical and structural change in many EU countries.

The individualisation of service provision

Against the background of these transformation processes, a plethora of motives for, and legitimations of, the individualisation of the provision of activation can be identified. The first is the need to cope with the heterogeneity of the groups at which activation is targeted. Being personal social services by nature, a one-size-fits-all approach is considered inadequate, as it would never be able to meet the diversity of needs and circumstances activation services are supposed to deal with. Because of this, activation has become more flexible and tailor-made over the years, devolving the power to decide on the activation interventions in individual cases to case managers. This is expected to produce effectiveness and efficiency gains: people will not be enrolled in programmes that they do not need, and will be referred to programmes that fit their situations and circumstances. At the same time, tailor-made services are expected to raise the motivation of programme participants, as they are now participating in schemes that are adapted to their needs, wishes and ambitions. Of course, these expectations are not free from contradictions and tensions. The actors involved – policy makers, programme providers, case managers, clients – may have different opinions on what effectiveness means, for example. In most cases, effectiveness is defined in terms of labour market entry; which does not necessarily have to coincide with the ambitions and wishes of clients. But even when it does, effectiveness can mean different things. Does it refer to sustainable employment? Does it refer to labour market inclusion in jobs that match the qualifications, skills, ambitions and wishes of the individual? Does it refer to placing people in a job as quickly as possible, irrespective of the sustainability or quality of the job? Here, the broader policy context in which individualised activation services are provided is relevant, as it guides the answers to these questions in individual cases.

A similar story about potential contradictions and tensions can be told regarding another motive for the promotion of individualised services: strengthening citizens' individual responsibility, which figures prominently in both the active welfare state and the new governance discourses. Both discourses do not necessarily have similar implications for what individualised service provision should accomplish. In the active welfare state discourse, individual responsibility often means that it is first and foremost the unemployed individual who is responsible for preventing unemployment and realising self-sufficiency through labour market participation. Individualisation against this background means that the responsibilities, obligations and entitlements of the unemployed person are determined on an individual basis. Subsequently, the person's behaviour is supervised on an individual basis in order to monitor compliance; if applicable, the individual may be sanctioned, or rewarded. In most EU countries, so-called individual or personal activation plans are used to write down the individual's responsibilities, obligations and entitlements: the Jobseeker's Agreement in the UK, the Integration Agreement in Germany, the Insertion Contract in France, and so forth. Often, these plans acquire the status of a quasi-contract, symbolising that they reflect an agreement reached between the case manager and the unemployed individual; although, in practice, the word 'agreement' is often far from an adequate designation of the process in which these activation plans are developed. This seems to be particularly so in the case of integration plans for social assistance recipients. For example, Ebsen writes on the German case that 'the statutory integration agreement model renders the agreements akin to commands, with the inclusion of the ideas and interests of the unemployed individual being dependent on the employment service staff's reasonableness and willingness to cooperate' (Ebsen, 2005, p 245; for a reflection on these contracts from a legal point of view, see Eichenhofer and Westerveld, 2005). In the new governance discourse, individual responsibility has a rather different meaning. There, it is embedded in a debate that emphasises the competence of service users in determining their needs and the interventions necessary to meet those needs. Individual responsibility means that the service user should have choice, such that, for example, they are given the option of exit (in a more consumerist notion of the service user) or voice (in a more participationist approach; also see Chapter Five), or – in a rather modest form of user involvement – the possibility to express their opinions on service providers by 'satisfaction surveys' or client panels. Obviously, Osborne and Gaebler's (1993) appeal to put 'customers in the driver's seat' can take various forms; and can be based on a range of motives, such as increasing the responsiveness of service providers, promoting the functioning of the market of social services, and putting the customer in charge in the process of service provision (see Chapter Two). Summarising, the process of individualising the provision of services may take place against the background of two rather different and potentially contradictory discourses: one focusing on enforcement and discipline, the other of a more empowering and enabling nature.

Reducing welfare state expenditure is a motive related to individualised service provision as well, in a variety of ways. Increased efficiency and effectiveness through individualised service provision may have favourable fiscal effects, for example because it prevents people becoming enrolled in programmes which they do not need, or which do not help them in promoting welfare state independence. Formulated more positively, it helps to provide more adequate support to those who are unable to re-enter the labour market on their own. From a somewhat different perspective, individualised service provision may also strengthen the gatekeeper function of social security systems, increase selectivity and promote fraud prevention as it generally increases the opportunities for behaviour surveillance, and introduces new ways of defining and distinguishing 'deserving' from 'non-deserving' clients. Both perspectives emphasise different priorities of policy reforms: the first focuses on the quality of services (prevent deadweight, promote adequacy), whereas the second primarily aims at restricting welfare state entitlements.

These brief comments reveal that we cannot start this study of the individualisation of activation services with the assumption that the meaning of the notion of individualisation is clear and unambiguous and requires no further analysis. On the contrary: unravelling the meaning of individualisation in concrete national contexts is one of the aims of this book.

Individualisation and the implementation process

As we argued earlier, the importance of the implementation process in shaping the nature and content of individualised social services should not be underestimated. This is especially so when we are dealing with personal social services, such as activation services, that aim to influence the conduct of their target groups, and can never be fully standardised. Therefore, what happens in the implementation process and in the face-to-face interactions between social workers and clients, as well as the conditions under which these interactions take place, are crucial factors in making social policies succeed or fail – which is of course not the same as saying that policy implementers are always to blame when policies fail.

The shift from passive to active welfare states and the introduction of new forms of governance have had – and still have – radical consequences, not only for policy users but also for those involved in delivering and providing social services: managers as well as social workers and case managers. Many of the institutions, agencies and organisations involved in policy implementation have to do very different things in the present day to what they did in the early 1990s – besides, many new institutions have entered the implementation and service provision arena. As Lurie (2001, p 5) wrote on the basis of a study of the implementation of Temporary Assistance for Needy Families (TANF) in the US: 'Once limited to impersonal clerical functions related to determining eligibility and benefits, frontline workers are now being asked to engage in more personalized conversations about their clients' lives, behaviors, and financial problems'. In other words, the 'products' of these institutions, and the primary process in which they are 'produced', have undergone major changes: from 'people sustaining' to 'people transforming' (Meyers, 1998), which asks for a new work culture, new routines, new attitudes towards clients, new ways of communicating and dealing with clients, new intervention strategies, and so on. In addition, frontline workers also have to do their work in very different ways: for example, they have to focus on efficiency and outcomes, contribute to the realisation of targets, negotiate and cooperate with partners in a network context, or contribute to 'client satisfaction'. In this context, the promotion of tailor-made and individualised forms of service provision adds to the challenges with which managers and social workers in service provision organisations are confronted, and to the turmoil in which these organisations have been for quite some time as a consequence of the almost continuous reforms of their work and organisations.

Social workers working at the front lines of service provision organisations have been characterised as 'linchpins in organizations that are difficult or even impossible to manage due to ambiguous goals, uncertain technologies, unlimited demands, and chronically limited resources' (Meyers, 1998, p 4). At the same time, they are the linchpins in putting the transformation processes in general mentioned earlier, and individualised service provision in particular, into actual practice: without transforming the work of managers and frontline workers, no welfare state or governance transformation is feasible. This raises questions concerning the conditions under which social workers do their work: the caseloads they have to deal with, the targets they have to meet, the availability of social services, the characteristics of target groups in terms of the nature of problems of exclusion and unemployment, the skills and capacities of case managers, their professional identities, and so on. It also raises questions about the coping strategies that the people working in the service-providing institutions develop; about the attitudes of social workers and managers towards the reform processes; about the ways in which the tensions that are likely to arise between the demands and directives of policy makers, the needs and demands of clients, professional identities and managerial concerns are dealt with; and about decisions that are made in the distribution of scarce resources, for example time invested in 'old' tasks (such as determining the eligibility of claimants of income support) and 'new' tasks (activation), support given to various groups of clients, and so forth. And finally, and most crucial for our purposes, it raises questions concerning the impact of all this on what the social policies designed by policy makers actually look like in practice. For it seems evident that Hill and Hupe's (2002) conclusion, that the process of policy making continues during implementation, certainly holds for the provision of individualised activation services and other personal social services.

Structure of the book

The aim of this book is to theoretically and empirically explore the rise of individualised social services in the area of activation policies and programmes. This is reflected in the structure of the book. The chapters in Part One deal with various issues that are relevant in the context of debates on individualised services from a theoretical perspective. The chapters in Part Two primarily adopt an empirical point of view: they are case studies of the introduction and development of individualised activation services.

Earlier in this chapter we argued that it is impossible to give a precise and unambiguous definition of what the notion of 'individualised activation services' stands for. It is used in various contexts and discourses, each of which renders it a different meaning. In Chapter Two, Ben Valkenburg tries to disentangle the concept of individualisation. He distinguishes five 'individualisation discourses' and explores the consequences each of them has for the meaning of individualised service provision. He argues that practices of the provision of individualised activation services often simultaneously embody elements of several of these discourses, which contributes to their inconsistency. The chapter pays specific attention to the issue of 'who is in charge' in the context of individualised service provision. This relates to the issue of the involvement or participation of service users in determining the objectives and nature of activation services, an issue that is picked up in some of the following chapters as well (see particularly Chapter Five), and is directly connected with the question of user voice, mentioned earlier.

A crucial part of the process of providing individualised activation services is the evaluation or assessment of the people at whom activation is targeted. This task is often carried out by local agencies and their frontline workers, and although it is sometimes partly standardised through the use of profiling procedures, it frequently involves room for discretion. In Chapter Three, Jean-Michel Bonvin and Nicolas Farvaque focus on the evaluative function of local agencies in the provision of activation services, and more specifically on the type of information that is considered relevant and taken into account when decisions on the nature of activation interventions are made: the so-called 'informational basis of judgement in justice'. In order to illustrate the importance of the informational bases that are used in service provision, and their consequences for the activation process, two approaches are juxtaposed: an employability approach, currently dominant in many EU countries, and a capability approach. The comparison of these ideal-typical approaches clearly reveals the implications that the selection of informational bases has for issues such as the objectives of activation processes and the role and responsibilities of actors (policy makers, policy implementers, policy users) involved in activation.

Chapter Four focuses attention to Ulrich Beck's theory of the risk society that has inspired many social policy scholars in analysing the erosion of the foundations of 'traditional' welfare states and in rethinking social policies. In this chapter, Håkan Johansson explores in what ways Beck's theory can be helpful in understanding the rise of activation and its various manifestations, as well as the introduction of individualised service provision. More specifically, he elaborates what Beck's notion of 'radicalised individualisation' could (and *should*) imply for individualised activation aimed at supporting citizens to become 'social entrepreneurs'. As a 'counterpoint' to Beck's analysis, the chapter discusses post-Foucauldian perspectives on individualisation, which interpret it as a disciplinary technique sustaining forms of 'governance at a distance'.

In the present chapter, the topic of user involvement is mentioned repeatedly as an important issue in the context of individualised activation services. In a very elementary sense, user involvement is a sine qua non condition for effective individualised activation: the service user is the subject of change that activation tries to accomplish, and they are the provider of information on the basis of which activation should be tailored. Simultaneously, the nature of user involvement is a crucial dimension in distinguishing various meanings of individualised service provision: it directly relates to the 'who is in charge' question (see Chapter Two) and to the service user's power in, and control of, activation processes. In Chapter Five, Ilse Julkunen and Matti Heikkilä reflect on user involvement in personal social services. They argue that several 'levels' or 'degrees' of user involvement should be distinguished, ranging from the user as provider of information about their situation, to the user as the person in charge of service provision. The chapter goes on to argue that the notion of user involvement has been adopted by various schools of thought, each of which defines the role of the user in a specific way, gives user involvement a specific meaning and promotes specific instruments for user involvement. Finally, the chapter raises the issue of the relevance of the social policy context in shaping the nature of user involvement, by exploring the links between type of social services on the one hand, and the kind of user involvement likely to develop on the other.

In Part Two of the book, case studies of individualised activation services are investigated. Rather than on new and original data, the case studies are based on a secondary analysis of data from existing studies of activation. Of course, this makes comparisons somewhat difficult, as the nature of existing data on activation in general, and on the individualised provision of activation in particular, differs from country to country. Nevertheless, each case study tries to address a similar set of questions:

- How did the debate on individualised activation services emerge and what are its backgrounds? To what degree and how is this debate embedded in broader debates on welfare state and governance reforms? What is the role of prior experiences with activation programmes in the development of individualised approaches in service provision? Does the EES play an important role?
- What does the individualised provision of activation services mean in the national context? Has this meaning changed over time, and, if so, how and why? Does individualisation mean different things in different contexts, for example in different activation programmes or in programmes aimed at different target groups?
- What have been the experiences with the implementation of individualised activation services? Does the implementation of individualised service provision mesh with, or deviate from, formal policy? What implementation and delivery conditions seem to be vital in determining what individualised service provision means in practice?
- What role is attributed to the actors involved in service provision (case managers and clients)? How does this actually work in service delivery?

The first chapter in Part Two (Chapter Six) deals with developments at the level of the European Union. For obvious reasons, the nature of this case study differs from the national case studies. In the chapter, Eduardo Crespo Suárez and Amparo Serrano Pascual provide a discursive analysis of some EU policy documents that are important in the context of activation policies: among others, documents produced in the context of the EES and the Lisbon Strategy. In Chapters Seven to Eleven, national case studies are analysed. These chapters deal with the following countries: the UK (Chapter Seven, by Bruce Stafford and Karen Kellard), Finland (Chapter Eight, by Elsa Keskitalo), Italy (Chapter Nine, by Vando Borghi), the Czech Republic (Chapter Ten, by Tomáš Sirovátka) and Germany (Chapter Eleven, by Dirk Jacobi and Katrin Mohr). With this selection of countries, the case studies cover the diversity of welfare state regimes that can be found across the EU: liberal welfare states (the UK), social-democratic welfare states (Finland), Southern European welfare states (Italy), welfare states in transitional countries (the Czech Republic) and corporatist welfare states (Germany). We do not want to suggest that each of the selected countries is exemplary or representative for the welfare regime type it belongs to. Nevertheless, the diversity of countries discussed in this book may give a good impression of the variety within the EU of policies and practices of individualised activation services and the contexts in which these policies and practices develop.

The final chapter of the book, Chapter Twelve, reflects on the case studies from a comparative perspective. Coming back to the general analytical framework developed earlier in the present chapter – which underlines the importance of welfare state and governance transformation processes as well as of processes of policy implementation/delivery in studying the individualised provision of activation services – Rik van Berkel attempts to identify similar and dissimilar trends in the way these services are developing in the countries discussed in the book.

References

Barbier, J.-C. (2004) 'Activation policies: a comparative perspective', in A. Serrano Pascual (ed) *Are activation policies converging in Europe? The European employment strategy for young people*, Brussels: ETUI.

Bredgaard, T. and Larsen, F. (2005) *Employment policy from different angles*, Copenhagen: DJØF.

Carroll, P. and Steane, P. (2002) 'Australia, the New Public Management and the new millennium', in K. McLaughlin, S. Osborne and E. Ferlie (eds) *New Public Management: Current trends and future prospects*, London: Routledge, pp 195-210.

Clarke, J. (2004) *Changing welfare, changing states: New directions in social policy*, London: Sage Publications.

Clarke, J. and Newman, J. (1997) *The managerial state: Power, politics and ideology in the remaking of social welfare*, London: Sage Publications.

Clasen, J. (2002) *What future for social security? Debates and reforms in national and cross-national perspective*, Bristol: The Policy Press.

Council of the European Union (2005) 'Council decision of 12 July 2005 on guidelines for the employment policies of the member states', in *Official Journal of the European Union 6.8.2005*, Brussels: EC.

Ebsen, I. (2005) 'Contracting between social services and their clients in the German concept of 'Fördern und Fordern'', in E. Sol and M. Westerveld (eds) *Contractualism in employment services: A new form of welfare state governance*, The Hague: Kluwer, pp 231-55.

EC (European Commission) (2002a) *Taking stock of five years of the European Employment Strategy: Communication from the Commission to the Council, the European Parliament, the Economic and Social Committee and the Committee of the Regions*, Brussels: EC.

EC (2002b) *Impact evaluation of the EES: Background paper: Prevention and activation policies for the unemployed*, Brussels: EC.

Eichenhofer, E. and Westerveld, M. (2005) 'Contractualism: a legal perspective', in E. Sol and M. Westerveld (eds) *Contractualism in employment services: A new form of welfare state governance*, The Hague: Kluwer.

Finn, D. (2000) 'Welfare to work: the local dimension', *Journal of European Social Policy*, vol 10, no 1, pp 43-57.

Giddens, A. (1994) *Beyond left and right: The future of radical politics*, Cambridge: Polity Press.

Giddens, A. (2000) *The Third Way and its critics*, Cambridge: Polity Press.

Gilbert, N. (2002) *Transformation of the welfare state: The silent surrender of public responsibility*, Oxford: Oxford University Press.

Goul Andersen, J. and Jensen, P. (2002) *Changing labour markets, welfare policies and citizenship*, Bristol: The Policy Press.

Goul Andersen, J., Clasen, J., Van Oorschot, W. and Halvorsen, K. (2002) *Europe's new state of welfare: Unemployment, employment policies and citizenship*, Bristol: The Policy Press.

Handler, J. (2004) *Social citizenship and workfare in the United States and Western Europe: The paradox of inclusion*, Cambridge: Cambridge University Press.

Hill, M. and Hupe, P. (2002) *Implementing public policy*, London: Sage Publications.

Jessop, B. (2002) *The future of the capitalist state*, Cambridge: Polity Press.

Johansson, H. and Hvinden, B. (2005) 'Welfare governance and the remaking of citizenship', in J. Newman (ed) *Remaking governance: Peoples, politics and the public sphere*, Bristol: The Policy Press, pp 101-19.

Levitas, R. (1998) *The inclusive society? Social exclusion and New Labour*, London: Macmillan.

Lødemel, I. and Trickey. H. (eds) (2001) *'An offer you can't refuse': Workfare in international perspective*, Bristol: The Policy Press.

Lurie, I. (2001) *Changing welfare states: Policy brief no. 9, October 2001*, Washington, DC: The Brookings Institution.

Meyers, M. (1998) *Gaining cooperation at the front lines of service delivery: Issues for the implementation of welfare reform*, New York, NY: The Nelson Rockefeller Institute of Government.

Mingione, E., Oberti, M. and Pereirinha, J. (2002) 'Cities as local systems', in C. Saraceno (ed) *Social assistance dynamics in Europe: National and local poverty regimes*, Bristol: The Policy Press, pp 35-81.

OECD (Organisation for Economic Co-operation and Development) (2003) *Managing decentralisation: A new role for labour market policy*, Paris: OECD.

OECD (2005) *Employment outlook 2005*, Paris: OECD.

Osborne, D. and Gaebler, T. (1993) *Reinventing government: How the entrepreneurial spirit is transforming the public sector*, London/New York: Penguin.

Pollitt, C. and Bouckaert, G. (2000) *Public management reform: A comparative analysis*, Oxford: Oxford University Press.

Pollitt, C. and Bouckaert, G. (2003) 'Evaluating public management reforms: an international perspective', in H. Wollmann (ed) *Evaluation in public-sector reform: Concepts and practice in international perspective*, Cheltenham: Edward Elgar, pp 12-36.

Saraceno, C. (ed) (2002) *Social assistance dynamics in Europe: National and local poverty regimes*, Bristol: The Policy Press.

Sol, E. and Westerveld, M. (eds) (2005) *Contractualism in employment services: A new form of welfare state governance*, The Hague: Kluwer.

Standing, G. (2002) *Beyond the new paternalism: Basic security as equality*, London: Verso.

Struyven, L. and Steurs, G. (2005) 'Design and redesign of a quasi-market for the reintegration of jobseekers: empirical evidence from Australia and the Netherlands', *Journal of European Social Policy*, vol 15, no 3, pp 211-229.

Van Berkel, R. (2006) 'The decentralisation of social assistance in the Netherlands', *Journal of sociology and Social Policy*, vol 26, no 1/2, pp 20-31.

Van Berkel, R. and Hornemann Møller, I. (eds) (2002) *Active social policies in the EU: Inclusion through participation?*, Bristol: The Policy Press.

Van Berkel, R. and Van der Aa, P. (2005) 'The marketisation of activation services: a modern panacea? Some lessons from the Dutch experience', *Journal of European Social Policy*, vol 15, no 4, pp 329-43.

Part One
Theoretical perspectives on individualised activation services

TWO

Individualising activation services: thrashing out an ambiguous concept

Ben Valkenburg

Introduction

Social policy almost by definition has to deal with the complex relations between general policies and the political process on the one hand, and individual people and their everyday lives on the other. We define problems and policies as *social* if they affect large groups of people. Social policies therefore are developed on a general, political level. They 'speak' in general terms (participation, employment, integration), 'address' large groups of people (the excluded, unemployed, migrants) and 'deal' with the redistribution of collective resources (money, the institutions of the welfare state). At the same time, social policy is aimed at individual people and their everyday lives, aspirations, competences, possibilities and impossibilities. It is national or local governments that draw up and deliver social policies. In the end, however, the goals of social policy can only be realised in and through the everyday actions of the individual people they address. Social policy, for example, can create conditions to prevent social isolation and to stimulate participation. In the end, success or failure is 'made' by the thoughts, decisions and actions of individuals. The relations between general policies and individual people, almost by definition too, have strong normative aspects. Social policies are not only about how things are, but also about how they should be and thus what people *should* do.

What goes for social policy in general, goes for activation policies in particular. The primary task for the institutions of the welfare state is to get people who are on benefits back into the labour market as soon as possible. These activation policies are not only based on more or less objective economic and financial considerations. They are also firmly based on normative ideas about 'work ethics', 'social responsibility', and so on. Thus activation policies require more from unemployed people than the fulfilment of bureaucratic duties. Social policies should give individual people the opportunity to work; individual people are supposed to take this opportunity. The success or failure of activation policies, in the end, depends upon and has to depend upon the people who are to be activated.

In recent years the tendency has been towards the individualisation of social policies, and of activation policies in particular. Those policies are giving increasing emphasis to the specificities of the everyday lives of individuals. This tendency, however, is neither clear nor unifocal. In most European countries it is an expression of various discourses. Activation policy measures often reflect several of these discourses. Although in some cases this is not a problem, in others it is, because some of these discourses contradict each other. They imply different meanings of individualisation and, in their translation into activation policies, have fundamentally different consequences for the relations between general policies and the individual citizens concerned.

This chapter will elaborate further on these different discourses. In the first part, the focus will be on what they stand for. This, of course, will not be an empirical exercise. It is an attempt to construct a typology and to offer theoretical concepts that may be helpful in the discussion on activation policies. In the second part, the issues raised by these different discourses are discussed. These issues differ, not only in terms of their content, but also in terms of their political implications. It is argued that the most fundamental issue in this discussion is whether or not the individualisation of activation policies enables people to be in charge of their own lives. The third part elaborates this issue and gives some arguments as to why it is fundamental. In the fourth part, the future of activation policy is considered. The normative argument will be that social policy *should* enable people to be in charge of their own lives and that the political process *should* do justice to the far-reaching consequences of this.

The concept of individualisation

There are at least five discourses related to individualisation that are relevant for activation policy.

The erosion of the traditional family

The first discourse focuses primarily on *the erosion of the traditional family as a social and economic unit*. At least in the Northern European countries this discourse has been going on since the 1970s. On an empirical level it relates to the growth of one-person households, the growing number of (new) marriages entered into by people through their life, the growing labour market participation of women and the general individualisation of relations within the family. On a more theoretical level it refers to the changing meaning of intimate relations. In spite of all the modern talk of the 'happy single', most people are still striving for stable, intimate relations. These relations, however, are no longer maintained against all odds. They are being more or less permanently evaluated. They are maintained for as long as they contribute to the emotional and affectional expectations people have of them. In general this is interpreted as a cultural development, resulting from the economic conditions of growing welfare, the participation of women in the labour market and the provisions of the welfare state (Beck, 1998). In this discourse, the individualisation of activation policies means that the provisions of the welfare state should not be aimed at families and their breadwinners, but at individuals, whether they are part of a family structure or not. In a situation where, historically speaking, the breadwinners were men, this implies a growing emphasis on the labour market participation of women. The 'choice' of women to give priority to their family life and to abstain from labour market participation is questioned. Giving priority to their family life, it is argued, makes them dependent on family conditions that may change in the short term (a divorce) or in the longer term (when the children leave home). To avoid the negative consequences in terms of benefit dependency they should remain active in the labour market. Activation policy should support them in this respect.

Differentiation and flexibility

Second, individualisation refers to *the differentiation and flexibility of social and economic life*. In modern society the individual lives of people are more and more characterised by differences. Furthermore, for most people flexibility and change have become an important part of their individual biography (Giddens, 1990, 1991; Beck and Beck-Gernsheim, 2002). As Bauman (2001) makes clear, sometimes this is voluntary ('rust never sleeps'), sometimes it is not ('a lifetime job is hard to find these days'). From the 1970s onwards this discourse has been the basis for growing criticism of the collectivist provisions of the welfare state. Traditionally, the welfare state offered provisions aimed at people whose lives were primarily characterised by what they had in common. What is needed today are flexible provisions that can be tailored to individual people and the situation in which they make use of them. In this discourse, the individualisation of activation policies primarily means striving for differentiated, flexible and tailor-made provisions.

The discourses on the erosion of the family and differentiation and flexibility primarily focus on cultural, social and economic changes and how these changes affect and individualise the lives of citizens. It is from such a perspective that they look at the provisions and policies of the welfare state. Overall, these discourses are still based on the idea that the welfare state is necessary and that, under the right conditions, the welfare state can meet the changing demands of modern cultural, social and economic life. While these discourses still play an important role, they are more and more overshadowed by discourses that focus primarily on the developments and problems of the welfare state as such (Pierson, 1998; Trommel and Van der Veen, 1999; Gilbert, 2002). This is expressed in the third and fourth discourses on the individualisation of social policy.

Privatisation and free market regulation

In the third discourse, the individualisation of activation policy is seen as part of *a broader policy of privatisation and free market regulation*. The argument is that the welfare state has created its own problems (paternalism, bureaucracy, inefficiency). These problems are seen as more or less inherent consequences of state regulation. This discussion on the problems of state regulation is anything but new. In the 1960s and 1970s it was part of a discourse of the left (Illich, 1973). The provisions of the welfare state were primarily seen as bureaucratic systems of power. Their formal goal was the emancipation of citizens. In practice they led to an enhancement of the state's power over its citizens, to paternalism and disciplination, and to a weakening of the competences of citizens themselves. From a Marxist perspective, they were seen as part of a strategy to alienate people from their real interests and from the social and economic struggles for socialist change (O'Brien and Penna, 1998). In the 1960s and 1970s, however, the struggle was not to get rid of the provisions of the welfare state. On the contrary, there were growing claims for enhancing the provisions for education, social welfare and healthcare. The struggle was aimed at politicising these provisions. The argument was that they should contribute to the autonomy of citizens, to their political awareness and to their social and economic struggle. From the 1980s onwards the discourse was increasingly dominated by neo-liberal ideas, in which state intervention and the freedom of citizens are seen as fundamentally opposed to each other (Hayek, 1976; for an overview, see Van der Brink, 1997). The solution is not to politicise existing provisions, but to privatise them and to subject them to free market regulation. This should offer people the choices they are looking for and create better conditions for non-bureaucratic and efficient provision. Individualisation in this discourse primarily means that the individual citizen is seen as a competent actor. Guided by their differentiated wishes, motives and needs, citizens are able to find their way in the market of provisions. Market regulation forces these provisions to serve citizens in such a way that their wishes, motives and needs are met. In some cases this also means that the budget available for activation policies should not be used to fund providing institutions that are then supposed to deliver services to designated target groups. Rather, money should be allocated to individual citizens, who then can use this to buy what they need in the market (for the Netherlands, see Bosselaar et al, 2002). Sometimes this discourse also means that the citizen is seen not as a client, but as a customer. A 'client' is a person with certain (social) problems, who should be supported by the provisions of the welfare state. This support is based on the central notions of solidarity, social justice and equality. A 'customer' is seen as a person who comes to the market to get what they want. The central notions to serve the customer are efficiency, rationality and a businesslike approach. Discussions on solidarity, social justice and equality are disqualified as old-fashioned and too fuzzy for running the welfare state in a modern way.

A shift in rights and duties

Closely linked to the third discourse, in recent years a fourth discourse has developed in which individualisation means *a shift in the rights and duties of the welfare state and citizens*. This discourse is currently dominating the political debate on social policies in many European countries. It is related to neo-liberalism, but includes an additional dimension of responsibility and morality. In neo-liberalism the citizen should be protected against the state. In the fourth discourse, the welfare state should be protected against the citizen. Theoretically inspired by authors who stress the role of the welfare state in the reproduction of an underclass (Wilson, 1987), the central argument is that the welfare state has given too much protection to its citizens. This has not only resulted in rising costs of the welfare state, bureaucracy and unverifiable provisions, but also in a situation where calculating citizens expect the welfare state to solve their problems for them, instead of solving them for themselves. This is primarily formulated as a moral problem with economic consequences. The moral problem is located at the level of individual citizens, who are assumed to have a questionable calculating attitude, to put unjustifiable and unsustainable claims on the welfare state, and to be unwilling to take care of themselves in a changing economy. The economic consequences are located at the level of the rising costs of the welfare state, overprotection and inflexibility in the labour market and, as an end result, economic stagnation.

This discourse is exemplified by the European Employment Strategy (EES; see Chapter Six). The EES stresses that the competitive position of the European economy needs to be reinforced by flexibilisation and deregulation of the labour market. A modern economy does not only demand flexibility from companies but also from employees. Outdated forms of security, and the forms of regulation that support them, stand in the way of modernisation. Modern employees must learn to live with permanent change, not only in their current jobs, but also in their relations with employers. They should be actively involved in their own adaptation to changing circumstances and the demands that these changing circumstances put on them. They should be permanently improving their own employability. Social security should not primarily be protecting people against loss of income as a result of the loss of paid employment. Rather, social security should aim to (re)integrate them into the labour market as part of a flexible, employable workforce.

This discourse adds a new element to the earlier shift from protection to activation. It implies a fundamental alteration of the social contract. The main responsibility for dealing with labour market problems lies with the individual. Citizenship in terms of financial protection is no longer an unconditional right of the individual, but has to be earned by visible individual efforts, aimed at reintegration into the labour market (Serrano Pascual, 2004). Citizenship is no longer described primarily in social terms, referring to protection against the risks of general (economic) developments. It is described in individual terms, referring to the risks the unemployed individual creates for themself in their relation to the labour market and to activation policies. The right to protection is determined by the behaviour, choices, attitudes and motivations of the individual. The emphasis shifts from the collective responsibility of the welfare state to the individual responsibility of the individual citizen. Here the discussion links up with the neo-liberal strategy. The welfare state *may* make citizens individually responsible for their own lives, because privatised, market-regulated provisions give them sufficient possibilities to take this responsibility. In other words: if they do not live up to it, that is their own fault.

In this discourse, the individualisation of activation policies also means that the welfare state turns into a distrusting welfare state, permanently screening individual benefit claimants for the extent to which they are assuming responsibility for their lives. Unemployment and related problems are no longer regarded as a consequence of social and economic developments (blaming the system), but as a result of the actions of the individual citizen (blaming the victim). Individualisation of activation policies in this discourse primarily means a stronger emphasis on individual responsibilities and obligations, sharper sanctions for individuals if they do not live up to them and enhanced control over individual actions and attitudes.

The growing reflexivity of individual and social life

In the fifth discourse, individualisation is primarily interpreted in terms of *the growing reflexivity of individual and social life* (Giddens, 1990, 1991; Beck and Beck-Gernsheim, 2002). In modern society knowledge is permanently used, discussed and developed in everyday practice, that is to say it involves a reciprocal process taking place in the context of everyday interaction. If the contexts are different, this reciprocal process may be different too. This changing meaning of knowledge is an important factor in, and at the same time the outcome of, processes of individualisation. Based on a permanent flow of new knowledge and in different contexts, people develop their individual identity and actions. In leading their everyday life, they further develop their knowledge. In this sense they are not only 'users', but also 'producers', of knowledge. In this reflexive process what is 'true' for their everyday life today may become 'untrue' tomorrow. Individual identity, and the everyday life people live, has become a reflexive project. In this discourse, the individualisation of activation policies primarily means that they should link up with and do justice to the reflexive projects of individual people.

This discourse tries to avoid the dualism between the everyday lives of individual citizens on the one hand, and the policies and provisions of the welfare state on the other. So far, the welfare state in its policies and provisions has failed to take account of the changing reflexive projects of citizens. Traditionally, it has been the political process that defines problems, analyses the causes and formulates strategies to solve them. Often the basis for doing this is knowledge that is seen as more or less objective (as compared to the knowledge of citizens) and general (as compared to the specific context of citizens). Only in the process of policy delivery does the individual citizen become part of the picture. In this stage of policy delivery the role of individual citizens is limited. They are supposed to cooperate in a process that is not primarily based on their own definitions of problems, analyses and strategies, but on those formulated by the political process at a central level. Usually there is little room actively to discuss these definitions, analyses and strategies, and to bring the two worlds of politics and citizens together.

One consequence is what Touraine (1997) has termed 'debased social policies', that is, policies that have little to do with the everyday reality they are aimed at. Unemployment, for example, is often politically defined as an 'objective' financial problem. Cuts in unemployment benefits are presented as necessities. They are legitimised by the assumption that unemployed people should and *could* find paid employment. Whether or not the unemployed individuals who have to find their way in the existing (instead of the desirable) labour market have a realistic chance to do so is left out of the political considerations. Another consequence is that the people responsible for the delivery of social policies are torn between what the politicians ask of them in terms of targets and caseloads on the one hand, and what is possible and desirable in the everyday lives of the citizens they are working with on the other. A final consequence is that political discussions play a minor, or at best a strategic, role in the everyday thoughts and actions of citizens. For many citizens political discussions and the way they are translated into policies and provisions is something that comes from 'outside'. They can neither deny nor escape from this situation. They are given little chance to bring in their own definitions, analyses and strategies, and thus they confront the situation in a more or less calculating way. Given their own definitions, analyses and strategies, they try to make the best of the situation.

In this fifth discourse, the lack of reciprocity between the political process and policies on the one hand, and the everyday lives of citizens on the other, is seen as a central element in the crisis of the welfare state. In a positive sense the individualisation of activation policy means strengthening this reciprocity. The starting point for doing this is not general, politically formulated activation policy *or* the everyday lives of the individual citizens. The starting point is where they meet, that is, in the dialogue between the professional who delivers activation policies and the individual citizen. The central aim should be to enable citizens to be in charge of their own lives, that is, to develop their own reflexive project of identity and everyday life, in an adequate way.

'In an adequate way' means that the way people take charge of their own lives should contribute to their integration and emancipation, and that there must be reciprocity between their individual perspective and the social perspective. The individual perspective is represented by the citizen as an individual person, with their social conditions, wishes, motivations, identity and possibilities. The social perspective is represented by society in general and, more specifically, the social context of the individual citizen (friends, relatives, and so on), the provisions of the welfare state that they deal with and the labour market.

In this reciprocal, client-oriented approach, realising the primary aim of enabling citizens to take charge of their own lives presupposes that they are enabled to take charge also of the process of activation. This in turn requires that the activation process takes into account the position from which the individual starts, their daily life and their strengths and competences. Individualisation in this discourse also means that the individual has a fundamental right to make decisions related to their own activation, without this being unduly constrained by the threat of financial sanctions. This does not mean that the individual has no obligations and responsibilities. In terms of rights and responsibilities, the correct approach for the assisting professional is to set up the trajectory for activation together with the individual citizen and in line with the position from which the individual starts. If this process is correctly followed then the citizen may be asked and expected to bear responsibility for the choices and decisions that have been made.

With its emphasis on the differentiation and flexibility of everyday life, this fifth discourse incorporates elements of the second. It takes the discussion a fundamental step further, however. Tailoring activation policy to the differentiated and flexible life is possible only if and when the individual citizen plays an active role in this process. This active role implies that the individual should be in a position to contribute their own definitions of problems, analyses and solutions to the process.

Different discourses, different discussions

As can be seen in the chapters on national case studies (Chapters Six to Eleven), many specific activation measures reflect more than one of the discourses mentioned above. There are, for example, policies that aim to increase the labour market participation of mothers on welfare with young children. These policies link up with the erosion of the traditional family, that is, with the fact that the number of single mothers has grown considerably during the last decades. Organisations that are to support them in finding a job are supposed to deliver their services in a tailor-made way. They must do this as part of a market of public, semi-public and private organisations. There is a lot of pressure on the mothers to find and to accept paid employment. At the same time all this should contribute to their taking charge of their own lives. On a political level the presumption often is that these different discourses can be combined in a consistent way. In practice this is a highly questionable assumption. If, in the above example, mothers on welfare were able to take charge of their situation, many of them might decide not to participate in the labour market. Many of them may feel that they already do a 'full-time job' bringing up their children and taking care of other members of their extended family. They see this not only as an individual but also as a social responsibility. The obligation to find a paid job, with the concomitant need to seek support, is seen as an externally imposed burden.

The heterogeneity of discourses also complicates the discussion on the individualisation of activation policy. Different discourses imply different discussions that cannot always be combined in a consistent way. In the current situation, the discussion is primarily characterised by confusion. A short summary of the main issues will make this clear.

Like most discussions on social security, the discussion on the erosion of the traditional family is concerned with financial aspects and the desirability of labour market participation. First and foremost, however, the discussion is a moral one. There is a lot of emphasis on what are seen as the negative aspects of individualisation, that is, on the erosion of social rules and values, social cohesion and solidarity. Critics, especially from the conservative end of the political spectrum, point to 'the Sixties' and to the erosion of the traditional family as the main causes of impolite and unsocial behaviour, egoism, lack of responsibility, unacceptable sexual behaviour, and so on. The solution is said to be the restoration of 'traditional family values' (whatever that may be) and thus, although not all representatives of this way of thinking dare to say this straightforwardly, of the nuclear family of man, woman and two or three children. From this conservative perspective, social policy to support single mothers is seen not as a solution, but as a contribution to the problem.

The notions of differentiation and flexibilisation lead on to a discussion on social justice (Fitzpatrick, 2003). There is a tension between striving for tailor-made provisions (individualisation) and adhering to the principles that all citizens should be entitled to the same rights (social justice) and that provisions should apply to those who really need them (social justifiability). In some countries, for example, the push towards tailor-made provisions has been one of the arguments for the decentralisation of social policies to local communities. This results in a growing influence of local political relations on the rights and duties of local citizens, and thus in politically determined differences in how these rights and duties are interpreted. Another discussion refers to the verifiability of social policies. The argument is that tailor-made provisions, in Lipsky's (1980) phrase, require a lot of discretionary space for the street-level bureaucrat. At the same time there are strong political forces that strive for greater control, by limiting this discretionary space through monitoring, standardisation, quality control, and so on. One of the arguments for this is the legitimacy of the welfare state as such. In 'modern society', citizens – in this case working people – are willing to pay taxes for activation policies only if the uses to which the money is put and their results are considered justifiable. In this argument one of the main causes of the 'legitimation crisis of the welfare state' is that in the past a lot of money was spent in a fuzzy, unverifiable way and without clearly monitored results. Last, but certainly not least, the discussion on differentiation has (multi)cultural connotations. In recent years most West European countries have witnessed a tendency whereby differentiation of lifestyles is, albeit sometimes reluctantly, accepted, with the exception of ethnically based differences.

The third discourse, on *privatisation and market regulation*, leads to a debate on whether or not social policy *can* be turned into a market. This is possible only if citizens are competent and powerful enough to find their way in the market. Furthermore, there must be a real choice. That presupposes that there should be more than one organisation that offers a specific service and that the citizen has the option of going from one organisation to another without being penalised. It also presupposes that the market is transparent. For the citizen, it must be clear which organisations are available to help them, how they function and the quality of services they can offer. Only under these conditions will a market contribute to the autonomy of citizens and to efficient provision of services. There are many doubts as to whether these conditions can be met in a realistic way. Furthermore, there is a debate on whether or not social policy *should* be turned into a market. The fundamental question is whether or not social issues like health and labour market participation should be subjected to the commercial interests that rule the market. In practice, it is clear that for commercial reasons private organisations focus on unemployed people with relatively good chances on the labour market, and give less attention to the really problematic cases. Last but not least, privatisation and market regulation go hand in hand with cuts in the budgets for social policy as such. This means that not only the providing organisations, but also the citizens who depend on them, should compete for their share of shrinking resources. In a more general sense there are good reasons to suppose that the citizens with 'the biggest mouth' will be served first, leaving no resources for others who might have more need of these resources. These discussions can be summarised as follows: those who are already socially and economically excluded are further excluded when welfare provision is privatised and regulated by the market.

Then there is also the discussion on verifiability and efficiency. In most countries privatisation and market regulation do not mean that central government is handing over control to the market, on the contrary. Up until now privatisation and market regulation led to more, instead of less, bureaucracy. In healthcare this means 'fewer hands at the bed' and 'more heads in management, coordination and administration'. Privatisation in some cases means that a lot of public money disappears into private organisations in an unverifiable way.

Many of the reflections on the third discourse apply to the fourth as well. As both are inspired by neo-liberal thought, this is not too surprising. More specifically, the fourth discourse gives extra weight to discussions on paternalism and on the shift from 'blaming the system' to 'blaming the victim'. As such both are not new. What *is* 'new' is that they are now more explicitly formulated and practically applied than ever before. Excluded citizens are not only further excluded, but stigmatised as well.

The central discussion in the fifth discourse, on a reciprocal, client-oriented approach, is whether or not citizens should be put in charge of their own lives and of their activation trajectories. Often this discussion is based on an exaggerated interpretation of this approach. It is interpreted as one in which the individual citizen may do whatever they want and in which the goal of social policy is to deliver whatever the individual wishes. Even if we leave this exaggerated interpretation aside, it raises a lot of questions. One issue is whether or not the citizens who depend on activation policies are able, and thus may be asked, to take charge of their own lives and of their activation trajectories. Another issue is, again, the verifiability of activation policy. A dialogue between the professional and the individual citizen that is more or less open-ended, not only in terms of policy delivery, but also in terms of definitions of problems, analyses and solutions, is said to make verifiability problematic. Furthermore, this dialogue requires an equality of power between professional and citizen, which is all but self-evident. Last but not least, this discourse explicitly raises an issue running through all the discourses on the individualisation of activation policy: who is in charge?

The fundamental issue: who is in charge?

In the first and second discourse the issue of 'who is in charge' is hardly at stake in a direct sense. To engage (or not) in intimate relations was and still is seen as a decision citizens have to make for themselves. The same goes for the differentiated and flexible ways in which people live their lives in other respects. Dealing with the consequences is a different matter. In this respect, these discussions are increasingly linked to the other three discourses. In all these three discourses, the issue of 'who is in charge' is explicitly dealt with, albeit in very different ways.

In the third discourse, citizens are supposed to find their own way in a market of provisions. This market puts them in the position of a customer, who will be able to find an offer that meets their demand. To a certain extent, this means that the citizens are put in charge. At the same time, however, there are severe limits to their role in the process. First, the problems that are to be solved are primarily defined by the political process: high unemployment figures, unemployment as the primary cause of other social problems like social exclusion, poverty, criminality, and so on. It is also the political process that determines the causes: an insufficiently competitive economy, owing to over-regulation of the labour market and too many people without a job, and too much emphasis on income protection. Finally, it is also the political process that formulates the solutions, that is, to stimulate employment and activate the unemployed, and that creates the instruments to implement these solutions in terms of education, subsidies and deregulation. For those citizens who agree with the political formulations of the problems, causes and solutions, this will not be much of a problem. The market may enhance their possibilities to do what they think should be done. However, for people who, for whatever reason, are not in agreement, the situation is different. Even if the market strengthens their position in relation to the organisations that deliver activation policies, the whole process remains firmly based on definitions of problems, causes and solutions that are *imposed on them*. If they are put in charge, their responsibility is limited to the process of policy delivery, and they face severe sanctions if they do not comply. Second, this discourse is strongly based on the general assumption that citizens are able to find their way in the market. As a general assumption this is not realistic. Many citizens who depend on the provisions of the welfare state are not able to find their way. For them, this discourse implies that they become part of processes and forces over which they have no control. This is more or less the opposite of being in charge. Third, this discourse goes hand in hand with cuts in budgets. This means that citizens have to compete with each other for shrinking resources and provisions. For the weakest groups this means they are 'put in charge to lose'.

As said above, the fourth discourse shares many elements with the third, including the way in which citizens are put in charge. The main difference is that there is a stronger moral element to the discussion and a more refined way to monitor what people do on an individual level in the fourth discourse. To a certain extent, 'being in charge' also has more negative connotations. Blaming the victim means that the problems citizens have are seen to be a result of the way they run their own lives. In this sense being in charge is not a goal for activation policy, but a cause of the problems this policy should aim to solve. For some groups this means that activation policy should limit the extent to which they are in charge of their own lives.

The fifth discourse, on a reciprocal, client-oriented approach, takes a radically different position. Here the individual citizen is explicitly put in charge, not only in the process of policy delivery, but also in defining the problems that are to be solved, and the ways in which this could be done. As a consequence, activation is to a certain extent seen as an 'open-ended process'. Participation in society can take various forms, in paid or unpaid work, and in economic, cultural and/or social participation. The point of departure is that people are entitled to social participation which accommodates their identity and daily life, contributes to the individual's management of their life and can be realised by the individual concerned in a realistic way. This means that participation is not restricted to paid work.

The question 'who is in charge?' is fundamental for several reasons. First, the question can only be answered in a consistent and, in that sense, fundamental way. There are many examples of activation policies that make clear what happens if the question is answered inconsistently. In the UK, for example, under the 'New Deal', individual case management has been introduced. The aim is to tailor activation trajectories to the needs of unemployed individuals as much as possible. In many situations this more individual approach is combined with a primarily top-down approach, in which the political process has already defined the problems that have to be solved and the ways in which this should be done. This situation is full of contradictions. It is far from hypothetical that the professional often talks with an individual unemployed person in a situation where the objectives to be realised have been set beforehand. In this situation the professional has far more power at their disposal than the unemployed individual. The options of the latter are in fact limited to agreeing to any proposal made by the professional. Experience with practice in the UK shows that in such a situation the professionals involved are soon caught between taking their clients and the ways they take charge of their lives seriously, and the objectives as defined from above that are translated into target scores. There are many other examples to be found. They make clear that different answers to the question 'who is in charge?' cannot be combined. If they are, activation policy not only becomes unclear and multifocal, but also full of contradictions. Either it is the case that it is the political process that defines problems, causes and solutions, and limits the active role of citizens to cooperating in the process of policy delivery. It then has to be explicit in *not* putting citizens in charge of their own lives. Or it is the case that policies put citizens in charge, and accept that this has consequences for the way problems are defined, solutions are found and social policy is delivered. Again, it must be stressed that this latter position does *not* mean that all the wishes of the unemployed individual are to be honoured without discussion. People are put in charge to strengthen the reciprocity between their individual perspective and the social and economic context they find themselves in.

Second, the question 'who is in charge?' is fundamental because the answer has far-reaching consequences. In this sense, it is not overly surprising that the political answers given so far are rather fuzzy. If politicians were explicitly to say 'we' are in charge and 'you' are only supposed to cooperate in the process of policy delivery, they would probably not survive the next elections. In a modern society this would be an unacceptable stance. On the other hand, if the citizen were, albeit in a reciprocal way, put in charge this would have far-reaching consequences at all levels of activation policy. It would require reciprocity in the primary process, where the professional and citizen meet. It would also require that the secondary process of the delivering organisation (management, organisation policies, and so on) should be fed by the primary process, and thus by the input of the citizens they are working with. In other words, it requires reciprocity between the primary and the secondary process of the delivering organisation. Last but not least, it requires that the political process not only tells delivering organisations what to do, but also listens to these organisations in order to know what should and could be done. In other words, it requires reciprocity between the delivering organisations on the one hand, and the politicians who are responsible for activation policy in general on the other.

Third, the answer to the question 'who is in charge?' is more or less paradigmatic in the sense that it determines the way we look at the different discourses on individualisation. If we follow dominant practice, where the political process is explicitly or implicitly in charge, it is legitimate to look for general criteria as a basis for conclusions. In the current situation this is what happens, for example in the discourse on the erosion of the traditional family. If, on a central political level, labour market participation is defined as 'the royal road' to inclusion, also for single mothers on welfare who have young children, activation policy is good when it contributes to this and bad if it does not. As a consequence such mothers may be forced to apply for and accept a job. It may even be supposed, and in practice often is supposed, that single motherhood is not a problem if the mother works, is in this sense part of mainstream society and thus able to raise her children in the appropriate way. In this case the results of activation policies can be monitored in terms of investments and scores (how many women have found a job?). If we take as a starting point that activation policy should contribute to the way people can take charge of their lives themselves, the conclusions in this discourse become more open-ended. From this perspective, for some mothers paid labour may contribute to their autonomy, for others it may not. In this situation mothers themselves may well have a lot to say with regard to the route that should be followed. This approach is based on the assumption that the consequences of single parenthood are not uniform for all, but different for each individual. Activation policy should take account of this differentiation. The results cannot be evaluated only in objective terms. They should also be evaluated from the subjective perspective of, in this case, the mothers themselves. Comparable remarks can be made for privatisation and market regulation. For some citizens this may strengthen control over their lives, for others it may not.

Last but not least this applies to the fifth discourse, which is strongly based on reflexive modernisation and individual identity as a reflexive project. For some people reflexive modernisation may result in more choices and possibilities becoming available. For others it may also mean more choices, but fewer possibilities (or more problems). Reflexive modernisation implies that to put people in charge of their own lives and their activation trajectories is a central aim. Their position from which they start as members of an individualising society, however, is very different. The same goes for activation policies that should enable them to be in charge in a more adequate way.

The question 'who is in charge?' turns the discourses on individualisation into what they should be in modern society: general discourses that should be discussed and investigated in their differentiated relevance for the lives of individual citizens. No more and no less. Only if these general discourses are connected to the differentiated lives of the citizens concerned, can they and may they be taken as an adequate basis for activation policies. This requires an active role for both the political process *and* citizens as individuals.

The debate on the future of activation policy

I round off this chapter with a few remarks about the debate on the future of activation policy. First and foremost, this debate should be based on the supposition that the individualisation of activation policy is not a temporary phenomenon. It is far more than a 'fashion of the day'. It is a response to fundamental economic, social, cultural and political changes. It can and it should be interpreted as a more or less necessary strive to modernise activation policy, and for that matter broader social policies, by giving increasing emphasis to the specificities of the everyday lives of individuals and to their active role in the policy process. This increasing emphasis is at the heart of all the discourses mentioned above, albeit in different ways and with different implications.

So far the strive to individualise activation policy leads to a situation that is primarily characterised by confusion, contradictions and unanswered questions. To a certain extent this is an unavoidable aspect of the process. It raises fundamental questions that cannot be answered overnight. It requires long-term experimentation, trial and error and debate. Even then, however, the 'individualisation' of 'activation policy' will be and should be a political and, thus, contested concept.

In this situation theoretical debates can be helpful to clarify concepts, to trace unanswered questions, to find answers for them and thus to clarify the political choices that have to be made. At the same time, the suggestion should be avoided that some of the discourses mentioned above are right and others are wrong. This would all too quickly turn into an unrealistic simplification. All of the discourses mentioned above relate to relevant economic, social, cultural and political changes. There are strong arguments in favour of activation policy being centred on people being put in charge of their own lives. These arguments refer not only to justice, but also to efficacy: it not only represents a decent way of treating citizens, but also stands for better results in the realisation of the objectives of social policy. Accommodating the requirements of the individual citizen, putting the individual in charge as much as possible and reciprocity are not just morally justifiable principles. In our modern societies they turn out to be important success factors for activation policies. This, however, is not the answer to all questions, but itself raises many new questions, that for the time being remain unanswered. Furthermore, this argument does not mean that all the other discourses are irrelevant.

Last but not least, the debate should be firmly based on what is actually happening in activation policies. If this is not the case, it quickly loses its political relevance. In this debate, theoretical questions and discourses can be helpful, no more and no less, and should be treated as such.

References

Bauman, Z. (2001) *The individualized society*, Cambridge: Polity Press.

Beck, U. (1998) *Democracy without enemies*, Cambridge: Polity Press.

Beck, U. and Beck-Gernsheim, E. (2002) *Individualization*, London: Sage Publications.

Bosselaar, H., Van der Wolk, J., Zwart, K. and Spies, H. (eds) (2002) *Vraagsturing: De cliënt aan het roer in de sociale zekerheid en zorg*, Utrecht: Van Arkel.

Coenen-Hanegraaf, M., Valkenburg, B., Ploeg, M. and Coenen, H. (2000) *Begeleid Werken; theorie en methodiek van een individuele, vraaggerichte benadering*, Utrecht: Van Arkel.

Esping-Andersen, G. and Regini, M. (2000) *Why deregulate labour markets?*, Oxford: Oxford University Press.

Fitzpatrick, T. (2003) *After the new social democracy*, Manchester: Manchester University Press.

Giddens, A. (1990) *The consequences of modernity*, Cambridge: Polity Press.

Giddens, A. (1991) *Modernity and self-identity*, Cambridge: Polity Press.

Gilbert, N. (2002) *Transformation of the welfare state: The silent surrender of public responsibility*, Oxford: Oxford University Press.

Hayek, F. (1976) *The road to serfdom*, London: Routledge and Kegan Paul.

Illich, I. (1973) *Deschooling society*, London: Calder and Boyers.

Lipsky, M. (1980) *Secret-level bureaucracy: Dilemmas of the individual in public services*, New York, NY: Russell Sage Foundation.

O'Brien, M. and Penna, S. (1998) *Theorising welfare*, London: Sage Publications.

Pierson, C. (1998) *Beyond the welfare state*, Cambridge: Polity Press.

Serrano Pascual, A. (ed) (2004) *Are activation policies converging in Europe?*, Brussels: ETUI.

Touraine, A. (1997) *What is democracy?*, Boulder, CA: Westview Press.

Transfer (2001) Special issue on 'Inclusion through participation', vol 7, no 1.

Trommel, W. and Van der Veen, R. (1999) *De herverdeelde samenleving*, Amsterdam: AUP.

Valkenburg, B. (2004) 'Activation policy: facing the dilemma', *Transfer*, vol 10, no 4.

Van Berkel, R. (2000) 'Activering in Nederland', *Tijdschrift voor Arbeid en Participatie*, vol 21, no 2/3, pp 95-108.

Van Berkel, R. and Horneman-Møller, I. (eds) (2002) *Active social policies in the EU: Inclusion through participation?*, Bristol: The Policy Press.

Van der Brink, B. (1997) *The tragedy of liberalism*, Utrecht: Department of Philosophy, University of Utrecht.

Wilson, W. J. (1987) *The truly disadvantaged*, Chicago, IL: University of Chicago Press.

THREE

A capability approach to individualised and tailor-made activation

Jean-Michel Bonvin and Nicolas Farvaque

For a couple of decades, employment and social integration policies have undergone significant transformations. In order to grasp the theoretical and practical meaning of these evolutions, new analytical tools and normative frameworks are needed. This is the very task that we pursue in this chapter. In the first section, the main evolutions are identified as well as their consequences in terms of analytical tools. Indeed, the contemporary transformations imply that the key locus of social policies is the local agency where the beneficiaries are assessed (as to the legitimacy of their claim, their degree of employability, and so on) and where active labour market programmes are actually designed and implemented. Therefore, new analytical tools are to be found in order to theoretically and critically assess these new modes of governance. The second section paves the road in this direction, by advocating the relevance of the capability approach (Sen, 1985, 1992, 1993, 1999) in such a context. In contrast with an employability (or human capital) perspective, which remains to a large extent entrapped in a technocratic or centralised conception of social policy, the capability approach genuinely takes into consideration what is the true goal of social policy, that is, the well-being and capacity to act of the beneficiaries. The concluding section takes a more policy-oriented view and identifies the main challenges faced by contemporary social integration policies in a capability perspective.

Individualisation and situated public action

New patterns of public action

Since the early 1980s there has been a threefold evolution of social policies in the field of labour market integration and the struggle against unemployment, which is by now well documented:

- first, a shift from passive measures (that is, benefits provided on the basis either of citizenship or of previous payment record, without further behavioural requirements on behalf of the jobseeker) to active programmes, in which the benefit payment is conditional upon the appropriate behaviour of the recipient, especially concerning their efforts to get back to the labour market as quickly as possible. In the literature, this first shift is captured as the move from decommodification to recommodification, where social policies are subordinated to labour market objectives as illustrated by the current focus on employability;

- second, a move towards individual measures, implying the substitution of the standardised programmes of conventional social policies based on predefined categories of social risk by individualised tailor-made policies. At the same time, macroeconomic Keynesian demand-side policies give way to supply-side interventions, be it that the cause of unemployment is considered to lie with the unemployed person or that the reform or the support of the labour market is thought to be out of reach of political will or capacity. Thus, servicing states (for example, training programmes or childcare) tend to complement, or sometimes even replace, welfare states and financial compensation, and they are envisaged as the main weapon to fight against unemployment and social exclusion;

- third, a territorialisation of social policies, that is, the increasing trend to give local actors in general (local civil servants, social partners, non-profit associations, private employment agencies and jobseekers themselves) more freedom of action in the policy process instead of envisaging them as mere executive tools in the hand of central government (in the case of civil officers) or as corporatist groups unable to take into account the collective good (Bonvin and Bertozzi, 2001). The pitfalls of the top-down procedure are abundantly documented, and local approaches are actively recommended by organisations such as the Organisation for Economic Co-operation and Development (OECD) (see the territorial flexibility advocated in OECD, 1998) or the European Union (EU) (see the first version of the European Employment Strategy recommending the setting up of a genuine local employment service in one of its guidelines), in order to mobilise local players' knowledge and goodwill and design more appropriate programmes. Thus, local actors are increasingly considered as partners in the definition of the common good.

This threefold change entails an in-depth reshuffling of the policy process: the classical distinction between the three stages of this process (that is, the *normative* step or policy design, the *pragmatic* one coinciding with policy implementation, the *evaluative* one or policy assessment), useful to describe a clear-cut policy process where the stages were neatly distinguished, does not hold in the new context. The strict functional and temporal separation and distribution of responsibilities characteristic of the previous period (that is, Parliament and central government in charge of designing appropriate legislation, civil officers confined to its implementation with very little margin for initiative, and assessment achieved only ex post mostly by independent actors) considerably reduced the capacity to adjust policies quickly. Indeed, evaluation resulted only ex post, and only after this stage could the policy process be triggered again in order to adapt legislation to changing circumstances. By contrast, the new pattern of social policy relies on the permanent interconnection and interdependence between the three stages, which allows a much quicker adjustment when necessary.

Furthermore, whereas the designing stage used to be the key to the whole policy process, implementation and evaluation are now playing the crucial part. As a matter of fact, the margin for interpretation left to local actors is much greater, and the new pattern of public action relies on a constant resorting to evaluating practices concerning both local agents (submitted to stringent contractual requirements monitored by evaluation procedures) and benefit recipients in order to check the appropriateness of their behaviour or the relevance of the measures designed for them. Follow-up and monitoring are essential components of such programmes, which accounts for the present trend towards benchmarks, indicators and the like. These evolutions coincide with the call for a greater adjustability of legislative provisions and practices.

Situated public action, individualisation and the evaluative tasks of local agents

Together, these three transformations point to a major change in the way public policies are designed and implemented in the field of employment and social inclusion. They form a coherent whole: the will to render public policies more 'active' entails a new way of thinking about the tasks of local agents and opens a space for individualised practices.

Activation and individualisation share common features, even if careful distinctions are to be made (see Chapter Two). In the context of social and employment policies, the activation motto originally meant a policy preference in favour of active expenses rather than passive ones.[1] However, the notion rapidly shifted to an idea of activating not only social expenses, but the *persons* themselves. This evolution was in line with the more encompassing goal of an active society, which called for a problematic individualisation of social policies. The principles behind the logic of individualised activation boil down to new practices of contractualisation and conditionality, which include behavioural requirements that might restrict the sense of social citizenship (Handler, 2003). Various policy innovations have modified the forms of public intervention, which resulted in a higher degree of individualisation and a blurring of traditional social categories of intervention. For instance, new categories of intervention, such as 'excluded' people, or young people with multiple 'difficulties', are explicitly requiring a situated evaluation of the individuals' needs and problems. This follows a twofold logic: on the one hand, in a social justice perspective, fairness and equity require taking into account individual circumstances by public institutions and policies; on the other hand, on the efficiency side, such a supply-driven intervention aims at giving incentives to quick professional reintegration. This supply orientation can take many different forms (for example, human capital policies, tax incentives, in-kind services such as care help) and the evaluation of its effects on the situation and well-being of the non-employed is a matter of debate.

Thus, the contemporary evolutions of social policies are deeply ambivalent when it comes to their impact on beneficiaries. A key issue in this respect is how potential beneficiaries of public action are evaluated by public agents. Which *informational basis of judgement in justice* is chosen by the latter in order to assess the former, that is, which *kind* of information (needs, lack of income, merit, motivation, past behaviour, and so on) is explicitly or implicitly considered as relevant when assessing jobseekers and designing active labour market programmes for them (Bonvin and Farvaque, 2005a)? The implementation of public schemes cannot be seen as a process of mechanical application, but rather as a complex process of multiple interpretations and learnings, at different stages, which relies on the public agents' evaluating competencies.

The evaluative tasks of local agents: pressures, selection criteria and dilemmas

Local agencies appear as a crucial locus in the new patterns of public action. With the new paradigms of decentralisation, partnership and individualisation – all of them consistent with the principle of subsidiarity – the role of these institutions has been exacerbated. Four main functions are conventionally attributed to the public employment service (PES): job-brokerage, labour market information, managing labour market adjustment programmes and administering unemployment benefits (Thuy et al, 2001). With the new pattern of public action, the role of the PES gradually shifted from its original mission of placement to managing employment policies targeted at the most deprived workers, and helping the most vulnerable or the 'hardest-to-place', who compose the major flows and stocks of these agencies (Erhel et al, 1996). Tensions and dilemmas emerge in consequence resulting from unavoidable conflicts between the pursuit of social justice and the obligation to be efficient in terms of a market-oriented basis of information only (that is, by increasing the placement and employment rates). According to Dean (2003), this search for economic efficiency in welfare-to-work policies directed at people with multiple problems and needs is consistent with, and might even be conducive to, a potentially corrosive culture of self-blame among the recipients. While many of their trajectories have remained beyond their control, these people nevertheless develop a vision of themselves as blameable and individually responsible for their situation. This representation or culture eventually triggers a negative dynamics, which restricts the domain of choice and constrains their capability to assess whether they are (physically, mentally and emotionally) ready to work. Dean emphasises the necessity to promote a more sensitive and flexible definition of job-readiness, and to check for the perverse use of activation schemes that exacerbate the insecurities experienced by these vulnerable people.

Conflicting evaluation procedures: New Public Management and local public action

This tension between economic efficiency and social equity is further aggravated by the increasing tendency to introduce performance targets in order to monitor and control the action of the PES (Walwei, 1996). This managerialist orientation gives clear indications to the staff members of the PES, and makes their action potentially more consistent. Indeed, quantitative outcomes are easier to apprehend from outside, and throw crude light on the efficiency of the policy process. However, at a micro-level, the respect of individual liberties risks being denied in order to produce good results. Performance aims at changing individual behaviours in order to make them comply with exogenous objectives. But this is not necessarily achieved in ways which improve service delivery (Wright, 2001), what eventually leads to 'making a good showing on the record as an end-in-itself' (Blau, 1963, quoted in Wright, 2001, p 247). When they become internalised by all actors involved in social integration policies, these performance targets result in perverse effects, for 'the behaviour of workers comes to reflect the incentives and sanctions implicit in those measurements' (Lipsky, 1980, p 51). That is to say, 'Staff make efforts to meet targets but these efforts are not necessarily of the kind intended by those who design the target' (Wright, 2001, p 247). To take an example, during the initial stage of the introduction of an 18-month programme for the less skilled youngsters in France, many staff members of special institutions acknowledged that they deliberately selected people not too far from employment, in order to respect the target of 50% beneficiaries in steady employment at the end of the programme. As the director of one of these structures said:

> There were strong pressures from the State on TRACE [the name of the programme]: obligation in terms of numbers of admissions in the programme, etcetera. At the beginning, in order to fulfil the State requirements, we had to produce exceptionally good figures. Only thereafter we could make room for quality, the development of activities. (quoted in Farvaque, 2000, p 188)

In Switzerland, at the beginning of the 2000s, all regional public placement offices (RPOs) were evaluated according to four indicators weighted in such a way as to privilege quick reintegration into the labour market. On this basis, a classification of all RPOs was established, and those in the second half of this hierarchy could be financially penalised. Such a procedure impacted on the placement officers' job and resulted in so-called creaming practices (focusing on the most employable) and in multiplying bad job offers to the most deprived, in order to improve the figures. Thus, the benchmarks used to assess the RPOs' performance ultimately shaped the jobseeker's evaluation in such a way as to exclude the most deprived from the potential benefits of active labour market policies. In this specific case, performance indicators acted as a factor of further exclusion and precariousness (Badan et al, 2004).

There is a plurality of possible legitimate evaluations of the jobseekers, but New Public Management (NPM) tools tend to impose a uniform informational basis of justice, that of efficiency in terms of employment rates or other similar indicators. In this case, the diversity of evaluation practices is erased in favour of one best way, often called a best practice. In an asymmetrical relationship such as the 'placement officer–unemployed person' one, NPM tools are used in order to impose a specific vision of how a jobseeker should behave and of what is expected from her. Under such circumstances, even if local actors do their best to help the neediest, performance targets established at the national level become self-defeating instruments, in that they prevent the achievement of the very objective of the active labour market policies, that is, professional and long-lasting integration.

Such a perverse impact of NPM tools can be observed from the very beginning of the relationship between the jobseeker and the PES. Studies, in the case of France, show the existence of such an evaluation bias immediately after the first interview. Confronted with very diverse cases, local agents rely on conventional rules of judgement that allow them to assess the jobseeker's distance from employment (Benarrosh, 2000). Such uniform rules result in distributing jobseekers into practical categories of action: those who can reasonably be helped – although to different degrees – and those who are unemployable, in the sense that they are not even capable of starting an effective job search. As a result, only the former are treated as effective jobseekers by the agency; for the others, the objective is to make them 'invisible', that is, to direct them towards other institutions (so that they are counted in other statistical categories), or simply to ignore them, for instance by ranking them in the category of the most autonomous jobseekers not needing specific help or repeated interviews, when they actually are the opposite. Thus, instead of helping the neediest, in line with the compensating logic of public action, social intervention by the PES contributes to reproducing and amplifying the discriminatory logic of recruiting practices in the labour market. Public and private actors are entangled in the same logic of competencies, thereby reinforcing the processes of social exclusion of the weakest and the least qualified.

In their day-to-day activities, local agents are constantly called to combine what can realistically be offered to jobseekers, and the national recommendations to activate all jobseekers with tailored measures. National guidelines demand agents to efficiently help unemployed people (that is, to raise employment and placement rates), and to fight against the growing exclusion of the most disadvantaged in the labour market. The everyday work of the agents is thus entrapped in the difficulty to make the placement mission assigned by the central authorities consistent with the real work, that is, the administration of considerable flows of poorly skilled unemployed people, for whom the adapted help is most often very close to case management practices typical of social work.

Performance targets do not adequately take into account jobseekers' personal circumstances. By integrating these quantitative criteria in their daily practices, local institutions give them further legitimacy, which tends to still deepen the phenomenon of social exclusion. As a result, individualised social policies risk being used as instruments to discipline the beneficiaries and make them comply with prevailing social norms. In our view, it is the responsibility of the State to prevent such pitfalls and design policies and assessment procedures requiring local actors to take into account unemployed people and their preferences, wishes, expectations, and so on, and forbidding any infringement on their human dignity. Our contention is that Sen's (1985, 1992, 1993, 1999) capability approach, which will be presented in the next part of this chapter, is an adequate normative and analytical tool to meet the challenge conveyed by local social policies. Against NPM tools and all the potential perverse effects of activation, individualisation and territorialisation, it claims that social integration policies should be elaborated with a view to promoting capability-friendly interventions, that is, interventions enhancing the beneficiaries' freedom of choice. This requires a genuinely bottom-up approach putting concerns at the micro-level at the very core of the policy process and evaluation practices, substituting many of the present practices where managerialist injunctions significantly limit the scope for taking seriously the beneficiaries' preferences and expectations.

Individualised activation and the capability approach

Following an intuition contained in Salais (1998) and elaborated elsewhere (Farvaque and Raveaud, 2002; Bonvin and Farvaque, 2003, 2005a, 2005b; Dean et al, 2005), we consider the capability approach proposed by Amartya Sen as both a useful theoretical tool in order to assess the meanings of individualisation at a situated level of public action, and a critical framework with regard to the NPM precepts and their imposition on local situations. We briefly present this approach in the next subsection.

The capability approach

The capability approach (CA) is a normative framework proposed by Sen in order to assess individual and collective situations (see Sen, 1985, 1992, 1993, 1999). The approach insists that individual freedom is the relevant 'informational basis' to be taken into account in public assessments. Indeed, in all practical issues connected to public action, Sen claims that the relevant information should concern what people are effectively able to do and be, rather than their resources or wealth (as standard economic evaluations do) or their subjective contentment (as the utilitarian tradition does). People's 'capability' (what they actually can do and be) stands for their effective positive freedom: for instance, in the case of work-related capabilities, the freedom to have decent employment, to work full time if this is one's wish, to have the right to change one's orientation and to get access to lifelong training, and so on. Such information on the individual's extent of freedom is not available if one relies on standard information.

In our view, the logic and practice of individualised activation ought to be questioned against this approach (Bonvin and Farvaque, 2005a). The CA raises two key questions in this respect: (i) the capacity to convert resources into real opportunities and (ii) the connected issues of choice and responsibility.

Conversion of resources

The CA relies on two major concepts: 'functioning' and 'capability'. The *functionings* of a person are her actual achievements. They represent the components of a worthwhile life if they are considered as valuable. Potential achievements are identified as the *capability set* of a person, and represent her real freedom to achieve valuable functionings. When assessing the well-being or agency of a person, capabilities should be the focal point: indeed the same functioning (for example, working part time) may be the result of constraint (compulsion to accept any job) or choice (for example, someone looking for a better work–life balance). Focusing on functionings does not allow the capture of this crucial difference. This implies that the development of capabilities is to be envisaged as the objective of all public policies: the normative perspective of the CA is not to impose outcomes (or functionings) but to provide the adequate environment for the development of capabilities (Sen, 1999).

The capability set of a person depends on the one hand on her entitlements, resources and commodities (that is, all goods and services that are available to her), and on the other hand on her ability to *convert* these into valuable functionings (Sen, 1985). Thus, entitlements and commodities form the material basis of the capability set, but they are not enough to guarantee the development of capabilities. The CA insists on looking at what people are really able to do with such cash or in-kind resources. When analysing individualised activation policies, this topic of the conversion is crucial: two people entitled to the same formal right (for example, the right to education or lifelong training) or the same resource (for example, a monetary allowance) do not necessarily convert them on a par. And they may not be responsible for such situations, which often result from inequalities in what Sen calls 'factors of conversion'. As a matter of fact, if someone lives in a deprived area where training centres are scarce or of bad quality, she does not enjoy the same opportunity set as another person living in a rich area with lots of high-quality training opportunities. There are different kinds of factors of conversion – for example, social, environmental, political, economic – which impinge on people's capacity to convert a resource into a valuable achievement, and most of these factors do not pertain to the field of individual responsibility. As a result, public action ought not to stop after the delivery of resources, rights or 'active programmes', if it aims at enhancing capabilities. It should also include an action on the conversion factors.

The role of local agencies and personal advisers can be analysed in this perspective: does their individualised action on beneficiaries go beyond the simple tasks of selection and administration of resources, and help them have more capability and freedom of choice? However, as important as it is, the role of local actors cannot be decisive on its own. Many studies have shown the limits of local action, precisely because available resources or entitlements are insufficient or not adapted to individual situations, or because in the absence of adequate conversion factors and enabling structures (for example, in terms of jobs or training opportunities), acting on someone's potential may turn into a vicious circle. Such perverse effects of individualised activation in a context of structural barriers preventing access to employment may drive local agents to adopt 'second-best' solutions such as teaching 'employable' persons how to accommodate themselves to unemployment or inactivity (Orianne, 2004). In these cases, medical or psychological intervention makes up for the inadequacy of the institutional environment in terms of conversion factors.

The CA requires struggling against obstruction factors that impede the conversion of resources or any other form of individual capital (be it income or competencies) into capabilities. Supply-oriented action can certainly enhance work-related capabilities through tailor-made interventions, but it needs to be completed by more comprehensive policies acting on the economic, social, political, and so on, context. The development of capabilities is not only an individual responsibility, but also and more prominently an issue of building adequate social structures. The focus on capabilities implies, then, a deep-seated reform of the traditional welfare state, with the double ambition of preserving social rights, that is, access to commodities and entitlements, and facilitating the translation of all resources and formal rights (to be understood very broadly as all the commodities available to the individual in terms of income, human capital and all other kinds of resources) into capabilities or real freedoms. In this perspective, individualisation of social programmes certainly allows taking into account people's heterogeneity, but it cannot be an end in itself, and cannot mask the need for interventions on social structures and factors of demand. The present trend towards activation and the notion of employability can be analysed in that perspective.

Choice and responsibility

The distinction between achievements (functionings) and freedom to achieve (capability) is also of great significance when considering the action of public evaluators. One can ask the following question: is their objective defined in terms of achievements to reach (either through incentives or via the systematic use of constraint), or in terms of capabilities, that is, the real freedom to do whatever one has reason to value? The CA emphasises the primary relevance of the capability sphere to evaluate individual situations and social arrangements, even though the dynamic expansion of a person's capabilities may in certain cases begin with interventions aiming at favouring some initial achievements. Indeed, a public action strictly focusing on functionings, that is, by imposing *any* kind of job on the beneficiaries, will be described as negating individual freedom.

In Sen's view, the respect of individual freedom goes hand in hand with a focus on individual responsibility, but this sharply contrasts with the Third Way and its ambition to transform 'the safety net of entitlements into a springboard for personal responsibility' (Blair and Schröder, 1999). Critics of this Third Way conception convincingly argue that such an exacerbation of individual responsibility curtails to a large extent the respect for the person as a human being, and enforces duties and constraints at the expense of an ethical vision of responsibility (Dean, 2002, p xvi). From a practical or 'street-level' point of view, such an appeal to responsible behaviour puts enormous pressure on the local agents, squeezed between insufficient resources and equipment (for example, both scarce financial means and lack of valuable job opportunities to offer their clients), and the necessity to take into account the jobseekers' legal claims and rights and to provide them with appropriate help and assistance. An ethnography realised in a Jobcentre in Scotland has documented the impossibility for the intermediaries of making use of their practical reason and knowledge, faced as they are with injunctions of short-term results and scarce adequate means (Wright, 2001). The lack of resources at their disposal often pushes them to act on people's *employability*, the best they can do as they cannot directly intervene on the level of *employment*. Their primary mission of matching jobs and people might result in a second best: the development of 'employability careers' for the people (Orianne, 2004).

By contrast, the CA insists that fostering people's responsibility is achievable only if adequate means and valuable opportunities, via the implementation of collective responsibilities, are defined and supplied. This is in line with a 'forward-looking' and 'task-oriented' perspective of responsibility, rather than a 'backward-looking' or 'blame-allocating' one (Goodin, 1998). Short-termist horizons imposed by performance indicators are not always adequate with such a forward-looking view of responsibility. Implementing collective responsibility in the field of labour market policies thus implies providing jobseekers with real capability for work, that is, with real access to a valuable job (which of course does not coincide with the elimination of any form of constraint or practical limitation, but with the necessity to build the most valuable combination of individual and collective responsibility: Bonvin and Farvaque, 2003).

Only if appropriate resources are on offer, is the individual able to behave responsibly. Following Bovens (1998, p 27, emphasis added):

> We will not easily accept the idea of bearing responsibility unless we have at our disposal *the possibilities of behaving responsibly.* We would be asking a lot of someone if we held him [sic] responsible in a situation in which he [sic] had no choice other than to behave in the way he [sic] did.

This conception of responsibility is certainly the main difference between the employability and the capability perspective. Indeed, even if both approaches put the emphasis on people's opportunities and potentialities, the ideas conveyed by the words employability and capability may in the end be radically opposed. The CA provides an ideal-typical conception of individualised policies, which emphasises the importance of an action on social structures (through the idea of conversion – see subsection above on 'Conversion of resources') and conceives individual responsibility against the standard of capabilities or real freedom to act (which represent the sine qua non condition for a genuine choice to take place). Following this normative framework with regard to contemporary individualised and tailor-made policies, it can be said that some employability-enhancing policies may prove to be capability-enhancing, but not necessarily all. The next subsection will explore the potential of the CA as a critical framework in order to assess individualised activation policies and their present focus on employability.

The informational basis of employability against the capability approach

The CA requires a complex and fragile equilibrium between policy objectives defined collectively (that is, the functionings conventionally defined as valuable or desirable) and the necessity to take into account individual and local circumstances. Raveaud (2002) aptly underlined the requirements of such an approach in the case of labour market policies. In his view the capabilities of the person who needs help should not be evaluated a priori, when she is precisely in a moment of vulnerability, as in the example of the 'unemployable' person. On the contrary, she has to be assessed when taking into account what she will do with the resources she will be provided with. The question is therefore not: 'Is this person entitled to anything, according to the capacities I can evaluate now?', but 'What is this person entitled to, in order to develop her capabilities best?'. The question is no longer to look for ways to restrict help and make it conditional, or to expect certain attitudes and actions from the poor and the unemployed. It is on the contrary to provide persons with what they need in order to restore and develop their capabilities.

Developing various empirical insights, we shall try to assess to what extent the notion of employability, which inspires today's active labour market policies, fits in this framework. In Europe, the recent coordination of national policies promoted by the European Employment Strategy (EES) recognises the collective responsibility of society in enhancing all individuals' capacities for work. The word 'employability' appears in the language of the European Commission circa 1997, and is correlative with the concern of rendering national systems of social protection more conducive to employment. The main goal is economic, that is, to transform passive benefit systems into active ones, with an expected 'double return': while expenditure for unemployed people is to be cut, more work-related resources drawn from more people in employment are expected. At the micro-level, such policies aim at enhancing the human capital of unemployed people, rendering them more adapted to the labour demand. At the macro-level, one can expect positive effects of active labour market policies (education, training, counselling and compulsion into work) on growth, as well as on the level of wages, inflation and employment. This latter goal – the improvement of the employment rate – has actually supplanted the issue of the struggle against unemployment. This coincides with a new conventional view concerning the respective valuation of work, unemployment and inactivity. Indeed, in the EES, work figures as the centrepiece, and inactivity is conceived of as an inferior functioning. By contrast, in the 1980s, two solutions to unemployment were available, namely inactivity (retreat from the labour market via early retirement or housework) or work. Thus, the focus on employability considerably restricts the informational basis for evaluation by asserting the indisputable value of work envisaged as the condition sine qua non of social integration. In terms of the capability approach, this could be legitimate, provided, however, that jobs of adequate quality are made available, which is far from being the case. Under such circumstances, the focus on employability may well act as a further factor of stigmatisation for all those unable to fulfil this requirement.

This vision of employability represents the trend followed by all EU countries, although at different paces (Raveaud, 2001). Nevertheless, employability rather appears as a buzzword covering distinct meanings over the 20th century and especially since the early 1990s. The most contemporary versions of this evolutionary notion are labelled 'initiative employability' and 'interactive employability' by Gazier (1999). The former considers that the person, that is, the jobseeker, holds full responsibility for her trajectory in the labour market, while the latter takes individual trajectories as entangled in an interaction between individual and collective responsibilities. The concept of 'interactive employability' indeed permits the taking into account of a broader conception of public action. Thus, the notion maintains its emphasis on individual initiative, but considers in addition the interactive dimension of the process leading to employment, where a plurality of actors – the State, regional or municipal councils, the third/non-profit sector, non-governmental organisations, firms, and so on – belong. The role of the entitlement system, as well as that of local institutions, which deliver and secure some of these entitlements, is of particular importance here. Such a version of employability would be close to the capability approach.

In our view, however, policies oriented towards 'initiative employability' do not qualify as enhancing capabilities. Some significant changes are needed to bridge the gap between 'initiative employability' and capability: especially with regard to completing action over individual human capital with the setting up of adequate labour market institutions. In the absence of such a capability-friendly institutional environment, human capital risks being nothing but a formal right. Thus, focusing on individual employability without providing the conditions for making meaningful employment available boils down to creating a modern and well-educated version of Marx's reserve army. Besides, initiative employability imposes a specific conception of employability that takes for granted the powerlessness of public institutions in front of market forces. By this token, it imposes a very restricted basis of information on local actors who lose most of their margin of manoeuvre and interpretation. In this respect, initiative employability, which is the currently prevailing version of employability, is very much in line with top-down modes of governance like NPM tools. As a matter of fact, such employment policies and public institutions act as factors of reproduction of discrimination and exclusion patterns observed in the labour market, as the case of the UK New Deal evidences:

> The notion of employability, at least as far as it is operationalised within the New Deal, tends to validate and even ossify extant patterns of labour market inequality.

Market-oriented welfare-to-work policies serve to facilitate access to the labour market on the basis of employability or job-readiness, prioritising low-cost placement of those near to the front of the employment queue while paying insufficient attention to those at the back. In contrast, an explicitly redistributive approach would concentrate resources and policy efforts on the most rather than the least excluded, seeking explicitly to overturn job-market inequities through anti-discrimination measures, targeted assistance, high-quality education and training, fair benefits, the extension of social rights in the workplace, and so forth. (Peck and Theodore, 2000, p 740)

The CA sheds light on the pitfalls of initiative employability. As an alternative, it calls for a reversal of the assessing logic in order to consider in the first place people's capabilities and to see how the environmental variables should be shaped in order to enhance them.

Table 3.1: Employability versus capabilities

	Employability	Capabilities
Common features	Partnership and role of local structures (decentralisation) Policies centred on the rebuilding of individuals' capacities	
Objectives	To increase the employment rate: the common good is predefined by means of a statistical reference against which the value of public action is assessed	Valuable functionings defined through social choice procedures Modalities of access to those functionings defined in situation
Type of responsibility	Individual responsibility Blame-allocating Backward-looking	Collective responsibility Task-oriented Forward-looking
Role of local agencies	Executive tools submitted to central objectives (ex post assessment)	Largely autonomous actors in charge of the in-context implementation of social policies

Table 3.1 summarises the main propositions of this chapter. The two columns should be read as ideal-types of local public action. As such, they are heuristic devices useful to analyse the concrete situation of local agents, which is always entangled between a logic of 'needs interpretation' (Fraser, 1989) and bureaucratic constraints.

Conclusion: solving the dilemmas of individualised activation – some lessons of the capability approach

We have tried to stress in this chapter the decisive evaluative function of local agencies in contemporary social policies. The question of how people are assessed in these institutions is crucial to understanding the new patterns of public action, broadly designed to enhance individuals' employability. The interaction between local agents and the recipients creates tensions and dilemmas between different bases of evaluation and action (economic efficiency and the objective of matching jobs and skills versus social justice and the help to be provided to unemployed people). Some of these models of evaluation and action prove more congruent with what the CA puts forward. In our view, at least three conditions need to be fulfilled for individualised activation to be capability-friendly:

- The setting up of a genuine discursive space guaranteeing that all partners' point of view is duly taken into account in the course of the public policy process. This requires both social choice procedures in the design of policies (in Parliament or other political arenas) and local deliberative democracy in the implementation and assessment of active labour market programmes, which implies that activated people are genuine partners of the activation process (and that quantitative targets such as the increase of the employment rate do not impede such participation).
- A long-term perspective is needed for the development of capabilities which cannot accommodate short-termist horizons. Cut-off dates may work very well for many unemployed people, all the same they push the most deprived to feel blameable and undeserving, and paralyse their capacity for initiative. By contrast, if time is considered as a resource (that is, looking forward) rather than a constraint, the jobseeker's evaluation follows a different logic, much more respectful of the individual circumstances and conducive to step-by-step social integration.
- An adequate articulation between individual and collective responsibilities, implying the need to considerably improve the tools of collective responsibility. If local institutions are not to act as disciplining agents whose main function is to guarantee social peace, then they should be equipped with adequate tools in order to efficiently pursue all jobseekers' integration. The present trend of social policies towards focusing on individual responsibility is not to be interpreted as evidence of moral deficiencies on behalf of the

jobseekers, but as a by-product of the political retreat from the field of macroeconomics and employment. Indeed, the increasing legitimacy of the use of so-called sticks and carrots points to the weakness of collective action in this specific domain. Furthermore, the insistence on individual responsibility clearly restricts the margin of manoeuvre of local agents. In contrast, the setting up of appropriate tools of collective responsibility would allow them to adequately play their part in the new pattern of social policies.

Hence, the CA does not suggest any quick-fix remedy. A plurality of informational bases of action may be resorted to in the course of public action. Instead of trying to predefine the best practices (what the employability approach in the sense of the OECD or the EU does), the CA suggests that criteria of action and evaluation should be established in situation by all partners involved, and that the possibility of their constant evaluation and redefinition should always be open. In the end, it is a very demanding approach, calling for the active and permanent involvement of everyone in order to guarantee to all members of society a real access to those functionings that are conventionally defined as valuable, and to enhance their real freedom to choose between these functionings. Local institutions in charge of labour market policies are then faced with an extremely demanding task. All the same, capability-enhancing practices feature as a realistic objective, provided local actors are equipped with institutional arrangements and collective frameworks (that is, macroeconomic and legal devices) more favourable to decent employment.

Note
[1] This distinction, far from straightforward, is strongly contestable, for passive expenses can enhance people's resources and budgetary capacities, as well as their consumption prospects. In a Keynesian perspective, passive expenses have 'active' multiplying virtues.

References
Badan, P., Bonvin, J.-M. and Moachon, E. (2004) 'Le rôle des acteurs locaux dans les nouvelles politiques de l'emploi', *Revue Suisse de Sociologie*, vol 30, no 3, pp 381-96.

Benarrosh, Y. (2000) 'Tri des chômeurs: le nécessaire consensus des acteurs de l'emploi', *Travail et Emploi*, no 81, January, pp 9-25.

Blair, T. and Schröder, G. (1999) *Europe: The Third Way/Die Neue Mitte*, London/Berlin, June.

Blau, P. M. (1963) *The dynamics of bureaucracy: A study of interpersonal relations in two government agencies*, Chicago, IL: Chicago University Press.

Bonvin, J.-M. and Bertozzi, F. (2001) 'Systems of collective action and learning capacities', in A. Serrano (ed) *Enhancing youth employability through social and civil partnership*, Brussels: ETUI, pp 129-56.

Bonvin, J.-M. and Farvaque, N. (2003) 'Towards a capability-friendly social policy: the role of local implementing agencies', Paper presented at the VHI conference: 'Transforming Unjust Structures: Capabilities and Justice', Von Hügel Institute, St Edmund's College, University of Cambridge, 26-27 June.

Bonvin, J.-M. and Farvaque, N. (2005a) 'What informational basis for assessing jobseekers? Capabilities vs. preferences', *Review of Social Economy*, vol 63, no 2, pp 269-89.

Bonvin, J.-M. and Farvaque, N. (2005b) 'Social opportunities and individual responsibility: the capability approach and the Third Way', *Éthique Économique/Economic Ethics*, vol 2, no 2, online: http://ethique-economique.org/Volume-2-Numero-2.html

Bovens, M. (1998) *The quest for responsibility: Accountability and citizenship in complex organisations*, Cambridge: Cambridge University Press.

Dean, H. (2002) *Welfare rights and social policy*, Harlow: Prentice Hall.

Dean, H. (2003) 'Re-conceptualising welfare-to-work for people with multiple problems and needs', *Journal of Social Policy*, vol 32, no 3, pp 441-59.

Dean, H., Bonvin, J.-M., Vielle, P. and Farvaque, N. (2005) 'Developing capabilities and rights in welfare-to-work policies', *European Societies*, vol 7, no 1, pp 3-26.

Erhel, C., Gautié, J., Gazier, B. and Morel, S. (1996) 'Job opportunities for the hard-to-place', in G. Schmidt, J. O'Reilly and K. Schömann (eds) *Handbook of labour market policy and evaluation*, Cheltenham: Edward Elgar, pp 277-307.

Farvaque, N. (2000) 'L'action publique située en faveur de l'insertion des jeunes: une tentative d'approche en termes de capacités: le cas d'une mission locale', Unpublished Masters dissertation, University Paris X Nanterre, France.

Farvaque, N. and Raveaud, G. (2002) 'Responsibility and employment policies: a 'conventionalist' view', Paper presented at the annual conference of the European Social Policy Research Network: 'Social Values, Social Policies: Normative Foundations of Changing Social Policies in European Countries', Tilburg University, 29-31 August.

Fraser, N. (1989) *Unruly practices*, Cambridge: Polity Press.

Gazier, B. (ed) (1999) *Employability: Concepts and policies*, Report 1998, Berlin: European Employment Observatory Research Network, European Commission.

Goodin, R. E. (1998) 'Social welfare as a collective responsibility', in D. Schmidtz and R. E. Goodin (eds) *Social welfare and individual responsibility*, Cambridge: Cambridge University Press, pp 99-195.

Handler, J. (2003) 'Social citizenship and workfare in the US and Western Europe: from status to contract', *Journal of European Social Policy*, vol 13, no 3, pp 229-43.

Lipsky, M. (1980) *Street-level bureaucracy: Dilemmas of the individual in public services*, New York: Russell Sage Foundation.

OECD (Organisation for Economic Co-operation and Development) (1998) *Vers des politiques de l'emploi plus efficaces: la gestion locale*, Paris: OECD.

Orianne, J.-F. (2004) 'L'État social actif en action: troubles de l'employabilité et traitement clinique du chômage', in P. Vielle, P. Pochet and I. Cassiers (eds) *L'Etat social actif: Vers un changement de paradigme?*, Brussels: PIE Lang.

Peck, J. and Theodore, N. (2000) 'Beyond "employability"', *Cambridge Journal of Economics*, no 24, pp 729-49.

Raveaud, G. (2001) 'Dynamics of the welfare states regimes and employability (a study based on the National Action Plans for Employment, 1998-2000)', in D. Pieters (ed) *Confidence and changes: Managing social protection in the new millennium*, The Hague: Kluwer Law International, pp 5-26.

Raveaud, G. (2002) 'Employability and social exclusion: a capabilities approach', in R. Muffels and P. Tsakloglou (eds) *Social exclusion in Europe: An empirical analysis*, Aldershot: Edward Elgar.

Salais, R. (1998) 'A la recherche du fondement conventionnel des institutions', in R. Salais, E. Chatel and D. Rivaud-Danset (eds) *Institutions et conventions: La réflexivité de l'action économique*, Raisons Pratiques No 9, Paris: EHESS, pp 255-91.

Sen, A. K. (1985) *Commodities and capabilities*, Amsterdam: North Holland.

Sen, A. K. (1992) *Inequality reexamined*, Oxford: Oxford University Press.

Sen, A. K. (1993) 'Capability and well-being', in M. Nussbaum and A. Sen (eds) *The quality of life*, Oxford: Clarendon Press, pp 30-66.

Sen, A. K. (1999) *Development as freedom*, Oxford: Oxford University Press.

Thuy, P., Hansen, E. and Price, D. (2001) *The public employment service in a changing labour market*, Geneva: ILO.

Walwei, U. (1996) 'Improving job-matching through placement services', in G. Schmid, J. O'Reilly and K. Schömann (eds) *International handbook of labour market policy and evaluation*, Cheltenham: Edward Elgar, pp 402-27.

Wright, S. (2001) 'Activating the unemployed: the street-level implementation of UK policy', in J. Clasen (ed) *What future for social security?*, The Hague: Kluwer Law International, pp 235-50.

FOUR

Placing the individual 'at the forefront': Beck and individual approaches in activation

Håkan Johansson

Introduction

The German sociologist Ulrich Beck has provided us with a broad analytical framework for how to understand *individualisation* as a general sociological process. Drawing on his risk society thesis, he emphasises that contemporary societies might provide individuals with new forms of opportunities, but also a new set of risks and insecurities. Due to modern industrial society's transformation into a risk society, each individual faces a situation in which they have to deal with risks such as environmental pollution, contamination of food and human and animal diseases, as well as social problems like unemployment or family breakdown. It appears as if the state is no longer willing – or has the capacity – to help citizens handle these risks. Instead risks are increasingly defined as *individual social risks*. But Beck refuses to reduce his understanding of individualisation to a threat for individuals and citizens. On the contrary, the core element of his individualisation thesis regards its potential to provide individuals with new opportunities and resources; to act, develop their life patterns and make their voices heard in relation to public authorities, social traditions and structures. In other words, citizens and individuals face an ambiguous situation in contemporary welfare societies, implying greater opportunities to develop individual identities, roles and careers, but also new forms of individual social risks (see Beck, 1992, 1994; Beck and Beck-Gernsheim, 2002; Beck and Willms, 2004).

This chapter addresses what students of activation can learn from Beck. The analysis is divided into two parts. The first sections map out the core elements of Beck's individualisation thesis. Analytical themes are identified, which both challenge and confirm current reasoning on activation. It is argued that the burgeoning activation discourse provides important empirical illustrations of Beck's sometimes broad analytical arguments. The following sections probe deeper into one aspect of Beck's individualisation thesis: the notion of *radical individualisation*. It is argued that Beck crosses an analytical line and becomes explicitly normative in his view on the role of the state and public authorities and how they could promote the form of individualisation that Beck is in favour of. These aspects of Beck's thesis have only rarely been addressed by the academic community. To help us understand the full implications of his arguments, these are contrasted with post-Foucauldian discussions that offer us divergent views on what the welfare state 'actually' does in contemporary societies. This challenges us to rethink Beck's individualisation thesis in general and individual approaches to activation in particular. The question raised is: are contemporary governance models that aim to install individual autonomy, choice and capacity, better defined as examples of new forms of discipline and control 'at a distance'?

Individualisation and social citizenship

Beck's writings concern changing conditions for welfare states, social policy discourses and models of social citizenship, and his risk society argument rests very much on similar propositions as much current reasoning on activation reform. He acknowledges that changing labour markets, modes of production and internationalisation have major significance for individual welfare states, and the status of 'the full employment society'. Due to open and international economies, national welfare states and national governments are required to adapt to market-oriented demands, regarding larger wage differentials and stronger work incentives, and develop public measures to strengthen unemployed citizens' qualifications and productivity. The question, which underlines much of Beck's writings and current discussions on activation reform, consequently concerns whether work – as we know it – has 'come to an end' and what implications this has for social citizenship, social protection systems and welfare states' ambitions to govern unemployed citizens (Van Berkel and Hornemann Møller, 2002; Goul Andersen and Jensen, 2002).

Exploring this in greater detail, Beck means that we can identify an individualisation of wage-earners' attachment to the labour market. In a historical perspective, work was an important social and economic integrative mechanism and provided individuals with a social identity. After completing training, individuals tended to stay in their designated profession throughout their entire working lives. Welfare states' ambitions to achieve full employment functioned as a key instrument for the struggle against poverty and unemployment, as well as for the integration of people into society. However, the usage of the 'full employment' model has not only been of concern for individuals' integration into society. It has also been a device for the state's control over citizens and had far-reaching consequences for how individuals lived their daily lives, as the 'daily rhythm of work, with its discipline, its values and its conception of personal responsibility and cooperation, corresponds to the demand made by the rulers of the work society upon their workers and employees' (Beck, 2000, p 10). In Beck's view, contemporary societies experience a shift regarding the ways in which industrial jobs constitute the model for a normal job, which naturally has several implications for both workers and unemployed citizens.

First and foremost, Beck proposes that the political and social rationale of 'full employment' is still important, yet subordinated to the principle of flexibility. Without going into details, flexibilisation of employment includes changes in, for instance, workers' contract arrangements (part-time, temporary or subcontracted work), the location of work activities (as people tend to work at different places) and the daily hours spent in work activities (as the demarcation line between work and free time is blurred) (Stråth, 2000). Several other scholars have made similar observations to Beck and addressed the social consequences of flexible labour market arrangements and modes of production (for example, Sennet, 1998; Gorz, 2000; Bauman, 2001). In correspondence, they identify an ambiguous situation for workers. On the one hand, changing labour market conditions might open up greater opportunities, for instance in terms of choosing a profession (Plougmann, 2002, p 34). But on the other hand, individuals face a situation in which they continuously need to develop their competencies and are generally requested to navigate their own 'risky' career. In that sense, if the 'full employment society' – as a historical model – presents the individual with a set of calculable risks, the late-modern flexible work society presents them with a set of uncertainties (Beck and Willms, 2004, pp 162-3).

The situation is perhaps even more ambiguous for unemployed citizens. Beck argues that it is important to have in mind that changing labour markets establish new patterns of social stratification. Unemployment has become a social problem that no longer only affects some social groups or classes. Instead, almost every citizen of a given community is in danger of becoming unemployed – at one time or another. The situation is most risky and insecure for those without marketable skills and Beck describes the situation as a transformation of unemployment, from being one based on collective responsibilities and solidarity, into an individual risk or a personal fate. In his usual tentative and provocative fashion, Beck acclaimed that individualisation of unemployment as a social problem implies that each 'individual becomes the waste basket of society's unsolved problems, and then is supposed to transform this garbage can he's [sic] been made into, into some kind of creative project' (Beck and Willms, 2004, p 74).

Several scholars have criticised Beck's unwillingness to address the implications of a changed labour market in greater detail. Alexander (1996) points out that his macro-sociological analysis has limited ground in detailed empirical studies. It rests on overly rationalistic and individualistic arguments and is combined with broad speculations about infrastructural processes that have little grounding in the actual processes of institutional and everyday life. Lash questioned the dynamics of flexibility and insecurity and asked: 'just how reflexive is it possible for a single mother in an urban ghetto to be?' (Lash, 1994, p 120). Furthermore, Beck did not deal with the consequences of his risk society thesis in relation to issues of citizenship, which is surprising as 'full employment' constituted the cornerstone in the institutionalisation of social citizenship in post-war welfare states (for general discussions see Allen and Henry, 1997; Ekinsmyth, 1999; Mythen, 2005).

However, some of Beck's unanswered questions are to a large extent handled by the burgeoning literature on activation, above all as the trend of activation illustrates how welfare states act in relation to unemployed citizens and a changed balance between collective and individual risk management. The activation discourse and installation of activation policies across Europe has imbued a changed status for social citizenship, and a changed balance between collective and individual social risk protection. Substantial changes in social citizenship are very much the analytical starting point for much current reasoning on activation, as activation policies imply that the duties side of the citizenship equation is enforced and made stricter. This is expressed in terms of a tightening of entitlements criteria in unemployment insurance and related changes in means-tested social assistance schemes. The precise development differs – naturally – between individual welfare states (for example, Lødemel and Trickey, 2001; Van Berkel and Hornemann Møller, 2002; Serrano, 2004).

Even though the population in general is affected by broader substantial changes in the status of social citizenship, this is even more so for specific groups. Those being considered as capable risk managers, with skills and competencies to develop in a flexible labour market, are often required to fulfil some broader duties and requirements. However, those identified as least capable and competent to enter the regular labour market are in focus for a set of policies that tend to be much more paternalistic, impose a stronger set of duties on the individual, limit the individual's scope for self-determination and build upon vague notions of normalisation and social control. In this least favourable category, unemployed people are considered as in need of being activated, conditioned to comply with public training, discipline and normalisation to become good citizens and workers. This differentiation between public intervention styles indicates that individualisation of unemployment policies might very well go hand in hand with limited opportunities for choice on the part of citizens.

These short comments indicate a goodness of fit between research on activation policy and Beck's individualisation thesis. Arguably, the activation literature provides empirical illustrations of Beck's broad and sometimes vague arguments on changing conditions for social citizenship, individualisation of social risk and individualisation of unemployment and unemployment policies.

Individualisation and citizens' activities

A second pillar in Beck's writings concerns the argument that individuals have stepped forward as social actors and questioned established social roles, cultural traditions and social structures. Following his propositions, living in contemporary societies implies that individuals have started to lose their contact with 'the traditional' and, in his usual style, Beck claims that individuals are *dis-embedded without being re-embedded*. He even argues that individualisation is the new social structure of second modernity, as a form of an *institutionalised individualisation*, but due to its character it is 'a non-linear, open-ended, ambivalent, and continuous process' (Beck and Willms, 2004, p 101).

This sometimes messy and general argumentation is not easy to grasp and pinpoint, which opens up the possibility for great flexibility with regard to how to interpret and use his general analytical propositions. Scholars emphasise that Beck fails to pay attention to issues of gender, ethnicity, age and nationality in his views on how people respond to risk and individualisation. Lupton and Tulloch conclude: 'the 'risk society' thesis is ethnocentric in its sweeping claims, failing to recognise the diversity of national and sub-national interests and concerns' (Lupton and Tulloch, 2002, p 333; also see Taylor-Gooby et al, 1999; Taylor-Gooby, 2001; Tulloch and Lupton, 2003). Beck's propositions are also criticised for being too optimistic about the opportunities people have to explore the new possibilities that a more individualised society might imbue (Dingwall, 1999; Scott, 2000; Mythen, 2004).

However, Beck's constitutive argument regards the firm belief that modern society was a society of pre-given roles, displayed in the set-up of, for instance, families or the labour market. In such a social structure, individuals had to follow certain roles and seek their success and happiness within them (Beck and Willms, 2004, p 64). Those individuals who transgressed established boundaries and challenged their designated roles could expect bitter critique and opposition from different institutions, such as the church or the state, as well as from fellow citizens and individuals. However, the sharp statement delivered by Beck is that this no longer holds true. In the backdrop of a turn towards a risk society and reflexive modernisation, individuals' biographies are no longer pre-given by society, social structures or cultural traditions. On the contrary, individuals and citizens can formally and practically have significant influence upon their lives and biographies.

One illustration of Beck's argument is naturally the structure of the family and the position of women in society (for example, Ostner, 2003). There is no need to be a trained social scientist to identify patterns of changing social structures and family roles in these respects. According to Beck, this is one key demonstration of the impossibility of deducing roles, careers or identities from broad social categories such as family and social class and Beck consequently claims that related roles and biographies have been dissolved and pre-given biographies torn up. This is a decisive feature of the process of individualisation, accompanied by a growing awareness among individuals that they have a biography of their own, a biography that they can design, change and model. Other scholars have put forward similar arguments and pictured the late-modern individual as a 'manufacturer' of personal identity, a designer of personal biographies or life as a form of 'do-it-yourself project' (for example, Bauman, 2001).

However, Beck's theory is sociological in nature. To understand the individualisation thesis, he reminds us that individualisation has been fostered by structural changes and welfare state arrangements. He specifically points to the relevance of public support structures and welfare state arrangements, which have provided citizens with social rights, and thereby opportunities to emancipate from previous social structures and roles. In an interview, Beck explains that 'individualization concerns the way that basic institutions like civil rights, education and equal opportunities produce and enforce individualization' (Boyne and Beck, 2001, pp 58-59).

However, the process of individualisation equally places the individual in an ambiguous situation, as each individual *has* to learn how to negotiate, to see their life as a project for continuous planning (Beck, 1992). At first glance, each individual appears to have a growing possibility to construct their own biography from a wider selection of elements than before. Yet these new role options are typified by their unknown outcome, as a general implication of what it means to be dis-embedded without being re-embedded (Beck and Willms, 2004, p 65). In that sense, an individualised society imbues not only that individuals face expanded opportunities of autonomy and choice, but also that they are – more or less – condemned to being active in designing their biography. Beck means that there is no option except to be an active, planning and reflexive individual. Even those who want to be inactive or follow a traditional role pattern have to do this actively, and choose their roles and identities.

These statements position Beck within a liberal tradition. However, in sharp contrast to neo-liberal views on individuality and freedom, he argues that his view on individualisation rests on the notion of *radical* individualisation. To flesh out this concept he explained that what:

> people are trying to realize in the small scale of their self-chosen lives is a cherished and internalized ideal that remains denied on the larger scale of society. They are trying to realize a more perfect democracy in miniature. They are willing to make the greatest possible efforts in order to redeem the key normative expectations of democracy – equality, justice, fairness, and the right of each individual to develop her individuality – and to accept and deal with all the consequences that necessarily flows from such efforts. (Beck and Willms, 2004, pp 66-7)

The quote exemplifies one important aspect of Beck's individualisation thesis. He establishes a division between society at large and the kind of 'small' social context in which people live their everyday lives. This naturally imbues a critique of the modern state and welfare state for not sufficiently opening up for citizen participation and autonomy and the right of each individual to develop their individuality, and above all a critique of the powers of the expert. But this form of individuality is not considered as in principal opposition to the society (as a neo-liberal position would be). Beck claims that his notion of radical individualisation has been misunderstood for being autarkic. Instead he means that the crucial message is a form of individualisation *with* other people. Generally stated, individuals construct their self-chosen lives by entering into a process of social interaction with other people, and that 'the idea of individualizing by oneself is a contradiction in terms. Individualization is a social concept or it is nothing. The idea of an autarkic I is pure ideology. Individualization is intrinsically defined by the normative claims of co-individualization' (Beck and Willms, 2004, p 67).

To further explain his position, Beck claims that acting in a boundless autonomy is an illusion and based on a neo-liberal conception of individuality. In contrast to this neo-liberal view on self-entrepreneurship, Beck proposes that his view on radical individualisation originates from a notion of *social entrepreneurship*, in that individuals socialise and possibly harmonise their lives with others.

Implications for activation research

Unfortunately, Beck did not explore these notions in any greater detail. But it is possible to extract some interesting analytical considerations from Beck's propositions that have great relevance for welfare state and activation studies. From my perspective, his individualisation thesis conveys a general message that long-established bureaucratic or paternalistic modes of administration, rigidity and inflexibility as well as arbitrary exercise of discretionary powers are challenged by citizens. What Beck proposes is that people have become more self-confident and conscious of their rights vis-à-vis welfare states, welfare services and professionals. Partly due to higher levels of education and training, citizens have greater competence than before to present their cases and claims vis-à-vis public authorities in general and more specifically the frontline staff of welfare agencies and services. At the same time, the increasingly accepted critique of authority and traditions gives individuals greater confidence to question judgements and decisions of the representatives of these authorities, agencies and services. This implies that, when it comes to welfare arrangements, citizens increasingly expect to play more active roles in handling diverse risks and promoting their own welfare. This includes marginal groups, for instance activated social assistance recipients, who expect to be given the possibility of influencing decisions relating to their own welfare, whether this is expressed through co-determination, user involvement or informed consent.

To what extent this form of individualisation actually is a 'reality', and a reality for 'all' segments of the population, is an issue that needs further intensive empirical studies (for example, Tulloch and Lupton, 2003). Most likely individuals' possibilities to explore the process of individualisation are unequally distributed across the population. Even though Beck was hardly interested in how people actually acted, he argued that an individualised society was not only for the richest and the well-off in society. He means that individualisation as a societal process opens up possibilities for *all* segments of the population, including poor, excluded and marginalised people, in terms of a possibility to seek biographical solutions to systemic contradictions (Beck and Willms, 2004, p 106).

Beck's propositions can be used for further considerations regarding the relation between citizens and welfare states and services in contemporary societies, above all as there is a growing ambition in welfare studies to consider the individual as a reflexive agent, with capabilities to make individual choices (Le Grand, 1997; Deacon and Mann, 1998; Hoggett, 2001; Fitzpatrick, 2002; Deacon, 2004). Some scholars have taken the notion of individualisation as a basis for new considerations for new considerations regarding the status of clients in welfare services, and developed new notions of 'welfare democracy' and 'welfare agency', which address the strategies and activities of clients. These models move away from seeing people as passive beneficiaries of state and professional interventions, not to mention as passive inhabitants of fixed social categories, for instance as 'the poor', 'the unemployed', 'clients' or 'diagnosed patients' (Williams et al, 1999). Similar research themes have only rarely been addressed in studies of activation policy or investigations of the interaction between activation worker and unemployed citizen. For instance, we know surprisingly little about the following:

- To what extent are citizens recognised as partners in contemporary welfare systems and activation programmes, with a potential to negotiate and make informative input into decision making?
- To what extent do professional groups and actors deploy methods based on dialogic or deliberative procedures in activation programmes?
- How does a 'democratisation' of welfare services and activation programmes change professional roles and practices, as an expert

with the right to define individual needs and to have the last say in issues regarding individual welfare?

Although a number of changes in activation policies and programmes are justified in terms of this trend towards participatory models, notions of user involvement and user perspectives, these issues have only been touched upon. Arguably, Beck challenges us to think of individual approaches in activation and the interaction between welfare services/professionals and citizens in a new manner. Some of these issues will be covered in this volume, as authors for instance address the significance of tailor-made individual action plans to accommodate public provisions to the particular needs and requirements of each person.

Can the welfare state promote radical individualisation?

The notion of radical individualisation is at the centre of Beck's analytical framework and although Beck rarely pays the welfare state or social policies any great notice, he actually develops a discussion on what the welfare state can do to help citizens to become social entrepreneurs and individualise radically, and even on what *welfare states ought to do* to promote successful agency and reflexivity of unemployed, poor and marginalised people. These discussions have not been presented in a coherent form, but drawing on recent interviews with Beck it is possible to extract three general themes that demonstrate his view on radical individualisation (Beck and Willms, 2004).

The first theme concerns new principles for welfare provision, in an age of social and economic insecurity. As demonstrated, changing conditions for social citizenship and individualisation of social risks is a cornerstone in much of Beck's reasoning. The acclaimed 'end of the full employment society' imbues a challenge to social citizenship as the main principle for a social contract in welfare states. Since unemployment is no longer a marginal problem and more flexible forms of working activities are replacing normal wage labour, Beck finds it unrealistic to use wage labour as the main integrative mechanism in society and as the general principle for social provision. Hence, the great challenge ahead is to develop principles for how welfare states can institutionalise new forms of basic social security, on a medium- or long-term basis. Discussing answers to these challenges, Beck argues that we 'have to ask seriously why we can't have *a de-commodified system of basic security*, one that is independent from paid labour' (Beck and Willms, 2004, p 83, emphasis added). Without going into details, Beck means that a similar system would provide not total security, but basic security, and this discussion naturally links up to the debate on basic income (Beck, 1999). In Beck's view, this would provide individuals with the necessary economic resources and security to give them both the confidence and possibilities to develop an experimental attitude in an age that is characterised by growing insecurity. It would also provide them with resources and opportunities to redefine established roles with regard to notions of work and wage labour, for instance to explore activities not necessarily linked to wage labour, but to other kinds of activities, such as self-organised work of different kinds.

The second theme concerns models of public governance, or how welfare institutions could be organised to take into account an experimentalist ambition among citizens. The greater picture outlined by Beck regards a challenge to develop models that could help citizens to live together as equals and yet be different. In this respect, Beck makes a distinction between *control norms* and *constitutive norms*. Unfortunately he did not clarify this distinction in greater detail, and only briefly commented that 'the central point to keep clear is that in the age of the self-chosen life, individuals can no longer be integrated by control norms and their pre-given either/ors' (Beck and Willms, 2004, p 89). As I understand, Beck means that control norms build on detailed social and legal rules and regulations, which too rigidly steer individuals and citizens and place them within fixed bureaucratic categories. In contrast, he argues in favour of constitutive norms, which 'encourage and provide security, which make the experiments of the self-chosen life possible, and which keep individualization from careering off into atomization' (Beck and Willms, 2004, p 89). Without explicitly relating these norm types to the role of the welfare state, Beck's comments have implications for how welfare states could interact with citizens. Arguably, Beck means that detailed rules tend to place citizens in fixed categories and steer professional activities and welfare services too rigidly. In contrast, constitutive norms such as governance by goals or frame-laws open up for more flexible services that – at least potentially – take individuals' needs and wishes as the starting point for any discussion on social welfare. Hence, a challenge for public authorities is to develop constitutive norms, in which lay knowledge has implications on the design and outcome of welfare services, in the meaning of giving citizens the opportunity to be equal and yet different.

The third theme brings forward another aspect of the notion of radical individualisation, concerning how welfare states can best involve citizens in decision-making procedures; in a broader and more dynamic manner than usually is the case. Beck discusses this point in greater length, as a general issue of democracy and participation. According to Beck, the great undertaking ahead concerns *establishing new ways for collective decision making*, for instance by empowering the civil society 'to open up an institutional space between the state and the market for the creativity and self-responsibility of individuals' (Beck and Willms, 2004, pp 96ff). In his account, welfare states need to sub-politicise politics, that is, to open up current democratic decision-making structures and practices to new subgroups, small groups, citizen groups, local forums and round tables. In Beck's view, these methods constitute important reinventions of the democratic and political system. His comments concern broader issues regarding democratic innovation, but, as indicated above, welfare research has also moved in a similar direction, regarding notions such as welfare democracy. Concepts of this kind aim to change the perspective in welfare (and activation) studies and shed light on what possibilities citizens have to express their voice in relation to public authorities and professionals: what room is there for negotiation, influence and participation on their behalf? Most likely, Beck would have considered these investigations as too narrow, user-oriented and not sufficiently analysing what alternative participatory models citizens develop in relation to the welfare state and its services. In that sense, user-oriented models might promote higher degrees of participation of clients, but a more complete understanding of radical individualisation would similarly draw on a broader involvement of actors and a broader recognition of what issues to discuss. Beck's perspective on sub-politicisation then includes, for instance, citizens' counter-strategies, collective mobilisation and forms of organisation that unemployed citizens develop in relation to their voluntary/involuntary participation in activation measures, as a way to express their agency.

To sum up, Beck identifies a set of themes that mark out the contours of how welfare states can organise activation services to best promote radical individualisation and social entrepreneurship. First, use wide definitions of work and valuable activities in the institutional set-up of income maintenance systems. Second, implement governance methods that draw on constitutive norms meaning that public authorities set up a broad regulative framework for engagement with citizens. Third, install decision-making procedures that rest on a broad involvement of actors and broad recognition of what issues are to be discussed.

These themes have corresponding significance for analyses of activation policy in general and individual approaches in activation in particular. First, what is the general profile of activation policies in a national and local context: does the activation offer mainly concern work-first-oriented policies or workfare policies, or does it include a broader variety of activities? Second, what kinds of governance methods are being used in national and local activation policies and projects: are these public interventions based on constitutive norms, or detailed regulations regarding how states and citizens will interact? Third, what kind of decision-making procedures are being used: is the content and planning of activation activities an issue designed and decided by public officials and experts only, or does the outline of activation involve a broad collection of actors, including the activated citizens, but also possibly civil society actors and third sector organisations?

New forms of disciplinary techniques?

Beck's normatively oriented propositions are thoughtful and provocative, but also somewhat surprising, since they stand in sharp contrast to the sociological criticism that constitutes the starting position for his investigations on risk and individualisation. It is possible to unpack this blind spot by using academic discussions that have updated Foucault's views on discipline and control (Burchell et al, 1991; Rose, 1996, 1999; Dean, 1999a). These discussions have much in common with Beck's individualisation thesis and his view on social risks, but there is a major discrepancy regarding the role of the welfare state and the potential of public action. The analytical challenge outlined in these post-Foucault analyses, concerns not the development of new normative models, but the identification of how contemporary societies *continue to govern* by using models that are linked 'to a form of governing that seeks to govern not through society but through the responsible and prudential choices and actions of individuals on behalf of themselves and those for whom they feel an emotional bond or affinity' (Dean, 1999b, pp 133-4).

Within this academic discourse, it is claimed that contemporary states increasingly govern by using means that operate 'at a distance', or by using what Foucault referred to as 'technologies of freedom'. The analytical intention with these propositions is to shed light on the ways in which states govern through, and not in spite of, the autonomous choices of individuals (Rose, 2000, p 324). The first step in similar governance methods is then to specify what constitutes (individual) agency and activity, and thereby to open up a new set of technologies that define individuals as prudent actors, supposed to plan and exercise responsibility. This naturally takes many different forms. Contemporary citizens are discursively constituted as responsible agents and encouraged and enforced to be capable and obliged to handle social risks of different kinds and their own future welfare (Dwyer, 1999). Welfare states increasingly interact with citizens and citizen groups using methods such as contracting, consulting, negotiating or creating partnerships. These governance methods then aim to 'empower and activate forms of agency, liberty and the choices of individuals, consumers, professionals, households, neighbourhoods and communities' (Dean, 1999a, p 165).

In other words, governing 'at a distance' includes methods that aim to reach a situation where individual subjectivity is constituted by individuals (or groups) themselves, that is, where citizens and individuals use different technologies of ethical self-formation, such as 'practices, techniques and rationalities concerning the regulation of the self by the self, and by means of which individuals seek to question, form, know, decipher and act on themselves' (Dean, 1995, p 563). Hence, governing 'at a distance' implies that welfare states and public authorities exercise control by setting 'norms, standards, benchmarks, performance indicators, quality controls and best practice standards, to monitor, measure and render calculable the performance of these various agencies' (Dean, 1999a, p 165).

Considering this analytical approach, the growing complexity in society demands that the conduct of citizens can only be controlled effectively if citizens operate under the illusion that they are autonomous, able to pursue individual preferences, make choices and influence how the decisions of others affect their lives. From this perspective, participatory dialogues with representatives of public activation agencies, instalment of individual action plans, or user involvement models have mainly a disciplinary function; that is, to persuade the citizens involved about the need for them to take responsibility for changing their own situation by thinking and behaving in the way that is desirable from the perspective of these agencies, or, specifically, complying with the norms of being an active and responsible citizen.

These propositions challenge us to think of individual approaches in activation in a new manner and that similar techniques of governance constitute possibilities for public authorities to govern, control and/ or discipline individuals beyond their capacity and formal authority as activation workers (for example, Sol and Westerveld, 2005). This not only makes our understanding of Beck's view on individualisation more precise, but we are also offered a different answer on what welfare states really do in the age of individualisation. Despite Beck's certainty that his welfare strategies, governance and decision-making models could promote social entrepreneurship and an experimentalist attitude among citizens, these could in addition be interpreted as examples of how states govern 'at a distance', as they all draw on the agency and participation of citizens and users.

However, there is a risk that these analytical propositions lead us into a dead end. Despite the illustration of how policies that aim to strengthen citizens' autonomy and capacity might represent new forms of discipline and control, this does not necessarily mean that similar policies fail to complete their objective. User-oriented services, partnership models or individual action plans might be tools that actually provide citizens with possibilities to have greater influence on their personal situation and on what kinds of services they are offered by public authorities, or instruments that provide them with greater confidence and courage to criticise and file complaints against public authorities.

Conclusions

This chapter has explored how Beck's individualisation thesis both confirms and challenges much current reasoning on activation. First and foremost, individualisation implies a new situation for welfare states *and* citizens. Due to several different challenges (which Beck barely touches upon), welfare states have started to redefine the social citizenship contract; social responsibilities nowadays tend to lie with the individual; and the right to social protection is increasingly determined by the behaviour, choices, attitudes and motivations of the individual, that is, an individualisation of social risks. As presented in this chapter, there appears to be 'a goodness of fit' between Beck's argument and the burgeoning literature on activation and this research discourse then offers empirical answers to the kind of criticism that Alexander (1996) was referring to. For students of activation, Beck's thesis is much more challenging when it comes to new forms of individual activities, as he claims that citizens (either willingly or reluctantly) act with greater confidence, competence and capacity in relation to welfare services and activation officers. He thereby directs attention to research themes that only moderately have been discussed in studies of activation. If we follow Beck on this point, we more seriously have to consider activated citizens' (counter-) strategies and the collective mobilisation that activation might imply in different contexts. Equally important is to study whether activation workers manage (or aim) to recognise the client, not only as a user, but as a full citizen with a right to have a voice and take part in discussions and debates regarding the profile of activation services.

This chapter has also explored the role of the welfare state in processes of individualisation. According to Beck, the welfare state has historically been an important actor to provide citizens with adequate resources and competencies to adapt an experimentalist attitude towards traditions and social structures. He believes that contemporary welfare states have a similar role to play, and if welfare states develop the right kind of strategies and models of governance they can promote the kind of social entrepreneurship that Beck is in favour of. Thereby students of activation are provided with a standard to assess activation programmes. However, one needs to be careful in adopting these standards, above all as they carry ambiguous messages to citizens. Even though it might appear as if the welfare state has stepped back from previous ambitions to control and discipline citizens, Beck's standards might also be considered as disciplinary techniques, resting on new forms of self-regulation and self-control, encouraged and perhaps even controlled by the state. Models of governance that aim to install individual autonomy, choice and capacity, could then be defined as examples of new forms of control 'at a distance'. However, which of these perspectives most accurately pictures what takes place between welfare states/activation officers and activated citizens not only needs more detailed analytical clarifications, but perhaps even more solid empirical investigations, in order to overcome the pitfalls of two broad and somewhat vague analytical perspectives.

References

Alexander, J. (1996) 'Critical reflections on '*Reflexive modernization*'', *Theory, Culture & Society*, vol 13, pp 133-8.

Allen, J. and Henry, N. (1997) 'Ulrich Beck's risk society at work: labour and employment in the contract service industries', *Transactions of the Institute of British Geographers*, vol 22, pp 180-96.

Bauman, Z. (2001) *The individualized society*, Cambridge: Polity Press.

Beck, U. (1992) *Risk society: Towards a new modernity*, London: Sage Publications.

Beck, U. (1994) 'The reinvention of politics: towards a theory of reflexive modernization', in U. Beck, A. Giddens and S. Lash (eds) *Reflexive modernization: Politics, tradition and aesthetics in the modern social order*, Stanford, CA: Stanford University Press, pp 1-55.

Beck, U. (1999) 'Goodbye to all that wage slavery', *New Statesman*, March, pp 25-7.

Beck, U. (2000) *The brave new world of work*, Cambridge: Polity Press.

Beck, U. and Beck-Gernsheim, E. (2002) *Individualization*, London: Sage Publications.

Beck, U. and Willms, J. (2004) *Conversations with Beck*, Cambridge: Polity Press.

Boyne, R. and Beck, U. (2001) 'Cosmopolis and risk: a conversation with Ulrich Beck', *Theory, Culture & Society*, vol 18, no 4, pp 47-63.

Burchell, G., Gordon, C. and Miller, P. (1991) *The Foucault effect: Studies in governmentality*, Chicago, IL: University of Chicago Press.

Deacon, A. (2004) 'Review article: different interpretations of agency within welfare debates', *Social Policy and Society*, vol 3, no 4, pp 447-55.

Deacon, A. and Mann, K. (1998) 'Agency, modernity and social policy', *Journal of Social Policy*, vol 28, no 3, pp 413-35.

Dean, M. (1995) 'Governing the unemployed self in an active society', *Economy and Society*, vol 24, no 4, pp 559-83.

Dean, M. (1999a) *Governmentality: Power and rule in modern society*, London: Sage Publications.

Dean, M. (1999b) 'Risk, calculable and incalculable', in D. Lupton (ed) *Risk and sociocultural theory: New directions and perspectives*, Cambridge: Cambridge University Press, pp 131-59.

Dingwall, R. (1999) '"Risk society": the cult of theory and the Millennium', *Social Policy & Administration*, vol 33, no 4, pp 474-91.

Dwyer, P. (2000) *Welfare rights and responsibilities: Contesting social citizenship*, Bristol: The Policy Press.

Ekinsmyth, C. (1999) 'Professional workers in a risk society', *Transactions of the Institute of British Geographers*, vol 24, pp 353-66.

Fitzpatrick, T. (2002) 'In search of welfare democracy', *Social Policy and Society*, vol 1, no 1, pp 11-20.

Gorz, A. (2000) *Reclaiming work: Beyond the wage based society*, Oxford: Basil Blackwell.

Goul Andersen, J. and Jensen, P. H. (2002) *Changing labour markets, welfare policies and citizenship*, Bristol: The Policy Press.

Hoggett, P. (2001) 'Agency, rationality and social policy', *Journal of Social Policy*, vol 30, no 1, pp 37-56.

Lash, S. (1994) 'Reflexivity and its doubles: structure, aesthetics, community', in U. Beck, A. Giddens and S. Lash (eds) *Reflexive modernization: Politics, tradition and aesthetics in the modern social order*, Stanford, CA: Stanford University Press, pp 110-73.

Le Grand, J. (1997) 'Knights, knaves or pawns? Human behaviour and social policy', *Journal of Social Policy*, vol 26, no 2, pp 149-69.

Lødemel, I. and Trickey, H. (2001) *'An offer you can't refuse': Workfare in international perspective*, Bristol: The Policy Press.

Lupton, D. and Tulloch, J. (2002) "Risk is part of your life': risk epistemologies among groups of Australians', *Sociology*, vol 36, no 2, pp 317-34.

Mythen, G. (2004) *Ulrich Beck: A critical introduction to the risk society*, London: Pluto Press.

Mythen, G. (2005) 'Employment, individualization and insecurity: rethinking the risk society perspective', *The Sociological Review*, vol 53, pp 129-50.

Ostner, I. (2003) "Individualisation': the origins of the concept and its impact in German social policies', *Social Policy and Society*, vol 3, no 1, pp 47-56.

Plougmann, P. (2002) 'Internationalisation and the labour market of the European Union', in J. Goul Andersen and P. H. Jensen (eds) *Changing labour markets, welfare policies and citizenship*, Bristol: The Policy Press, pp 15-38.

Rose, N. (1996) *Inventing our selves*, Cambridge: Cambridge University Press.

Rose, N. (1999) *Powers of freedom: Reframing political thought*, Cambridge: Cambridge University Press.

Rose, N. (2000) 'Government and control', *British Journal of Criminology*, vol 40, pp 321-39.

Scott, A. (2000) 'Risk society or angst society? Two views of risk, consciousness and community', in B. Adam, U. Beck and J. van Loom (eds) *The risk society and beyond: Critical issues for social theory*, London: Sage Publications, pp 33-46.

Sennett, R. (1998) *The corrosion of character: The personal consequences of work in the new capitalism*, New York: W. W. Norton & Company.

Serrano, A. (ed) (2004) *Are activation policies converging in Europe? The European Employment Strategy for young people*, Brussels: ETUI.

Sol, E. and Westerveld, M. (2005) *Contractualism in employment services: A new form of welfare state governance*, The Hague: Kluwer Law International.

Stråth, B. (2000) *After full employment: European discourses on work and flexibility*, Brussels: P. I. E. Peter Lang.

Taylor-Gooby, P. (2001) 'Risk, contingency and the Third Way: evidence from the BHPS and qualitative studies', *Social Policy & Administration*, vol 35, no 2, pp 195-211.

Taylor-Gooby, P., Dean, H., Munro, M. and Parker, G. (1999) 'Risk and the welfare state', *British Journal of Sociology*, vol 50, no 2, pp 177-94.

Tulloch, J. and Lupton, D. (2003) *Risk and everyday life*, London: Sage Publications.

Van Berkel, R. and Hornemann Møller, I. (2002) *Active social policies in the EU: Inclusion through participation?*, Bristol: The Policy Press.

Williams, F., Popay, J. and Oakley, A. (1999) *Welfare research: A critical review*, London: UCL Press.

FIVE

User involvement in personal social services

Ilse Julkunen and Matti Heikkilä

Introduction

Focusing on the user in the welfare service sector has been emphasised since the 1990s. Governments throughout Western Europe have encouraged users to contribute to the planning and development of social and health services (Crawford et al, 2005). There is also a growing user movement dedicated to promoting rights-based access to social care and a changing role for human services users (Fisher, 2002). Interest in service user perspectives and participation still appears to be episodic, however. In the 1970s service user studies were linked to the growing claims of enhancing the public sector (see Chapter Two). Social commitments had increased as well as problems of bureaucracy. User studies were performed to get an overview of the problems inherent in the interaction between authorities and users. In the 1980s the focus was more on developing the administration and finding more flexible forms of service (for example, Grönroos, 1987). Interestingly, however, studies were rather provider oriented and user perceptions gained only marginal focus and were at most indirectly investigated.

The early 1990s witnessed an audit explosion, at least in Britain, driven by 'reinvention of governance', through an increasing interest in quality management that produced a plethora of quality audits (Power, 1997). In the late 1990s and at the beginning of the 2000s an increased emphasis on user involvement can be seen as a means of modernising welfare services, at least in the Nordic countries. In Denmark, the modernising programme (www.moderniseringsprogram.dk) states that by modernising the public sector, the government aims to focus services on the needs of citizens. The government is committed to creating public services that are coherent, accessible and responsive, rather than organised for the provider's convenience. Similarly, in Norway the modernising programme emphasises that citizens are able to participate, to know their rights and their responsibilities, to feel secure in front of the authority, and to receive good-quality and accessible services. On a European level, recent policies addressing unemployment in general and the integration of disadvantaged groups in particular have stressed a shift to active labour market policies and the need to mobilise individuals to engage more in their own processes of social inclusion and labour market integration. This is reflected by two key policy trends: a shift towards activation, and individual plans as a fundamental means of activation policies.

Hence, currently the focus on user perceptions is grounded in an ideological shift that emphasises the responsibilities of the individual and the reshaping of welfare services. User involvement is, thus, considered important in assuring the quality of services, in developing existing services and in shaping new forms of services. The underlying assumptions are that involving users leads to more responsive services and better outcomes. Including the users in evaluations of welfare services is seen as an appropriate tool for generating standards that reflect the rationality of the users (Krogstrup, 2004). Still, the idea of user involvement is overlain by contrasting and often conflicting aims and expectations. At the practical level, user involvement is exploring different forms of involvement, given that service providers are uncertain of the 'how and what' of user involvement.

Reflecting user involvement

With an increased emphasis on involving service users in the welfare service sector, there is a clear need to explore the rhetoric of what user involvement entails. How is user involvement defined and argued and what elements and levels can be found?

Although there is a high degree of interest in user involvement it has not entailed any consensus on the conception of that involvement. Karen Healey (2000) has, for instance, claimed that there is no universal definition of user participation or user involvement. The concept must always be placed in a context. User involvement is thus construed and perceived differently in different contexts. In the context of welfare services, user involvement is often perceived as the possibilities of users to affect the content and quality of public service. User involvement is not one-dimensional, however, and one can distinguish between collective and individual, and indirect and direct user involvement. There are, for instance, collective forms of user involvement such as formalised boards of users and involvement can be indirect through user feedback or direct when users actively take part in the planning and development of the services. It is also essential to distinguish between different levels of involvement (Truman and Raine, 2002), in other words: (1) at a national and local level; (2) in the planning, organisation and management of public services; and (3) in the organisation of individual services.

User involvement and user participation are sometimes regarded as synonymous. In spite of this, however, it is useful to remember that *user involvement entails preconditions that the users' activity has an impact on the service process in some way*. Therefore distinguishing between user involvement and user participation is helpful, as user participation means that users are only taking part in some activity or only serve as informants. A distinction needs also to be made between involvement and participation and more far-reaching empowerment strategies. On the other hand, Shaw (1997) argues that it may be misleading to use the language of empowerment to describe participation and involvement. Empowerment is seldom mentioned in statutory and official guidelines but when it is, what is usually intended is enabling in the sense of promoting participation and involvement, not empowerment in the sense of professionals giving up their power and control. In many cases it is clear that the initial motivation and enthusiasm for empowering activities has come not from users themselves but from professionals concerned that this would be good for users. To some extent, however, the idea of professionally led empowerment can be seen as a contradiction in terms. It assumes that the professional knows best about the particular dimension of the customers' lives for which empowerment is needed as well as about the particular ways in which empowerment will be achieved. All too often users are seen as the passive recipients of mentoring, and any failure to comply with its agenda is interpreted as deviancy.

Involvement and participation have frequently been classified and typologised, beginning with a ladder of participation indicating different levels of participation (Arnstein, 1969). The ladder of citizen participation has been a useful way of characterising levels of public involvement, ranging from the ideal of citizen control to manipulation by officials and powerful interest groups. It has been used successfully in many studies and also other forms of typologies have been developed. Essentially, user involvement is seen as a continuum and an extending process, from weaker to stronger or from more passive forms towards more active forms of involvement (Figure 5.1).

There is, however, a need to reflect on the term 'user' and to disaggregate the broad category of user. User participation may have a different meaning for different users, for voluntary and involuntary

Figure 5.1: User involvement as a four-stage process

1	**User management** Users at the leading level; define, formulate and frame the service
2	**User influence** Users as independent and competent individuals or groups in developing quality
3	**User involvement** Users as involved in contributing to changes in the provision of services
4	**User participation** Users as informants

users, long– and short–term users and current and potential users. It is underpinned by, for instance, very different views about the nature of power and the relationship between those who possess power and those who do not, as Valkenburg points out in Chapter Two. The power relation between users and service providers can be conceptualised by using the concepts of 'exit' and 'voice' (Hirschman, 1970). Hirschman's theory has been used, for instance, to study whether the present reality of welfare pluralism lives up to the expected merits (de Campo, 2005). It raises such questions as: to what extent does the user of social services have the possibilities of choice, and can users be regarded as consumers or as clients? While exit and voice options can co–exist in the same organisation they are fundamentally different. According to Burns et al (1994) the market model gives, in theory at least, individuals the power of exit. The democratic process again relies on individuals or groups having the power of voice while dissatisfied customers obtain a response by taking political action. Shaw (1997), on the other hand, argues that in the language of consumerism the distinction between involuntary and voluntary service users is given too little recognition and addresses the problem that passive consent is too often taken to mean agreement. The context has a great impact on how exit and voice can be materialised. Hence, the way services are organised and funded may play a major role when determining the rationale and the degree of freedom, or independence, of the individual user.

What then are the arguments for increasing user involvement? Dahlberg and Vedung (2001) account for some motives:

- The organisation provides better-quality services (service adaptation argument).

- There is higher efficiency while goals are achieved (efficiency argument).
- The imbalance between users and the administration is rectified (empowerment argument).
- The system achieves a higher acceptance and support (legitimacy argument).
- Involvement as such is positive and strengthens self-reliance among participants (expression argument).
- There is education in democracy (citizen education argument).

The service adaptation argument is based on the connotation that the basic aim and target of services is to serve the users. The users' preferences and needs should be the basis of the service. This relationship is of course not that straightforward; it is connected to how services are defined, whether there are social rights or not. Users of social services are also not customers as such, they do not usually pay directly for their services (although they do indirectly through taxes) and they are seldom in a position where they can choose their service. Nevertheless, the service should be adapted to the users' needs and requirements and their preferences is one way of evaluating the services. Effective consumerism depends on the possibility of active consumers. Hence, user involvement that is committed to any degree to empowerment should include the development of quality and performance measures based on criteria owned by service users (Shaw, 1997).

The citizen education argument suggests that participation will educate the participants on civic virtues so that they will become better members of the community in the future. This democratic schooling is expected to occur as a side-effect. The participants will acquire civic skills, which they may use later on and in other contexts (Vedung, 2004). Krogstrup (2004) states that it is important to distinguish between different inherent understandings. The efficiency argument is linked to a top-down understanding. The citizen education argument, the expression argument, and the empowerment argument are, on the other hand, linked to a bottom-up understanding.

Looking at the knowledge base on user studies, we can argue that studies to date have been more concerned with consumers' rights, such as with quality assurance, customer care and the rights of redress and exit (Taylor, 1991). Also the model for service user questionnaires seems to be generally based on models from market research in the private sector (Lehto, 1994). The critics point out that user satisfaction surveys are not providing a valid image of user satisfaction. The argument is that the users are responding to questions considered relevant by those determining the criteria and these questions are not necessarily the same as those the users consider to be relevant (Krogstrup, 2004). It also seems that the basis of service user studies has been poorly grounded and lacks a coherent theory. Most studies appear to have a fixed preconception of welfare services. Services are services which exist today and not future services which could be created on the basis of the expectations and needs of community members. Some studies have proven that involving users has contributed to changes in service provision, but the effects of these on the quality of services have not been reported (Crawford et al, 2005). Truman and Raine (2002), for instance, claim that there has been a long tradition within the voluntary sector of centring the planning and delivery of services on the needs of users. However, when it comes to incorporating democratic approaches into mainstream social care this approach is rather rare.

Different strands and routes to user involvement

Croft and Beresford (1996) have elaborated on the politics of participation and defined two different approaches to user involvement: the consumerist and the democratic approaches. Beresford (2002) points out that while it can be argued that the two approaches to involvement may blur into each other, with overlapping interests and objectives, they can also be seen to be based on distinct and different philosophical and ideological approaches. The emergence of consumerist thinking on welfare services has coincided with the expansion of commercial provision and political pressure for a changed economy of welfare in the 1980s. Welfare services were criticised for their inefficiency and bureaucracy. The pressure towards creating cheaper services grew. The roots of the democratic approach extend further back than the welfare state 'crisis'. In its broader sense the roots of the wider discussions of democracy extend back nearly 3,000 years, although the seeds of the current discussion are traced to the early 1970s when concrete forms of participation were being created (social planning, community development). Thus, the consumerist and the democratic approaches reflect different philosophies and objectives. The consumerist approach stems from service providers. Their interest is in improving management to achieve greater economy and efficiency, but also to give consumers a choice. The democratic approach, on the other hand, has largely been developed by service users and their organisations. Their primary concern has been with empowerment, improving the power to influence and providing the possibility of a voice.

If we look more closely into these approaches, other forms of thinking can also be found. Evers (2003) has developed a model of five strands, which are based on a document entitled 'Current strands in debating user involvement in social services' written for the Council of Europe Group of Specialists in Social Services (CS-US). According to Evers the strands cannot be considered as being on the same level. Labels like 'welfarism' and 'consumerism' are pointing to widespread ideologies that refer to society as a whole, while professionalism can be seen as a more limited and specific hallmark that has been brought about along with the development of the welfare state. The same may be said about managerialism and its link to consumerism: the extension of market-based concepts and thinking has changed the vocabulary and points of reference within the administration of social services. Framed mainly in market research terms of 'improving the product' through market testing and feedback, the consumerist approach has so far mainly been based on consultative and data collection methods of involvement. Still, as Beresford (2002) argues, these may include participatory initiatives, having effective outcomes for service users. Finally, what is summed up under the term 'participationism' can be seen as a set of beliefs that can to some degree overlap both with more traditional welfarist concepts (that give a strong role to politics and thereby to users as citizens) and with consumerist concepts (that want to upgrade the role of markets and thereby the role of users as consumers). These different strands may be very helpful dimensions that visualise different focuses and different tools and show also how these strands hold both traditional and modern elements.

Thus, when examining the realities of user involvement in different countries it is important to distinguish between different approaches and thinking and also to take into consideration what role user organisations have in developing user involvement in social services. At the same time the figure visualises that different approaches and different mechanisms serve different purposes. What is important, however, is to be clear about our understandings of involvement and to recognise differences in the thinking and objectives of these approaches (Figure 5.2).

What services and what users?

Although we limit our focus in this chapter to personal social services, the internal variation of the concept (kinds of services) is still remarkable

Figure 5.2: User involvement in social services: various strands of thinking, elements and tools

Welfarism	• hierarchical governance of service systems • full coverage/uniform services • equal standards • boards and commissions for corporate governance • quality control by state inspection • social rights and patients' charter
Professionalism	• case management • upgrading of educational levels • upgrading of professional advice and consultancy • quality control through professional self-control • public service ethos
Consumerism	• competition • individual choice • market research • vouchers • customer orientation • consumer lobbying • consumer protection
Managerialism	• managed care • target setting • upgrading managerial and economic concerns • external quality management • complaint management
Participationism	• collective self-help • volunteering • strengthening user- and community-based service providers • strengthening local embeddedness • orientation towards empowering users • more service dialogues • more user control in designing and running services

Source: Evers (2003)

when it comes to user involvement. The whole question of user involvement or the formal and actual position of the client vis-à-vis the service provider can be considered in a different way: in standard universal services of childcare than in social work practices linked to social assistance, for instance.

When reflecting upon this issue of various kinds of social services and its impact on involvement we might need a limited number of key dimensions along which the basic distinctions can be made. The 1980s and 1990s were full of intelligent rhetoric and also empirical research about welfare regimes and models, but almost none of them were based on services. The dominant position of transfers has been and still is remarkable. The same is reflected in the social protection policies boosted by the European Union. Among the few exercises trying to develop models, regimes or classifications in the field of social services and/or social care, one can mention Alber (1995), Anttonen and Sipilä (1996) and Rostgaard (2002). One useful distinction that can be made when examining various kinds of social services is based on the following two fundamental questions:

- Are the services responding to an individual (social) problem or need, or to a dependency due to old age, disability or young age (small children)?
- Are there clearly defined criteria for accessing services (eligibility criteria) or are the services to a high degree discretionary (needs or means tested)?

Dependency-oriented versus problem-oriented services

A lot of confusion has emerged around the duration of need. In countries where there is a relatively large public responsibility in welfare, considerable public service systems have been created to compensate for the missing functional capability caused by permanent disability and old age. The same goes for child protection. Essential for these types of dependency-oriented services is that they tend to be permanent or at least long-lasting solutions from the user's point of view and that the whole idea of the service intervention is to respond to a permanent, sometimes even increasing, dependency. These services then are seen as remedies aiming at compensating for the insufficient functional ability. They can be organised in different ways and by different actors – that is, by the public sector, family and even the market. Very often the term (social) care has been used as a synonym for this type of services.

The street-level understanding of social services is often problem-orientated. They are by their nature targeted. These services are meant for relieving some individual or family problem that has been collectively defined as a problem. In these services there is a tendency towards problem solving, they tend to be curative and normalising. The ultimate aim is to get the client back into mainstream society and the labour force, with the rehabilitation or the return of their own life management skills. Typical target groups of this type of services are drug addicts, alcoholics, ex-criminals, minority ethnic groups (integration services), lone mothers, immigrants, problem families (in child protection activities), long-term unemployed people, and poor people in general. In an ideal case, the duration of the need (and use) of service is limited. Problem-oriented social services are often seen as a part of the general regulating system of deviance and non-coherence.

Why is it then so important to recognise the distinction between the two types of services? It is because their underlying logic is so different. The often-heard phrase is that the basic aim of social work is to make its own services less necessary. In this sense the need and use of social services can be seen as an indirect indicator of social problems and disintegration in a given society. But this holds only when talking about problem-oriented services, and definitely not when talking about the dependency-driven services. The dependency services are, with good reason, called the middle-class services. This is why in ageing societies the political and financial weight of social services is on the increase.

Strong service rights or strong discretion?

A basic characteristic of almost all social services is that access to services is up to professional discretion. The perceived need of the client is decisive and interpreted by the professional. In a positive way discretion means interpreting individual circumstances and tailoring services to the needs of the individual. Discretion can also be seen as an opposite pole to strong social rights particularly with regard to means testing the individual's need for social assistance. However, the new element of economic constraints has put professionals in a new situation. An important factor preventing more objective criteria for service delivery is budgetary constraints. In this context, targeting may mean cost-effectiveness but above all it means cost management. Cost-effectiveness is also related to neo-liberalism and shifts the responsibility of the welfare state to the individual's responsibility.

From a user's perspective the obvious discretionary nature of services – sometimes even arbitrariness – creates uncertainty and decreases the predictability of personal options. This lack of reasonable, strong service rights is especially obvious in problem-oriented services – for children in need of custody, but also for dependency services and frail older people. Services for unemployed people can also be placed under problem-oriented services. For this group, services may mean new obligations, contracts or requirements to alter their behaviour (Julkunen, 2001).

The lack of clearly defined rights to access is also the key difference to social benefits, especially insurance-based benefits. Statutory subjective rights to services are relatively rare. However, in Finland there are three examples – childcare services for all children under school age, certain housing services for disabled people and a flat-rate, means-tested social assistance for everybody meeting the national minimum income norm. The problem with strong rights is that they tend to be very expensive, even if the client fees could cover some 15%–40% of the total costs. A recent tendency on the way towards stronger rights is to define fixed time intervals (maximum number of days from the first contact) within which the client has a right to have their needs adequately assessed.

The dimensions of rights or discretion on the one hand and dependency-oriented and problem-oriented services on the other can create a sort of quadrant (Figure 5.3). This quadrant is welfare-regime specific as it exemplifies the situation in the Nordic countries and more specifically in Finland.

What are the consequences of these distinctions for user involvement? First we have to ask whether there is any dependency or correlation between these two axes and dimensions and what kinds of services tend to be located in each field of the quadrant. From a Nordic welfare-regime perspective we can see that services for homelessness, drug addiction and child protection are underpinned by weak rights, professional discretion and needs targeting. Social assistance on the other hand is more clearly defined as a social right.

Figure 5.3: Coordinates of social services

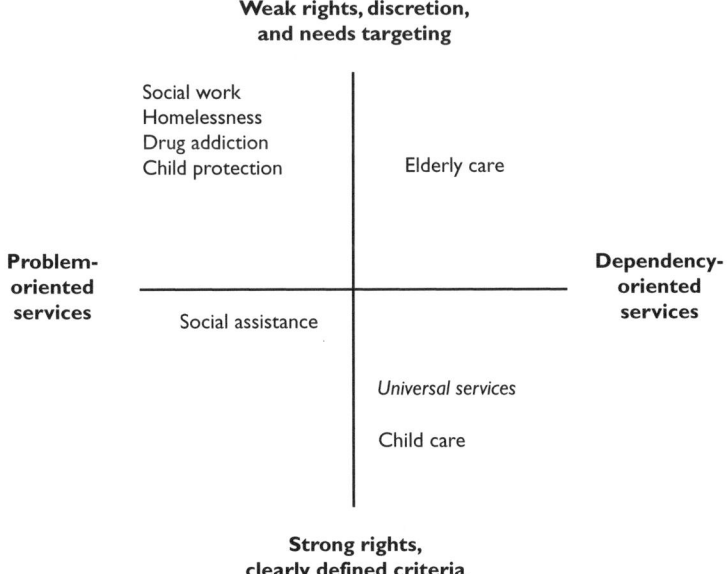

We can argue that:

- Problem-oriented services tend to imply more professional discretion (when it comes to access) than dependency-oriented services.
- An interesting exception in some welfare regimes is the case of social assistance. If the national or regional norms for calculating the right to and the amount of this benefit are clear and 'universal', one can talk about strong social rights of poor people even if the whole concept of social assistance implies the idea of needs and means testing.
- In the dependency-compensating category of services there is more pressure to ensure that clear criteria of access are defined.
- In this category belong most of the so-called universal services like child care, elderly care, especially home help, whereas social services and social work in a narrow sense fit in the high discretion–weak rights class.

Having said this we can put forward some hypotheses regarding the possibility of user involvement in the different types of services outlined above. At least tentatively one can argue that:

- The more there is one-sided (professional) discretion both in regulating access to services and in internal implementation, the weaker the rights of users/clients, even potential users, and the more vague the base for proper user involvement and participation.
- The users of services entailing high discretion and needs assessment and a problem orientation tend to be disadvantaged, poor people whose voice is weak and whose political weight is small.
- Many of the services characterised here as dependency-oriented are meant for all who can demonstrate a proof of need and therefore they can be called middle-class services. Even if this is not true in all societies (where public care services are provided only for poor people), the role of users can approach that of consumers and consumers can become mobilised and can also constitute a remarkable actor politically.

Coming back to user involvement we can assume that the need to define the formal position, rights and obligations of the user is especially urgent in services where the dependency is comprehensive, such as in institutional/residential care. In practice, in elderly care the clients may lack the capabilities to participate and advocate their interests and therefore need external support. In childcare services the whole question of user involvement concerns the parents. In traditional, social work-oriented services (homelessness, addiction, child protection and those for underprivileged people) the unequal negotiation setting is inherent between the client and the professional and thus new efficient mechanisms are needed to increase user involvement.

Rhetoric and realities?

Croft and Beresford (1996) argue that when we look at the substantive purposes that participatory arrangements may actually serve, we discover that they are not consistent with people's effective involvement and increased say. Instead, other functions are identified, such as, for instance, *incorporation*: people are drawn into participatory arrangements which limit and divert their effective action; *legitimation*: people's involvement is used to give the appearance of their agreement and consent, and thus participation serves as a public relations exercise and window dressing.

As Munday (2001) has stated, until very recently the users of most public services had very little involvement in decisions about services they received. In the old-fashioned spirit of paternalistic social work, the main approach has been to provide social services with well-meaning social workers and other professional staff believing they knew what was best for their clients. Paternalism has thus been one of the main driving forces. Hence, critical feedback of users is still of recent origin within personal social services and has a long way to go before becoming part of the fabric of routine practice (Shaw, 1997).

One factor that may limit user participation in a face-to-face context is the lack of information, skills and opportunities to implement the rights to participate. One may also argue that sometimes the staff members of a given service can feel professionally threatened by the increased interest of their clients to participate – not only in their own case but also on an institutional level. When it comes to professionals, Fisher (1983) has, for instance, asked how far we can be confident that social workers will be open to an idea that may raise uncomfortable questions about their established routines. An activation of service users can be seen and felt as an extra burden for hard-working professionals. This is a cultural issue as well. If the professional identity and position of staff members is not strong enough, the sense of threat when exposed to questions may emerge. Hence, professionalism can be seen as a barrier. There is a risk that social workers are used to being in control and therefore may have problems in letting users decide for themselves.

On the level of the service institution the active participation of users may take on collective forms. The key client groups can be organised at a local and very often also a national level. The lack of tradition and institutional encouragement can be an obstacle here. Much depends on the initiatives and willingness of the professional staff and especially the management of the service. Nevertheless, both the non-governmental organisations and user organisations have proved crucial in developing and increasing user involvement in social services. This can be seen as the Third Way in politics, beyond the old paternalism and the new consumerism.

It has been supposed that the result of a participatory process itself may be that the position of the user may shift from strictly a consumer role at the beginning of the process towards an adviser to the professionals' role at a later stage in the process – and even end up in the role of a semi-professional. This possible process may be seen as undesirable as well.

A lack of clear legislative measures, that is, law-based definitions of users' (clients') position, rights and obligations may form an obstacle to active participation. At least in the Nordic countries there is relatively advanced legislation – both for patients' rights in healthcare and for clients' rights in social services – that can guide practices and serve as a minimum level. In Finland there are also statutory social ombudsmen at the local level (in each municipality) whose aim is to advocate the needs of service users. On the other hand, there is legislation that creates obstacles to user involvement, for example, coercive laws. However, legislative measures are not sufficient and efforts should be made to develop formal structures and practical measures. This may involve financial support for user organisations and the founding of user boards.

Personal barriers can be traced to different attitudes and different views on involvement. A Swedish research study (Boem and Staples, 2002) has argued that users and professionals have different views on what empowerment entails. The most important aspect for users was concrete outcomes – financial independency and decent living conditions. The professionals, on the other hand, put more emphasis on outcomes such as gained activity and self-reliance of the users. Personal barriers can also be seen when it comes to certain vulnerable groups, such as persons with impaired autonomy. Researcher Barbro Lewin (1998) has, for instance, argued that when the old paternalistic forms are abandoned they should be replaced with a new active interpretation of needs and support in dealing with the authorities. Also Healy (2000) warns that an erroneous interpretation of the participation or involvement concept may in fact lead to the authorities renouncing action in a situation where it would be necessary from a user's perspective. As was stated earlier, the user's participation takes place from a very unequal position. The professional provider holds the position of power; it is the provider who can decide how far participation goes. This is especially true in cases where the client can choose only one single offer and has therefore no consumer choice. The same is true in activation policies, where the right to benefits is determined by the behaviour and motivations of the individual.

In relation to activation policies a more accurate understanding of an individual's disposition could offer a great deal to policy and practice. It would help account for individual agency, including the pragmatically rational aspects of career and lifestyle decisions. The availability of meaningful options that allow for biographical progress may be a cornerstone for future services. This means embedding activation into the personal counselling process where negative incentives prevail and also acknowledging the social and economic factors that influence individual situations and perspectives. Such a perspective avoids the danger of self-blame when the labour market is not easy or attractive to enter.

New structural frameworks and continuous support are then needed. The need for support is evident whenever people are not aware of what is possible and how to get involved. Without clear structures and support there is a risk that only the most confident and well-resourced people become involved. Support may be needed to increase people's expectations, to build up their skills (the educational argument; see Vedung 2004) and to develop alternative approaches to involvement. Support is also needed at the professional as well as at the user level. This continuity in the encounters with users can be seen as 'triggers for learning' (Krogstrup, 2004) or as the emergence of a new reflexive working culture.

We can then assume that increased involvement and participation in personal social services can be obtained in a win-win situation. User involvement is an extending process, ranging from more passive forms towards more active forms. This means taking users beyond the role of passive suppliers of opinion and enabling their role as active negotiators of change. But to be able to step beyond mere rhetoric, different stages of implementing social services (design, delivery, monitoring and evaluation) should be defined and made more concrete in terms of user involvement. All in all, it is a question of developing multiple tools and new reflexive structures and guarantees that protect users' rights.

References

Alber, J. (1995) 'A framework for the comparative study of social services', *Journal of European Social Policy*, vol 5, no 2, pp 131-49.

Anttonen, A. and Sipilä J. (1996) 'European social care services: is it possible to identify models?', *Journal of European Social Policy*, vol 6, no 2, pp 87-100.

Arnstein, S. (1969) 'A ladder of citizen participation', *Journal of the American planning association*, vol 35, no 4, pp 216-24.

Beresford, P. (2002) 'User involvement in research and evaluation: liberation or regulation?', *Social Policy and Society*, vol 1, no 2, pp 95-105.

Boehm, A. and Staples, L. (2002) 'The functions of the social worker in empowering: the voices of consumers and professionals', *Social Work*, vol 47, no 4, pp 449-61.

Burns, D., Hambleton, R. and Hoggett, P. (1994) *The politics of decentralisation: Revitalising local democracy*, London: Macmillan.

Crawford, M., Rutter, D., Manley, C., Weaver, T., Bhui, K., Fulop, N. and Tyrer, P. (2005) 'Systematic review of involving patients in the planning and development of health care', *British Medical Journal*, no 325, p 1263.

Croft, S. and Beresford, P. (1996) 'The politics of participation', in D. Taylor (ed) *Critical social policy: A reader*, London: Sage Publications, pp 175-98.

Dahlberg, M. and Vedung, E. (2001) *Demokrati och brukarutvärdering*, Lund: Studentlitteratur.

di Campo, E. (2005) 'Exit and voice of care: service users in Austria, Belgium, Italy and Northern Ireland', ESA-RN: Ageing-Torun, www.ageing_in_europe.de

Evers, A. (2003) 'Current strands in debating user involvement in social services', Document written for the Council of Europe Group of Specialists in Social Services (CS-US), www.coe.int

Fisher, M. (ed) (1983) *Speaking of clients*, Sheffield: University of Sheffield.

Fisher, M. (2002) 'The role of service users in problem formulation and technical aspects of social research', *Social Work Education*, vol 21, no 3, pp 305-12.

Grönroos, C. (1987) *Hyvään palveluun: Palvelujen kehittäminen julkishallinossa*, Valtionhallinnon kehittämiskeskus. Helsinki: Valtion painatuskeskus.

Healy, K. (2000) *Social work practices: Contemporary perspectives on change*, London: Sage Publications.

Hirshmann, A. (1970) *Exit, voice and loyalty*, Cambridge, MA: Harvard University Press.

Julkunen, I. (2001) 'Individual strategies and job chances: a comparative perspective', *European Journal of Social Work*, vol 4, no 3, pp 275-89.

Krogstrup, H. (2004) 'Evaluation from a user perspective', in I. Julkunen (ed) *Perspective, models and methods in evaluating the welfare sector: A Nordic approach*, FinSoc Working Paper, Helsinki: STAKES, pp 71-82.

Lehto, J. (1994) 'Kunnallisen hyvinvointipolitiikan kysymyksiä', *Dialogi*, no 8, pp 34-6.

Lewin, B. (1998) *Funktionshinder och medborgarskap: Tillkomst och innebörd av de två rättighetslagarna*, Uppsala: Uppsala Universitet.

Munday, B. (2001) 'Key issues in European social services', Paper presented to the conference: 'The Role of Social Services in Sustainable Social Development', Berlin, 25-26 October.

Power, M. (1997) *The audit society: Rituals of verification*, Oxford: Oxford University Press.

Rostgaard, T. (2002) 'Social care regimes: the configuration of care for children and older people in Europe', *Policy Studies*, vol 23, no 1, pp 51-68.

Shaw, I. (1997) 'Engaging the user: participation, empowerment, and the rhetoric of quality', in A. Pithouse and H. Williamson (eds) *Engaging the user in welfare services*, Birmingham: Venture Press.

Truman, C. and Raine, P. (2002) 'Experience and meaning of user involvement: some explorations from a community mental health project', *Health and Social Care in the Community*, vol 10, no 3, pp 136-43.

Vedung, E. (2004) 'Evaluation models and the welfare sector', in I. Julkunen (ed) *Perspective, models and methods in evaluating the welfare sector: A Nordic approach*, FinSoc Working Paper, Helsinki: STAKES, pp 13-39.

Part Two
Individualising activation services:
Case studies

Political production of individualised subjects in the paradoxical discourse of the EU institutions

Eduardo Crespo Suárez and Amparo Serrano Pascual

Introduction

The social policy strategies pursued by the national governments in Europe are inspired, to a considerable extent, by proposals issued by the supranational institutions of the European Union (EU). Analyses of the employment strategy drawn up by the European institutions have been presented in various studies (Goetschy, 1999, 2003; de la Porte and Pochet, 2003; Foden and Magnusson, 2003; Mósesdóttir, 2003; Barbier, 2004; Crespo Suárez and Serrano Pascual, 2004). The purpose of this chapter is to examine certain structural features of the European social policy discourse and, more specifically, the discursive production of individualised subjects in its use of the concept of activation. Our study is conducted on the basis of a theoretical stance that regards the production of discourse as a political and social practice that generates significant forms of action and social effects.

One of the features of discursive practices with regard to social policies consists of the political construction of the targeted subject of intervention (citizen, customer, patient). This construction of the subject implies a justification and legitimation of a series of intervention practices which can, in some cases, be understood as a redistribution policy aimed at redressing what is considered unfair, or else as policies adjusted to redress 'personality deficits' (change of behaviour and attitudes). This is the case with activation policies. Intervention policies focused on activation are based on and, at the same time, produce two opposite models of the subject – active and active-able subject – which foster two very different social policies. In the first case, with the active subject, the provision of an institutional framework is required which enables the capacity of agency as citizen. In the second case, with the active-able subject, practices are based on the concept of the 'patient's deficit': therapeutic action on behalf of the 'curing' state is necessary. Therefore, activation policies, rather than individualising practices, should be regarded as practices of subjectivation or, in other words, policies aimed at producing subjects.

We see the EU social policy discourse as constituting something of a paradox. What we mean here by paradox is rather close to its meaning in classical rhetoric, namely, a statement purporting to be true yet which contains, or conceals, a contradiction. What is happening, to some extent, is that this paradoxical discourse is unilaterally setting itself up to present as a matter of indisputable fact something that is in reality the outcome of a political process that entailed confrontation between differing positions. The paradox is constituted as the monological, unilateral and authoritarian manifestation of a reality which, insofar as it is a political reality, should be understood as dialogical, plural and conflict-ridden.

The principal technique whereby European discourse is made monological is via an economics-driven discourse, which presents as the conclusion of a scientific and positivist analysis a state of affairs that, in actual fact, is the outcome, at a given point in time, of a process of political negotiation and decision making. The hegemony of this economics-driven approach has been described as 'one-dimensional thought'. The paradox which prompts this kind of discourse is that which gives rise to monological and unilateral speech, namely, that while one knows or intuits – by means of common sense – that things are not as they are claimed to be, it is very difficult to put one's finger on the contradiction contained in the paradox, since the authority implicit in the statement deprives us of the tools to conceive of things in any other way. Accordingly, the paradoxical discourse is imposed as a hegemonic ideological practice. This is a practice consisting of the production of unquestioned and unquestionable evidence which comes to form the substratum of beliefs about the world in which we live and the type of understanding required for dealing with the problems that face us in it. These beliefs have today acquired an all-encompassing character and they configure not only a mode of representing reality but a means of explaining it and an implicit rationale concerning the kind of action that can be taken.

In order to tackle these questions, in this chapter we will proceed in two stages. First of all, we will briefly describe some features of the political status of European discourse and of the regulatory activity of the European institutions. Then, we will go on to posit the major structural features of the European discourse on activation/social intervention. This discourse might be labelled a discourse of 'active policies for active subjects'. Accordingly, we will present, first, the concept of activation peculiar to the social policies and the paradox inherent in this concept and, second, the concept of the active subject for whom the policies are intended. The main paradoxes of the European discourse on social policy relate to these two aspects of activation: some have to do with the *justification* of the social policy itself and others with the political production of *citizen subjects*. The justification is bound up with the paradox according to which, on the one hand, the declared aim is to preserve a self-styled European social policy identity while, on the other hand, what is being promoted in actual fact is the abolition of the EU social model in question and its transformation into its opposite. The paradoxes of the subject relate to the assertion that the aim is the autonomy of the subject while the policies designed to promote this aim entail the passive conditioning of subjects through strategic recourse to welfare benefits.

We will focus on the contribution of the European institutions to a process of political production of subjects on the basis of the paradigm of activation. This intervention model is not only marked by action of a technical nature in relation to unemployment, but also particularly by a political intervention that is characterised by a proposal of a new concept of citizenship. The activation discourse goes beyond a proposal regarding social exclusion. This intervention focuses on defining the problem of unemployment. In other words, there is a subversion of the problem: intervention with regard to the object (unemployment) is turned into action aimed at the subject (the unemployed person).

Therefore, these policies foster economic participation (in the labour market). At the same time, however, they contribute to refraining from potential political participation. Instead of providing the political conditions for exerting the social rights to which they are entitled as citizens, policies of this kind are transformed into therapeutic policies, on behalf of a clinical state, focused on 'curing' the motivation and attitudes of jobseekers in order to achieve their compliance with their duty as citizens: to be in charge of themselves.

The political status of the European discourse: persuasive regulation and ideological articulation

The processes of seeking responses to the crisis in the labour market have been taking on an increasingly European dimension. They involve coordination between the European, national and regional levels, in the context of a common strategy to promote employment and fight exclusion. The strategy is characterised by what has come to be known as 'soft regulation'. This form of regulation is 'open', in order to adapt to the new economic conditions, to the tremendous variety of situations within Europe, and to the principle of subsidiarity which underpins the whole approach. Accordingly, it is a question not of drawing up detailed rules but rather of introducing general 'procedures'[1] which allow greater flexibility, variation and choice.

The 'open method of coordination' has been defined by some authors as a post-regulatory state and by others as a new paradigm for social regulation. A large number of researchers have criticised the regulatory power of the European strategy to fight unemployment (see, for example, Keller, 2000; Jacobsson and Schmid, 2001). It has been claimed that this open method of coordination is excessively open in that, rather than enacting strict sanctions designed to ensure compliance with the policies in question, it is dependent on governments' attitudes to the possibility of social policy cooperation. Similarly, the concepts to which the strategy refers, such as employability, activation, the European social model, and so on, are vague and subject to polysemic[2] interpretation, encouraging governments applying the European guidelines to do no more than translate already existing policies into the terminology proposed by the European institutions. Accordingly, as has been pointed out by some authors, the drafting of National Action Plans by national governments turns into an exercise in rhetoric rather than constituting a technical and well-thought-out reformulation of earlier social policies. Some of the studies undertaken thus demonstrate how the central concepts of the European Employment Strategy (EES) are so general as to lend themselves to accordance with various differing forms of welfare state and political philosophy (de la Porte, 2002; Serrano Pascual, 2004). Nonetheless, it is important to recognise the significance of this rhetorical and discourse-based activity since, even though there are no sanctions for failure to comply with precise standards, there exist other more subtle and effective forms of regulation, which may take the form of pressure from the peer group or from public opinion.

Even the simple exercise of reclassifying existing policies within the conceptual framework supplied by the employment guidelines has an important ideological impact since, as a result of this exercise, the national policies are increasingly approximating to the discourse of the European institutions. A certain vocabulary – 'employability', 'partnership', 'activation', 'gender mainstreaming', and so on – has gained currency in national policy discourses (Behning and Serrano Pascual, 2001; Serrano Pascual, 2001, 2004; Barbier, 2005). This adoption of the 'language' proposed by the European institutions has had a major impact on the construction of the terms of the problem of unemployment and/or poverty, thereby influencing the general boundaries within which the debate is conducted and the ways in which the problems are described. The European institutions did not invent these concepts, but it is by them that they have been popularised, so that they have become official terms in standard usage for the structuring of discussions and naming and understanding of the problems.

The paradoxical rhetoric of European social discourse

The 'soft regulation' which is such a feature of European social policy coordination is, as explained above, of considerable significance in configuring a common mode of understanding social problems within the EU. As we have stated, it is less a question of regulating by recourse to a legal framework than of setting a defining cognitive framework around reality in accordance with which the measures to be adopted will then be devised. This European regulatory discourse, understood as a social practice, is characterised by a definition of the reality of employment in Europe, of the causes which give rise to it, of the reasons for avoiding it and of the mechanisms for dealing with it.

What we see is that, in the European social discourse, the characterisation of the current situation as a *knowledge-based society* becomes a basic fact, the laws of the *market* a law that is not to be questioned and *active adaptation* a value about which there can be no doubt. From this angle, the function of the public authorities is to assure the adjustment of the subjects to new productive rules.

This European discourse has, what is more, a certain *paradoxical* character: while presenting itself as a social discourse, geared to a concept of the active subject, it also defines, in purely technocratic terms, a field of possible practices in which politics is reduced to managing adaptation to situations regarded as fixed and not open to question, and within which the citizen subject is viewed as a client requiring motivation by the provision of incentives.

The citizenship concept is watered down as it is restricted to its clinical assistance dimension and stripped of the social and political dimension of citizenship. It is about economic participation in the process of modernisation and adjustment to the new rules of the productive system, at the expense, however, of the political participation of the citizen.

To some extent, the paradoxical nature of the EU discourse arises as a consequence of a process of intertextuality[3] in which discourses from different ideological spheres (basically social democrat and liberal) and different social welfare traditions are conjoined in a process of negotiation and consensus. Accordingly, it is a discourse that retains a hybrid position, entailing recourse to registers that appeal to the empowerment of the subject vis-à-vis institutions, and so on, while at the same time advocating intervention models that offer no greater decision-making power than submission to the imperatives raised by an exclusive belief in the virtues of the market. As such, although the discourse may seem to reinforce a concept of an independent and autonomous subject, on the other hand, this concept of a subject as a morally autonomous being is simultaneously called into question. Accordingly, this paradoxical character of the European discourse is explained not only by the peculiar character of the governance of the European institutions[4] but also by the contradictory nature of the ethical demands inherent in the new stage of capitalism which requires the participation and compliance of the worker while also placing the subject in a vulnerable and isolated position.

According to our understanding, the function of this current hegemonic discourse is not to negate or repress alternative discourses but rather to produce certain ideas and conceptions of reality (about social exclusion, unemployment, and so on) which will become accepted as constituting self-evident and incontrovertible facts of life. Accordingly, it is posited that the European construction of the concepts which articulate the problem – or the risk – of being without work directs us towards a reading of this social question in individual and moral terms, by contrast with the political interpretation of the problem applicable to the concepts that articulated the social question during other periods of the development of capitalism. Accordingly, we consider that while this discourse advocates, on the one hand, the 'economic activation' of subjects, it encourages them, by the same token, to become 'politically passive' (Crespo and Serrano Pascual, 2004), thus contributing to the re-marketisation of society, insofar as the market is restored to the status of dominant regulatory imperative. These discourses reinforce the individualisation of society, but this individualisation is not a means whereby subjects can emancipate themselves politically as citizens but, on the contrary, a process of individualisation at an ethical level.

Our analysis will be conducted in two stages. We begin with an analysis of the underlying justifications and reasons used to explain the intervention paradigm based on activation. The second stage will consist of an analysis of the conception of subject implicitly and/or explicitly conveyed by this activation discourse. The two aspects are complementary insofar as the attempt to legitimate the policy proposals is founded on a set of arguments structured around metaphors and concepts constructed in the manner of incontrovertible facts.

The paradoxes of active adaptation

The deep changes that have taken place in the capitalist model of production call, as explained by Boltanski and Chiapello (1999), for new justifications to secure the mobilisation, commitment and support of individuals in relation to the production process. These justifications are characterised by an appeal to rational argument and ethical reasoning concerning the advantages of participation in these processes, both at the individual (personal motives) and collective (common gains) levels. These justifications, insofar as they are sufficiently substantial, acquire the status of self-evident facts. At the present time, this impression of substance is created by a continual appeal to economics, which is endowed with an appearance of political and ethical neutrality. This is particularly true of the discourse used by the European institutions.

The justifications encountered in the discourse of the European Commission and Council entail reference to a twofold register: on the one hand, adaptation to the new situation of the knowledge-based economy is presented as an inevitable necessity; on the other hand, there is something in the nature of a self-imposed demand to maintain a so-called European approach to the conduct of social policy.

Adaptation to the knowledge-based economy

The definition of the situation comes to constitute an important tool of discourse insofar as, once accepted, it becomes established as non-problematic. In the case of European social discourse, the situation within which the policy proposals are framed is defined, according to our understanding, as the knowledge-based society. The knowledge-based society is presented as a scientific fact to which adaptation is inevitable. The laws of the economy are naturalised as autonomous processes. Political action consists, accordingly, not so much in questioning the economic situation as in guaranteeing the optimum conditions for adaptation and economic competition, a state of affairs described by Weiss and Wodak (2000, p 3) as follows: 'contingency is transformed into necessity and necessity into virtue'. The new ideologies of capitalism grant a central role to explanatory factors of a technological, macroeconomic or demographic nature (Boltanski and Chiapello, 1999), in a manner such that they are presented as forces alien to intervention by society or the individual and which, as such, are imposed and suffered, so that the only choice open to the subject is between adaptation or exclusion.

In the European discourse the knowledge-based society operates as both an inevitable starting point and a desirable ideal. It is presented as an inevitable fact – or 'quantum shift' – by means of the claim that, alongside globalisation and demographic change in Europe, it is a reality that has to be faced urgently and which represents a challenge: 'The European Union is confronted with a quantum shift from globalisation and the challenges of a new knowledge-driven economy. These changes are affecting every aspect of people's lives and require a radical transformation of the European economy' (European Council, 2000, p 1).

Within the terms of the discourse, the new situation is a challenge that cannot be avoided and, at the same time, an opportunity to develop a new type of society. As such, the knowledge-based society is also an ideal: 'an emerging new society which is more adapted to the personal choices of women and men' (European Council, 2000, p 2). The change to this new society is endowed with a certain utopian character since, 'it will be capable of improving citizens' quality of life and their environment' (European Council, 2000, p 3). This way of viewing the knowledge-based society as a utopian goal is not limited to the technical and economic aspects; it is also social, so that active preparations are required for the transition to this new state of affairs.[5]

Once reality has been defined as a knowledge-based society, and the strategy to be followed within this context has been laid down, anything that does not accord with the ideal definition becomes an obstacle and barrier to modernisation. The knowledge-based society makes demands to which individuals must seek active adaptation, relying on the strength of the EU.

Implicit in the discourse of modernisation is the idea of progress and the characterisation of all that opposes it as retrograde. At the Stockholm Summit in 2001 this modernisation was presented as 'the modernisation of labour markets and labour mobility ... to allow greater adaptability to change by breaking down existing barriers' (European Council, 2001, p 16).

The European discourse on active adaptation to the knowledge-based society contains a number of paradoxes that, as already pointed out, operate discursively in a monological mode, preventing the underlying contradictions from coming into view. The definition of the situation in terms of a knowledge-based society, insofar as it is turned into a statement of fact – something that is self-evident – prevents, first of all, its political and strategic character from emerging into the open. To define current society – and the society of the future – as a knowledge-based society is a strategic decision that may, in the current European situation, be politically appropriate and correct, but *never* can it be self-evident. The fact that it is nonetheless made to seem self-evident means that the consequences are presented as inevitable and policies as ways of coping with the task of adaptation. What the discourse sets up as subject to debate is the process of adaptation, which is defined as modernisation, and not the appropriateness of the definition given. The knowledge-based society is reified as a concept and imposed as applicable to all categories of the population, however diverse they may be and however much their interests may conflict.

Defence of a self-styled European social policy

Adaptation to the new situation is justified not only by an appeal to its inevitability but also by recourse to an interest in constructing a so-called collective identity, faithful to its values, characterised by the European social model (ESM), and which is to be defended for reasons of social cohesion and democratic governance: 'The Union must shape these changes in a manner consistent with its values and concepts of society and also with a view to the forthcoming enlargement' (European Council, 2000, p 1). This discourse is constructed under the umbrella of a self-evident collective identity, of a 'we' (the EU, Europe, and so on), the distinctive feature of which is supposed to be shared acceptance of a set of values and cultural features. These values which 'we' supposedly share are nonetheless – so the argument goes – threatened by new economic, demographic and social situations. This situation means that the ESM has to be transformed in order to ensure its preservation (Jepsen and Serrano Pascual, 2006). Paradoxically, however, the transformations envisaged themselves call into question the ideological foundations of the socialisation of solidarity that is supposed to characterise the ESM.

The demands of the new knowledge-based economy will entail a transformation of the ESM, mobilising already existing resources and practices, the legitimacy of which is already guaranteed but which will receive a new meaning, geared to the demands of the new productive model. The paradox arising here consists in the fact that, to preserve the model, it is necessary to transform it in a manner that may entail the disappearance of its fundamental underlying principles. Employment is no longer so much a social right – and unemployment a failure in relation to the rights of citizenship – as the result of a calculation, the calculation which – so it is supposed – unemployed persons perform in relation to the advantages and disadvantages of working. Social policies are no longer geared to guarantee citizenship rights but to provide incentives and devise situations in which 'work pays':[6]

> The system of financial incentives is one of the main determinants of participation in the labour market.… The balance between income from work … against income in unemployment or inactivity determines the decision to enter and to remain on the labour market. (European Commission, 2003, p 11)

> these systems need to be adapted as part of an active welfare system to ensure that work pays. (European Council, 2000, p 9)

One of these changes has to do with the socialisation of risk.[7] While, in the traditional welfare system, risk is conceived of as a characteristic external to the subject (unemployment, sickness, and so on), in the neo-liberal and technocratic discourse the main risk is located within the individual (the risk that they may not be active). The redistributive logic that has characterised the tax and benefit systems and which is the pedestal around which the principle of socialisation of risk has become institutionalised in our industrial societies must, so it is claimed, be transformed and become *individualised*, becoming dependent on the economic and moral behaviour of the person (individual response to incentives). Rather than as a set of tools for the redistribution of wealth, the tax and benefit system comes to be conceived of as a set of 'dis/incentives', implying important transformations of the legitimacy underpinning its existence: 'reforms in tax and benefit systems and their interaction, so that they promote participation in the labour force and tackle poverty and unemployment traps, and increase labour demand and participation, in particular of those with low earning prospects' (European Council, 2003, p 25).

The ESM, as it is being constituted in the rhetoric, is characterised by an interest in social cohesion based on labour market activity and on the participation of the various social actors, now described as social partners.

Social inclusion is directly linked to employment and to its quality. Ever since the Lisbon Summit (European Council, 2000) it has been stated that social cohesion must be linked to full employment. Yet now – any last vestiges of Keynesianism having been cast to the wind – full employment becomes exclusively dependent on market dynamics, turning the intervention of the public authorities into a set of measures designed to drive the labour force into action:

> The fight against social exclusion is of the utmost importance for the Union. Paid employment for women and men offers the best safeguard against poverty and social exclusion.... Active labour market policies promote social inclusion, which combines the pursuit of social objectives with the sustainability of public finances.... (European Council, 2001, p 20)

Although questions linked to employability have been central to the EES, in the case of the quality of work, which would enable these emancipatory promises to be fulfilled, it is present in a much more fluid and vague manner.

Social inequalities, like social cohesion, are interpreted principally in terms of economic participation and of access to technological knowledge (the digital divide). Equal opportunities policy has been translated fundamentally in terms of the activation and incorporation of women into the labour market. This notion of equality has inspired a range of policies, such as those directed to reconciling paid and unpaid work (development of public day care, parental leave, the family-friendly organisation of work, flexible promotion of part-time work) or positive discrimination measures intended to promote the employability of women (improving women's access to the educational system, giving financial incentives to firms which recruit members of the under-represented sex, trying to influence the incentive to participation in employment).

Nevertheless, the notion of social inclusion is different in nature from that of equality. It focuses on the division between an excluded minority and the included majority, so that the stress is not so much on the differences and inequalities within this 'included' majority in society but on the division between the included and the excluded (Levitas, 1998). The type of strategy inspired by a discourse based on social exclusion is 'to become an insider rather than an outsider in a society whose structural inequalities remain largely uninterrogated' (Levitas, 1998, p 7). This notion thus implies a dichotomous vision of society (included–excluded) which obscures the social inequalities among the apparently included subjects. The emphasis on a gender inequality dimension, for instance (integration of women into the labour market), without calling into question the origin of this inequality, merely helps to reinforce the unbalanced social relations that are at the origin of this subordinate position of women.

This approach thus entails two main weaknesses: on the one hand, its tendency to focus on social divisions rather than on social differences, or on how differences become inequalities; and on the other hand, its failure to call into question the social and power relations in which social inequalities originate and to consider the underlying causes of inequality and social exclusion. As stated in the Lisbon Council declaration: 'The new knowledge-based society offers tremendous potential for reducing social exclusion' (European Council, 2000, p 10). In this new society towards which it is claimed that we should be moving, social differences are differences of access to knowledge: 'at the same time, it brings a risk of an ever-widening gap between those who have access to the new knowledge and those who are excluded' (European Council, 2000, p 10). It is claimed that the explanation behind social exclusion is a question of access to or participation in these tools of knowledge, relegating to a lower level any political interpretation of inequality and social exclusion.

Labour problems in Europe are dealt with, accordingly, as problems of adjustment, adaptation, promotion, and so on. If instability is presented as a given, the personal (in)ability to cope with uncertainty is defined as the real problem (see Chapter Two). Rarely are they presented as conflicts of interest among groups and sectors. The term labour exploitation is unknown, as is that of abuse of power or confrontation. There is more talk of imbalances than of inequalities and, insofar as this is a discourse about ways of fighting unemployment, it is surprising to find that the concept of social justice and citizenship rights is virtually absent.

When it comes to corporate participation in this collective project, the appeal is fundamentally to moral criteria (confidence, corporate responsibility, readiness to learn), which, even so, do not call into question the autonomy and freedom of companies. Meanwhile, what is being proposed, in parallel, is a reordering of the logic inherent in those systems of welfare benefits that have enabled the worker (or jobseeker) to retain some degree of autonomy vis-à-vis the laws of the market. In this context of asymmetrical imbalance in power relations between the two sides, it may seem something of an irony to speak of 'social dialogue'.

The paradox of the 'active' subjects

Rhetorically speaking, the European discourse takes as its point of departure the development of individuals: 'People are Europe's main asset and should be the focal point of the Union's policies. Investing in people and developing an active and dynamic W[elfare]S[tate] will be crucial to Europe' (European Council, 2000, p 7). This conception of the individual posits the need for personalised intervention in accordance with the specific needs of the subject: 'Making the right offer to the right person at the right time. Such an approach would rely upon an early identification of the needs of each jobseeker and the design, at an early stage, of a personalised action plan, with a view to a sustainable integration in the labour market' (European Commission, 2003, p 11).

The paradox of the discourse of the 'active' subject is that it conceals the contradiction between an explicit model of the autonomous subject and an implicit distrust in this subject's motives which make them vulnerable to the potential snares represented by welfare benefits that have not been earned as a reward for honest labour. The explicit conception of the human being is that of a formally free, autonomous and responsible subject, governed by free will. The search is less for discipline than for participation (not only productive but also ideological and attitudinal). Personal attitudes will thus come to the fore and 'social risks' (unemployment, social exclusion) will be regarded as 'individual traps' (lack of employability). As stated by Valkenburg (Chapter Two), unemployment and inactivity are constructed as a moral problem, the individual's failure to be in charge of their own lives.

Citizens are turned into 'clients' who need to be regarded as individuals in order to offer them the recipe best suited to their individual characteristics. It is a question of offering them the appropriate resources to develop their employability (personal adaptability). This is presented as a paradigmatic change in intervention, compared to earlier models which are disqualified on the grounds that they promote 'passivity' and 'dependence'. The discourse is accordingly geared to encouraging the subject's potential in such as way that they will become 'his/her own entrepreneur' or in the words of Johansson (Chapter Four) *'condemned to be active in designing their own biography'*.

The snares of inactivity

The problem of unemployment becomes a problem of individual activation: it is people who have to be helped, motivated and activated so that they will avoid the 'snares' into which they might otherwise fall. Unemployed people are no longer victims of unemployment but of poverty, which operates as a 'trap' (European Council, 2002). One of the paradoxical features of this trap seems to be the lack of determination to find a way out of it. In its neo-moralistic endeavour, European discourse claims that the public services are to be used as incentives to encourage people to regard work as something desirable.[8] In this way, as stated by Johansson (Chapter Four), this type of policies aims to ensure self-discipline.

Persons disappear from the discourse in their capacity as citizens – who have to be respected with their rights and, at any rate, protected in the exercise of these rights – in order to become objects to be dealt with and processed, that is, 'clients'. This shift from a conception of citizens as *subjects* with rights to one of citizens as clients and *objects* of intervention constitutes one of the main political transformations wrought by neo-liberalism.

Personal autonomy, as the political goal of a democratic society, may be understood as a demand for citizen freedom. Accordingly, autonomy is part of the conception of citizenship, which is enshrined not only in civil and political rights and freedoms but also in social rights. However, there are numerous different ways of understanding personal autonomy, as developed by Valkenburg and Johansson in this volume (Chapters Two and Four). The hegemonic conception is that present in neo-liberal discourse where it predominates as an individualistic concept of the person and of citizenship. Neo-liberal individualism is characterised by an asocial notion of the subject according to which autonomy is exclusively the consequence of the behaviour of the individual, being something that persons achieve on their own (possibly with help from outside in the form of support and incentives). This conception of the subject and of autonomy, which is hegemonically presented as self-evident, conceals the fact that autonomy is not a property of individual subjects but of social relations. As stated by Johansson in Chapter Four, social cooperation is the key condition for constructing a self-chosen biography. In this sense it is perfectly possible to suppose that there will be relations in which it makes no sense to speak of autonomy in individual terms since the subjects involved cannot become autonomous unless there is a change in, for example, the relations of exploitation or oppression.

Social protection is disqualified on the grounds that it generates dependence. This notion of unemployment as dependence is sustained by a concept of a weak subject, in a sense that is both cognitive and moral. Such a subject has, so it is argued, to be driven into action by the strategic use of public resources as incentives. In this way, social subsidies come to be used to reinforce a conditioning process guided by an elementary logic of calculation: that it is better to work than not to work ('work pays').

The use of the concept of dependence, as the criterion used to disqualify previous forms of social intervention, is, nonetheless, just one mode of understanding dependence. The social protection systems, which were developed as a condition of the autonomy of the worker in the face of asymmetrical relationships that characterised the market, are cast into disrepute because they encourage individual dependence and irresponsibility. 'Autonomy' is to be promoted in this way, but it is an autonomy vis-à-vis institutions, one achieved at the cost of increasing 'dependence' on the market and its laws. As such, it is a question less of fighting dependence than of transforming the object of the dependence.

The conjunction of autonomy and individualism leads to a paradox that has been summed up by Culpitt (1999, p 156): 'This is the paradox: only those who can be 'saved' by their own efforts will get the help they need'. The metaphors of activation, present in the European discourse, are configured in this paradoxical manner: they set autonomy and citizen emancipation as the goal and their design is as strategies to achieve individual (psychological) change, such as change in motivation, in attitude and in behaviour. The concern for the possibility of preserving social protection systems in the future translates into a goal which is in turn a definition of reality: there are persons who, for whatever reasons, do not wish to work/adapt and the purpose of social policies is to bring them to wish otherwise. This is the key to the process of activation.

Conclusions

European social policy discourse has in some countries an important ideological impact, given the type of regulation that characterises these policies, one that is based more on persuasion than on the laying down of specific regulations. This influence takes concrete shape in the configuration of the framework used for interpreting and discussing the problem of social exclusion at the national level. As such, this discourse is a fundamental component of the configuration of the social question at the European level.

In this chapter we have developed the conceptions of the 'client', or 'target subject', of these so-called 'active' social policies, as well as the type of intervention that is being advocated by means of this cognitive framework as promoted and disseminated by the European institutions. It is our contention that these conceptions are setting the terms of the debate conducted at the European level concerning the goals, nature and strategies of social policy.

One of the main conclusions of this analysis of the discourse of the European institutions relates to its *paradoxical* character. In this chapter we have sought to show some of the paradoxes contained in this discourse, on the basis of the initial idea that a paradox is a statement presented as true but which contains or conceals a contradiction. The main paradoxes relate to the discursive function of the concept of activation. Within the discourse concerning 'active policies' for 'active persons' are subsumed contradictory positions and conflicting realities. And yet conflict is, paradoxically, the first concept to disappear from the discourse.

The main paradoxes of the European social policy discourse spring from these two aspects of activation: some have to do with the very manner in which European social policy seeks to justify itself as an 'active policy'; others relate to the political construction of the citizen subject – an 'active person' – whom they are geared to assist.

From the standpoint of the 'active policies', the main paradoxes have to do with the disappearance of *politics* – as an arena for confrontation between conflicting interests and positions – and its replacement by *policies* – as tools for managing a situation that is not called into question and which is stipulated in the manner of a technical/scientific assertion. These 'active policies' are thus articulated around the paradox according to which a claim is made about the need to preserve a so-called European social policy-making identity while what is being promoted, in fact, leads in the direction of abolishing the main principles which underpin this identity, thereby turning it into its opposite.

From the standpoint of 'active subjects', the main paradox relates to the way in which the individual is regarded as autonomous and responsible, yet in a manner which causes the disappearance of the very conditions whereby this autonomy and responsibility can be exercised (labour insecurity and exploitation). Social and labour conflicts are turned, paradoxically, into personal problems and policies into moral procedures of motivation and activation. In European discourse the main risk run by the unemployed person lies within themselves, in the form of the danger of falling into dependence and the 'trap' of inactivity and poverty. The paradox of the discourse of the 'active' subject conceals the contradiction between an explicit model of the autonomous and responsible subject and an implicit distrust in the motives which guide this subject and make them vulnerable to the possible snares of welfare benefits that are not the rewards of honest labour.

This paradoxical character of the European discourse may be attributable to the European institutions' need to translate into policy discourse their complex position, faced as they are with the requirement to merge within a single policy stance the different – and potentially opposed – political traditions that have prevailed within different parts of the continent. One component of this rhetoric might well be the attempt to merge, within a concept like the 'European social model', different ideological traditions which are conceptually articulated in consensual terms, thus causing the disappearance of the conflict-ridden and, in some cases, mutually contradictory nature of the political and ideological philosophies. This rhetorical use of concepts stemming from different ideological traditions does not, however, serve to prevent a situation in which the terms of the 'new social question' here being advocated amount to a deeply individualistic and moralising neo-liberal ideology based on a belief in all-out productivity as the overriding regulatory principle.

These paradoxical features of the European discourse may equally well be explained as resulting from the contradictory demands emanating from the emerging 'knowledge economy' since, on the one hand, this new economy calls for and demands, more than ever, the enthusiasm and commitment of the workers while, on the other hand, it endorses, to an unprecedented extent, increasingly non-standard and insecure forms of labour.

Notes

[1] This method consists of the following stages:

- The European institutions propose a series of guidelines, consisting of general measures and aims, frequently grouped together under concept headings ('activation', 'employability', and so on).
- The guidelines are referred to by the member states in drawing up their national and regional policies (National Action Programmes).
- A series of benchmarks are identified, designed to serve as tools for synchronic (between countries) and diachronic (over time) comparison with a view to identifying 'best practices'.

- There takes place a process of evaluation, revision and monitoring by the peer group and the European institutions.

[2] Polysemy refers to a word that has different meanings.

[3] Intertextuality could be defined as the way a text alludes and is interconnected to other texts.

[4] Given the EU's characteristic structure and dynamic as a set of countries with governments of different complexions yet seeking to promote common policies.

[5] 'To act now to harness the full benefits of the opportunities presented....' (European Council, 2000, p 1).

[6] 'by removing obstacles and disincentives to take up or remain in a job' (European Council, 2001, p 16).

[7] On the relation between social policies and risk see Culpitt (1999) and Johansson (Chapter Four, this volume).

[8] 'Enhancing job opportunities and providing adequate incentives for all those willing to take up gainful employment' (European Council, 2002, p 64).

References

Barbier, J. C. (2005) 'The European Employment Strategy, a channel for activating social protection?', in L. Magnusson, P. Pochet and J. Zeitlin (eds) *Opening the method of coordination: The case of the EES*, Brussels: Peter Lang, pp 417-46.

Behning, U. and Serrano Pascual, A. (2001) (eds) *Gender mainstreaming in the European Employment Strategy*, Brussels: ETUI.

Boltanski, L. and Chiapello, E. (1999) *Le nouvel esprit du capitalisme*, Paris: Gallimard.

Crespo Suárez, E. and Serrano Pascual, A. (2004) 'The EU's concept of activation for young people: toward a new social contract?', in A. Serrano Pascual (ed) *Are activation policies converging in Europe? The EES for young people*, Brussels: ETUI, pp 13-47.

Culpitt, I. (1999) *Social policy and risk*, London: Sage Publications.

De la Porte, C. (2002) 'Is the open method of coordination appropriate for organising activities at European level in sensitive policy areas?', *European Law Journal*, vol 8, no 1, pp 38-58.

De la Porte, C. and Pochet, P. (2003) 'A twofold assessment of employment policy coordination in light of economic policy coordination', in D. Foden and L. Magnusson (eds) *Five years' experience of the Luxembourg employment strategy*, Brussels: ETUI, pp 13-69.

European Commission (2003) Communication from the Commission to the Council, the European Parliament, the Economic and Social Committee and the Committee of the Regions, 'The future of the EES and strategy for full employment and better jobs for all', COM (2003)6 final: Brussels: EUR-OP.

European Council (2000) *Presidency Conclusions, Lisbon European Council*, 23-24 March 2000, Brussels: European Council.

European Council (2001) *Presidency Conclusions, Stockholm European Council*, 23-24 March 2001, Brussels: European Council.

European Council (2002) 'Council Decision of 18 February 2002 on guidelines for member states' employment policies for the year 2002', *Official Journal of the European Communities*, 1 March, p 64.

European Council (2003) *Presidency Conclusions, Brussels European Council* (www.eu2003.gr/multimedia/pdf/2003_3/729.pdf).

Foden, D. and Magnusson, L. (2003) (eds) *Five years' experience of the Luxembourg employment strategy*, Brussels: ETUI.

Goetschy, J. (1999) 'The European Employment Strategy: genesis and development', *European Journal of Industrial Relations*, vol 5, no 2, pp 117-37.

Goetschy, J. (2003) 'The Employment Strategy and European integration', in D. Foden and L. Magnusson (eds) *Five years' experience of the Luxembourg employment strategy*, Brussels: ETUI, pp 69-111.

Jacobsson, K. and Schmid, H. (2001) 'Real integration or just formal adaptation', Paper presented at the Conference of the European Sociological Association, Helsinki, 28 August-1 September.

Jepsen, M. and Serrano Pascual, A. (2006) (eds) *Unwrapping the European social model*, Bristol: The Policy Press.

Keller, B. (2000) 'The new European employment policy, or, is the glass half-full or half-empty?', in R. Hoffman, O. Jacobi, B. Keller and M. Weiss (eds) *Transnational industrial relations in Europe*, Düsseldorf: Hans Böckler Stiftung, pp 29-44.

Levitas, R. (1998) *The inclusive society? Social exclusion and New Labour*, London: Macmillan Press.

Mósesdóttir, L. (2003) 'Moving Europe towards the dual-breadwinner model', in D. Foden and L. Magnusson (eds) *Five years' experience of the Luxembourg employment strategy*, Brussels: ETUI, pp 183-205.

Serrano Pascual, A. (2001) (ed) *Enhancing youth employability through social and civil partnership*, Brussels: ETUI.

Serrano Pascual, A. (2004) (ed) *Are activation policies converging in Europe? The EES for young people*, Brussels: ETUI.

Weiss, G. and Wodak, R. (2000) 'European Union discourses on employment: strategies for depoliticising ynemployment and idealogising employment policies', *Concepts and Transformations*, vol 5, no 4, pp 29-42.

SEVEN

Reforming the public sector: personalised activation services in the UK

Bruce Stafford and Karen Kellard

Introduction

The Labour government since its election in 1997 has sought to tackle poverty and social exclusion in the UK and ensure that the UK is competitive in the global economy by virtue of a skilled and flexible labour force. It has introduced a number of policies, including active labour market programmes, which promote work as the best means of reducing poverty and social exclusion. The design of these programmes has changed over time, and this chapter discusses the degree to which the delivery of welfare and employment services is being made more personalised.[1] These trends will be illustrated by the two largest activation programmes in the UK: the New Deal for Young People and the New Deal 25 Plus. Both these programmes are aimed at unemployed people, that is, recipients of Jobseeker's Allowance. However, as there are New Deals aimed at other client groups – for instance, lone parents – the chapter also touches on the experiences of recipients of other benefits. The chapter begins by placing these developments in their policy and economic context.

Policy and economic context

The key policy and economic factors that have influenced the development of active labour market policies are the Labour government's employment policy, levels of employment and unemployment in the UK, the main characteristics of unemployed people, the government's proposed reforms of the public sector and its reform of welfare-to-work policies.

Employment policy

Tackling unemployment is central to the government's long-term objectives of economic growth and rising living standards. The aim of the government's employment policy is 'to ensure a higher proportion of people in work than ever before' (HM Treasury, 2005, p 3). The Department for Work and Pensions, which has responsibility for employment and benefit policies, has targets agreed with the Treasury for the period 2005-06 to 2007-08 to: increase overall employment rates over the economic cycle; increase the employment rates of disadvantaged areas and groups (such as disabled people), taking account of the economic cycle; and reduce the number of children in workless households (DWP, 2005).

Associated with this has been a desire to secure a cultural shift in the contract between the individual and the state (Blunkett, 2000). Within a policy agenda that emphasises rights and responsibilities, the government has sought to convert what it saw as a passive system to an active one, whereby the right of individuals to get support from the government when looking for work is balanced by the responsibility to seek training and work if able to do so. The one set of policies that stand out as active labour market policies are the New Deals, which are central to New Labour's welfare-to-work strategy and its modernisation of the welfare state.

Employment and unemployment in the UK

In recent years, the UK labour market has been relatively robust and unemployment has been maintained at comparatively low levels. Although the rate of employment does vary with the business cycle, at the end of September 2005 there were 28.8 million people in employment, the highest since records began in 1971 (National Statistics, 2005). Since 1959 the rate of employment has varied between 70% and 75%, and at September 2005 it was 74.9%. Unemployment in the UK rose following the 'oil crisis' of the 1970s and the recessions of the 1980s and early 1990s. Since 1993 the trend has been downwards. As at September 2005 the unemployment rate, using the International Labour Office definition,[2] was 4.7%, with 1.43 million people unemployed. According to the government the strong performance of the labour market has been achieved through working towards five main principles (HM Treasury/DWP, 2003):

- macroeconomic stability;
- flexibility in the labour market, within a regulated framework;
- tax and benefit policies that make work pay;
- ensuring an adaptable, flexible and productive workforce through training and education; and
- activation policies that aim to prevent people becoming detached from the labour market.

As unemployment levels have fallen, attention has focused more on those unemployed people who are harder to reach and on the, now larger, population of benefit recipients who are economically inactive. Differences in the composition of the workless population, such as having a disability, and of the wider economically inactive population, have affected the design of labour market programmes such as the New Deals. Different New Deals have been developed for distinct client groups, for example young people and disabled people (see Stafford, 2003a). These programmes reflect differences in both key characteristics of the target groups and benefit status (with mandatory programmes for those claiming Jobseeker's Allowance as they have to be actively seeking work as a condition of benefit entitlement, and voluntary programmes for groups in receipt of other benefits, such as Income Support [lone parents] and Incapacity Benefit [people with a disability or health condition]).

Public sector reform

In recent years, the Labour government has placed a renewed emphasis on the delivery of public services. For political reasons the reform of public services has been given predominance by ministers, including the Prime Minister. Central to the political and policy debate is the concept of choice – of allowing individuals to choose a service from different providers – and that services must be responsive or customer-focused. Choice is believed to drive up standards and empower customers. Introducing market-led approaches to the public sector is not new in the UK – initiatives such as competitive tendering of services and internal markets date back to the 1980s and 1990s. However, the current emphasis on customer-focused public services is a step change in policy development. It is under Labour that the notion of the demanding 'citizen customer' has gained ascendancy.

The 1999 White Paper, *Modernising government*, included a commitment to provide responsive public services (Cabinet Office, 1999). The aim was that service users, not providers, would be the focus of public services, so that customers' needs are met. A raft of measures to modernise government was announced, many were existing initiatives, such as the planned establishment of a one-stop shop for benefit claimants of working age – Jobcentre Plus.[3] In a speech on modernising the Civil Service, Tony Blair declared: 'Consumer expectations of government services as well as others are rising remorselessly. People no longer take what is given them and are grateful. They want services that are responsive to their needs and wishes' (Blair, 2004).

The government's reform agenda is controversial both within and outside of government. The nature of this debate is not outlined here, rather it is sufficient to note that there is a wider debate in the UK about individual and collective choice and about the extent to which the provision of public services should be personalised.

Welfare reform

In general, the debates about public sector reform, and about choice in particular, centre on education and the health service. However, some of the ideas now given more national prominence underscore both earlier and current reforms of the welfare state. The 1998 Green Paper *New ambitions for our country: A new contract for welfare* (DSS, 1998a) outlined the government's principles and 'vision' for reform. The Green Paper outlined the case for 'developing flexible personalised services to help people into work' (DSS, 1998a, p 3). In part this reflects ministers' criticisms of the way in which benefits had been delivered; speaking in 1997 the then Secretary of State commented:

> The way that social security is delivered at the moment is resented by the public who pay for it, the clients who use it, and the staff who run it. For many people, the current system is fragmented, reactive, inflexible and confusing....
> I am determined to overhaul the service that we have inherited. I want to develop a modern integrated system that is simpler, streamlined and more efficient. (Secretary of State, 1997)

The service was seen as not keeping 'pace with rising expectations of service quality' (DSS, 1998a, p 71). Indeed, one minister described it as a 'second class service', claiming that it does not meet individuals' needs (Eagle, 1999). Instead, customers ought to have 'the right to good quality, convenient and responsive services which both help them with their individual needs and enable them to fulfil the obligations which go with receiving benefits' (DSS, 1998a, p 71).

Indeed, independent research supports ministers' critical comments of the 'traditional' method of delivering benefit and employment services (for a summary see Stafford, 2003b).

The Green Paper sought to extend the then personal adviser service available to lone parents under the New Deal for Lone Parents and to young people under the New Deal for Young People to other client groups of working age. The aim was to provide a tailor-made, personalised service that would be summarised in an Action Plan for each customer. Personal advisers were to meet with customers and to discuss work aspirations and options, to assist with job search, to explore training needs and provision, to produce indicative calculations of whether a customer would be better off in work and to advise (as appropriate) on childcare provision and the availability of specialist referral services (for example to deal with drug or alcohol abuse).

While a caseworker approach with lone parents had been piloted by the Conservatives (Vincent et al, 1998), Labour developed and extended the concept to other client groups. Indeed, the personal adviser model is not only inherent in the design of the New Deals (see below), but also a feature of the 'work-focused interviews' conducted in Jobcentre Plus offices. On 1 April 2002 the Employment Service and parts of the Benefits Agency were merged to form Jobcentre Plus, which delivers employment and benefit services to people of working age. Jobcentre Plus provides services to unemployed people claiming the UK's unemployment benefit, Jobseeker's Allowance, and to other people claiming social assistance and incapacity benefits. The national rollout of this new service meant that by March 2006 over 700 integrated local offices had been established. This new organisational structure is complemented by the introduction of mandatory work-focused interviews for all new claims, including those made by unemployed people, lone parents, sick and disabled people and widows. These involve personal advisers and customers discussing the latter's work aspirations, and their barriers to and opportunities for employment. While, formally, there is no requirement to seek work or be available for work for non-Jobseeker's Allowance claimants, there is increasingly a focus on getting people, whether or not they are unemployed, into employment.

The New Deals

There is a 'family' of New Deal programmes (see Table 7.1) that differ in terms of the client group targeted, whether participation is mandatory and the nature of the intervention. They are 'labourist' activation policies, because they assume that social inclusion is achieved through labour market engagement and employment. There is a New Deal policy paradigm with:

- a focus on paid work as 'the single most effective' or 'surest route out of poverty' and social exclusion and the best means for securing independence (DSS, 1998a; HM Treasury, 2000a, 2002b);
- a belief that welfare-to-work policies are necessary to prevent unemployed and economically inactive people becoming detached from the labour market (HM Treasury, 2002a);
- an expectation that increasing the supply of labour will increase the pool of (skilled) labour available to employers, which will increase production and productivity (Blunkett, 2000; HM Treasury, 2000a);
- a belief that movements into work can be assisted by:
  - delivering a proactive benefit system founded on a flexible, integrated, personalised (or caseworker) service backed by investment in information and communication technology (DSS, 1998b);
  - providing enabling services and support that tackle people's barriers to work and improve their employability;
- a stress on the rights and responsibilities of individuals and of the state (DSS, 1998a); and
- a willingness to work in partnership with the voluntary and private sectors in delivering benefit and employment services.

The New Deals are very much a supply-side policy. There is an aspect of the 'democratisation of activation' in the New Deals (see Chapter Four, this volume) in that they extend the range of client groups to be covered from unemployed people (Jobseeker's Allowance recipients) to lone parents and disabled people claiming other benefits.

The personal adviser model

In general, customers and staff like the personal adviser model. In the New Deal for Young People, for instance, claimants like the one-to-one contacts they have with their adviser (Bryson et al, 2000) and tend to be satisfied with their personal advisers (Bonjour et al, 2001).

Table 7.1: Summary of New Deal programmes

New Deal	Participation	Commenced	Target group	Content
New Deal for Lone Parents	Voluntary	Prototypes: October 1997 National: October 1998	(From 2001) lone parents on Income Support who work less than 16 hours a week or not at all, and their youngest child aged under 16 years	Consists of an initial interview with a personal adviser, a review meeting after six and 12 months and annual meetings subsequently (if they remain on Income Support). The personal adviser discusses work options and provides support while lone parent is looking for work and once they are in work
New Deal for Young People	Mandatory	Pathfinders: January 1998 National: April 1998	Individuals aged 18 to 24 and claiming Jobseeker's Allowance for at least six months	Includes a 'gateway' period of advice and support followed by one of four Options (subsidised employment, full-time education and training, voluntary work, environmental work). In April 2004, a 'flexible' Options stage was introduced: customers can 'mix and match' Options and the minimum required length of stay on all Options is reduced from 26 to 13 weeks. There is a review of progress at week 10 of the Option period
New Deal 25 Plus	Mandatory	National: June 1998 Pilots: November 1998[a]	Jobseeker's Allowance claimants for 18 out of the last 21 months	Personal advisers offer a 13-week Intensive Activity Period, which can be extended to 26 weeks at the adviser's discretion, or to 52 weeks for full-time education or training
New Deal 50 Plus	Voluntary	Pathfinders: October 1999 National: April 2000	Claimants of work-related benefits aged over 50	Personal advisers provide support for job search, work, financial advice regarding transition into work and an 'in-work' training grant

(continued)

Table 7.1: Summary of New Deal programmes (continued)

New Deal	Participation	Commenced	Target group	Content
New Deal for Partners	Voluntary	Pathfinder: February 1999 National: April 2000	Partners of recipients of Jobseeker's Allowance, Income Support, Incapacity Benefit, Severe Disablement Allowance and Carer's Allowance	Those aged 18 to 24 and without children can choose to join the New Deal for Young People. For parents aged 18 to 24 and those aged 25 plus, there is access to a personal adviser to provide information regarding help and support available to find work, including financial incentives and childcare
New Deal for Disabled People	Voluntary	Pilots: October 1998 National: July 2001	Those receiving disability or health-related benefits	A network of job brokers provides advice and support to find and prepare for work. Job brokers are paid on their outcomes – registering participants, job entries and sustained employment
New Deal for Musicians	Voluntary	Pathfinder: October 1999 National: Spring 2000	Those already on New Deal for Young People or New Deal 25 Plus	If, in these New Deal programmes, an individual can demonstrate a genuine interest in working as a musician, personal advisers will make a referral to a music industry expert to be a mentor and provide support and advice

[a] Innovative schemes were piloted in selected areas after the programme had been introduced in 28 areas.

Source: Taken from: Hasluck (2000, table A.1, p 71); Millar (2000, table 2.1); updated from www.newdeal.gov.uk

Six months after programme entry 91% of respondents in a survey said they got along very well or quite well with their personal advisers (Bryson et al, 2000). However, the quality of the relationship varied by programme Option (see Table 7.1). Those attending Options that were closer to the labour market (the Employment Option, 60%) were more likely to get on very well with their personal advisers than those on Options further from the labour market (the Environmental Task Force, 47%) (Bonjour et al, 2001).

Notwithstanding evidence that claimants and staff have had positive views about the personal adviser model (see, for instance, Legard et al, 1998; Arthur et al, 1999; Atkinson, 1999; Finch et al, 1999; Legard and Ritchie, 1999; Woodfield et al, 1999; Lewis et al, 2000; Kelleher et al, 2002; Osgood et al, 2002), there are (inevitably) some shortcomings in the personal adviser model, and some claimants have mixed views about the service received.

The extent to which claimants' needs and barriers to work are identified can vary between advisers. Some adopt a 'holistic' approach that explores the broader social and economic needs of individuals, while others are more narrowly focused on work-related issues (Lewis et al, 2000). Although claimants' demand for a more comprehensive service might vary, some customers do value the interest shown in them as individuals by some personal advisers (Finch et al, 1999; Legard and Ritchie, 1999; Lewis et al, 2000). However, personal advisers typically provide a service that is more narrowly focused on work outcomes for unemployed people (that is, those claiming Jobseeker's Allowance), whereas those claiming other benefits, especially those with complex needs, often receive a limited service (Kelleher et al, 2002). Frequently, there is a focus on sorting out the benefit claim and not on work aspirations or barriers to participation in the labour market (Kelleher et al, 2002).

Moreover, despite the emphasis on employment in the government's welfare reforms, an evaluation of a pilot version of Jobcentre Plus showed that the delivery of work-focused interviews can be problematic (Kelleher et al, 2002; Osgood et al, 2002). Time pressures meant that early meetings with claimants tended to concentrate on their claim for benefit, and work-related issues were generally neglected.

In principle, personal advisers are encouraged to caseload claimants to appropriate services or support. However, there is some qualitative evidence of personal advisers 'creaming' the most job-ready claimants (Arthur et al, 1999; Loumidis et al, 2001; Kelleher et al, 2002) (see also Chapter Three, this volume). This is partly a response to a lack of resources, an unintended consequence of increasing numbers of claimants and limited staff making the scheduling of follow-up meetings problematic, in particular for customers with complex or long-term employment issues. It is also partly because personal advisers can lack the skills and experience to deal with claimants with particularly complex or sensitive personal circumstances and job placement targets encourage staff to focus on those most job-ready. To cope with this situation, more difficult cases can be referred to internal or external specialists (such as lone parent advisers or disability employment advisers), deselecting cases from the caseload and/or team working.

Finally, personal advisers have an advocacy role, of championing their customers' needs with, for instance, service providers and employers. However, personal advisers are 'gatekeepers' to resources and other services, and, if necessary, refer cases for decisions on benefit sanctions. Ultimately the relationship between personal advisers and claimants is not one of equals; the relationship is asymmetrical with the advisers in charge (see Chapter Four, this volume). There is a potential tension between these two roles that limits the rapport that personal advisers can establish with their customers.

Other measures

The New Deals operate within a wider policy climate of work incentives, tax and benefit changes and Employment Service initiatives and schemes aimed at specific disadvantaged client groups or geographical areas. Measures include reforming National Insurance (that is, social insurance) contributions and the introduction of tax credits for working families and for people with disabilities (in October 1999) and of a national minimum wage (in April 1999). As well as steps taken to improve pay for those on low incomes, other measures have been put in place to ease the transition into work. Work incentive measures such as Job Grant, Lone-Parent Benefit Run-on and Housing Benefit Run-on are designed to assist those who undergo the transition from benefit receipt into paid employment.

Targeted geographical initiatives include area regeneration schemes such as the New Deal for Communities and a 'family' of Action Zones for Health, Education and Employment. The New Deal for Communities, for example, was launched in September 1998 and is a key programme in the government's strategy to help some of the most deprived neighbourhoods in the country. The programme aims to bridge the gap between some of the poorest members of society and the rest of England. By focusing resources on small deprived areas, and working with other initiatives operating in the areas, it seeks to achieve maximum impact.

Making it more personal

In summary, the Labour government's welfare reforms have entailed from the very beginning a degree of personalised service delivery through the personal adviser model as typified in the New Deals. The model has also been adapted and will be the 'norm' as Jobcentre Plus is rolled out nationally. Notwithstanding some criticisms of the personal adviser model (see above), there is evidence that it is becoming more personalised and the New Deals being made more flexible. There are two main reasons for arguing this. First, the evolution of, and the interactions between, the New Deal for Young People and New Deal 25 Plus are leading to more 'flexible' services, which by their nature are more tailored and so personalised. Second, there are several other policies and schemes aimed at the harder to reach, which in order to be effective have to be more personalised in their approach.

Evolution of programme design: the New Deal for Young People and New Deal 25 Plus

The New Deal for Young People is a mandatory programme for young people who have been claiming Jobseeker's Allowance for six months. As originally designed it entailed (Chatrik and Convery, 1999):

- A Gateway period of up to four months where a personal adviser (or staff from a specialist external agency) provides advice and support to help claimants secure unsubsidised employment. Claimants are given help with job search, careers advice and preparation for the following Options stage. Sanction for refusal to participate in the programme is a time-limited withdrawal of Jobseeker's Allowance. To make young people more prepared for work and to improve their job-search skills an Intensive Gateway (the 'Gateway to Work') was piloted in 12 areas in August 1999 and rolled out nationally in June 2000 (HM Treasury, 2000a). This offered more intensive help from personal advisers with job search and assistance with developing individuals' soft skills including punctuality, team working, and so on. In addition, since July 1999 the last month of the Gateway has been made more intensive, whereby participants are made aware that remaining on benefits is not an option and are prepared for the next stage of the programme

(Options). Nonetheless, some participants remain in the Gateway for longer than four months.

- After the Gateway, employment and work experience Options for those still unemployed. The Options comprise: a subsidised job for up to six months or help starting their own business; work in the voluntary sector for up to six months; a job with the Environmental Task Force for up to six months; or full-time study for up to 12 months for people with no or only basic educational qualifications. There is an expectation, although no guarantee, that subsidised placements will lead to permanent positions. Each Option involves at least one day per week (or equivalent) off-the-job training leading to an accredited qualification. This is a compulsory phase of the programme; and those refusing to participate may face benefit sanctions.
- A follow-through phase of further intensive job search for those not in unsubsidised employment.

Claimants who have not found a job or other opportunities at the end of these stages may return to claim Jobseeker's Allowance.

Evidence of the evolution of a more personalised programme is that the government is changing the Options stage of the programme. The 'Tailored Pathways' pilot was introduced in 17 Jobcentre Plus areas in 2002, to test the impact of a more flexible approach to the Options stage of the New Deal for Young People. The pilot enables New Deal personal advisers to put together a modular package of support that could include periods of training, work experience and subsidised employment. A flexible Option period was intended to better enable provision to be tailored to the needs of employers and individual young people. The pilot has recently been evaluated, and was found to produce small but significant increases in job outcomes in pilot areas (Griffiths et al, 2003). In the 2003 Budget the Chancellor of the Exchequer announced that a more flexible Options period would be introduced. Since April 2004, personal advisers are able to 'mix and match' Options and define the length of stay of each customer. The minimum length of stay has been reduced from 26 to 13 weeks (although the full-time Education and Training Option can still last for a maximum of 52 weeks in exceptional circumstances). The customer's progress is reviewed at week 10 at a Job Readiness Review. At the review the personal adviser determines whether the customer's length of stay on New Deal for Young People will be extended, for a period of up to 13 weeks. At any point during the Options period a customer is able to access the full 26 weeks of the Employment Option.

This more flexible, personalised version of New Deal for Young People is in part a response from the lessons learnt from the New Deal 25 Plus. The New Deal 25 Plus has undergone more radical change than the New Deal for Young People. Its evolution, which is outlined below, reveals the implementation of a more personalised (yet work-focused) service.

The target group for New Deal 25 Plus has changed over time. Initially, jobseekers (or those with National Insurance contributions) aged 25 and over and who had been unemployed for at least two years were eligible for the programme. However, in design and funding the programme was less developed than the New Deal for Young People. There was no Options stage, guaranteed training for the participant or training grant for employers. It also follows that the opportunity for subsidised employment was not a mandatory part of the programme. Overall, the programme's duration varied, depending upon customers' circumstances, and ranged from several months to a year.

This early version of the New Deal 25 Plus was a relatively modest programme; in effect it comprised additional sessions with a personal adviser and a repackaging of existing programmes for long-term unemployed people (such as Jobclub, Work Trials and Access to Work). It was developed in haste by ministers and compared unfavourably with the 'flagship' New Deal programme for 18- to 24-year-olds. The relatively small size of the funding compared to the size of the client group meant that resources were spread thinly among participants and there would only be a modest number with subsidised jobs. The programme was in danger of appearing to offer more than it could in practice deliver.

In practice, the early version of New Deal 25 Plus lacked 'pace and purpose' and the advisory period lasted too long (Hasluck, 2002). Most participants left the programme after the advisory stage and returned to Jobseeker's Allowance.

In November 1998 an enhanced version of New Deal 25 Plus was piloted in 28 areas in Britain and in the whole of Northern Ireland. In the pilots in Britain jobseekers became eligible for the New Deal 25 Plus at either 12 or 18 months of unemployment. A mix of public and private sector (partnership) organisations, including the then Employment Service, delivered the programme. The pilots were meant to be innovative and they tested a number of different measures and models of delivery. They also drew upon the New Deal for Young People, in particular they incorporated a Gateway. The pilots ran until March 2001.

In April 2000 the Gateway in New Deal 25 Plus was further

intensified, with more contacts with clients and additional support provided. However, an evaluation assessed the overall impact of these changes to be marginal, possibly because the frequency of contacts between personal adviser and clients did not increase, and that for the 'hard to help' a more radical intervention was required (Hasluck, 2002).

More significant changes were introduced nationally in April 2001. The government described these changes as a 'step change', with the programme 're-engineered' to make it more flexible and intensive. The New Deal 25 Plus now more closely resembles the New Deal for Young People; the changes being based on lessons learnt from the latter and the November pilots. Compared to the previous national and pilot versions of the programme, more measures are available, and personal advisers work more intensively with participants to ensure that barriers to work are discussed adequately. Previously, claimants thought that there had been an overemphasis on getting 'any job' (Bivand, 2000). The intention was to tailor provision to participants' needs and for claimants to spend less time on the programme. Staff were very supportive of the change in the programme (Winterbotham et al, 2002). This re-engineered programme comprises:

- A Gateway period lasting up to four months where participants meet their personal adviser weekly. Early on an Action Plan is produced that outlines the steps to be taken to get the claimant a job. Personal advisers provide initial help to find unsubsidised employment, advice on the actions needed to find work (including screening for basic skills), access to independent careers advice, and when required access to specialist services in, for example, drug dependency, debt management and self-employment. After four weeks the option of subsidised employment is available to participants. Those without unsubsidised employment at the end of the Gateway are referred to the Intensive Activity Period (IAP).
- An IAP is a period of full-time activity that provides individually tailored packages of support to meet the needs of clients and help them move into paid work. It lasts for 13 weeks, and can be extended for a further 13 weeks. This package is agreed between the personal adviser, the provider and the client. The package can include Basic Employability Training (BET) for up to six months to overcome barriers to work; support for self-employment; work experience placements; and education and training courses that last for up to one year and lead to a recognised vocational qualification. Ongoing job search is also a key feature of every IAP.

- Follow-through: participants without employment after the IAP return to Jobseeker's Allowance and continue to receive support from a personal adviser. This stage can last for six weeks, but can be extended to three months. Participants not securing employment become re-eligible for the programme after 18 months of claiming Jobseeker's Allowance.

Initially, people aged 25 and over and who had been unemployed for 18 or more months were eligible for the re-engineered programme; this was later revised to those who had been unemployed for 18 out of the previous 21 months. The New Deal 25 Plus is not the only provision available to those aged over 25. At six months of unemployment jobseekers can receive basic skills training (BST) and soft or key skills training (Soft Job Focused Training, SJFT). At 12 months there is Longer Occupational Training (soft and key skills training of a longer duration than SJFT) and for the over fifties there is New Deal 50 Plus. Those on the New Deal 25 Plus also have access to the New Deal for Musicians.

In the 2002 Budget the Chancellor of the Exchequer announced two reforms to the New Deal 25 Plus, namely that:

- pilots would be established to test extending on a mandatory basis the eligibility of jobseekers who had been unemployed for 18 months out of the previous three years (as opposed to 18 out of the previous 21 months). This measure is designed to address those with repeated spells of unemployment, because they are at risk of long-term unemployment; and
- the introduction of more intensive mandatory Gateway to Work courses for all participants in four locations (Dundee, London, Manchester and Swansea). Mirroring the New Deal for Young People, Gateway participants who have not found unsubsidised employment can be referred to courses to provide assistance on CV writing, job-search methods and interview techniques.

An objective of the April 2001 changes was to provide a service that was tailored to the needs of the customer. The programme did (eventually) deliver earlier interviews and more frequent contacts between personal advisers and clients, and a form of case conferencing where staff discussed individual cases. The latter was seen as a positive development by staff, although not fully implemented in all (case study) areas (Wilson, 2002). These measures serve to intensify participants' job-search activities and possibly the likelihood of them obtaining work. Qualitative research with staff suggests that the weekly interviewing regime during the Gateway improved their relationships with clients (Hasluck, 2002). The Gateway was seen as being effective for customers who were work-ready; there were more mixed views on its benefits for 'harder-to-help' participants (Wilson, 2002). Participants are reported as finding the revised Gateway a positive experience (compared to their usual experiences of the service) (Hasluck, 2002).

Claimants do discuss with providers and their personal advisers the nature of their IAP. However, the improvement in personal adviser–customer relations did not extend to the IAP. There were fewer contacts between personal advisers and participants during the IAP than was originally envisaged, because personal advisers lacked the time and were reluctant to visit employers and training providers (Hasluck, 2002; Wilson, 2002). Possibly as a consequence of this, participants undertook less job-search activity during their IAP.

The extent to which the New Deal 25 Plus delivers a flexible and personalised service appears to depend upon the skills of the personal adviser and the provider (Wilson, 2002). While Jobcentre Plus is involved in the delivery of New Deal 25 Plus in all areas, much of the programme (including assistance with job search) is provided by contractors. Early on there was some tension between personal advisers and training providers, arising from different interpretations about the extent to which New Deal 25 Plus was focused on job outcomes, and lack of clarity about who had responsibility for deciding the provision for clients (Winterbotham et al, 2002). This tension appears to have diminished as personal advisers and providers have reached a common understanding on the primary purpose of the programme.

Case studies of the re-engineered programme demonstrate a wide variation in delivery (Wilson, 2002). The length and management of the Gateway and the type of provision can vary (Winterbotham et al, 2002). For most participants there is even access to the New Deal for Young People's Gateway to Work, courses that typically last two weeks and focus on soft skills and motivation. However, qualitative studies show that access to more services, such as drug counselling and financial advice, is more limited, because of its specialist nature or lack of provision (Hasluck, 2002). Similarly, there were differences in the local delivery of the IAP.

Discussion and conclusion

This chapter has sought to demonstrate that the welfare reforms introduced by the Labour government have become more personalised over time. Here 'personalisation' reflects the 'differentiation and flexibility of social life' and the 'rights and responsibilities' discourses outlined in Chapter Two. The possible reasons for this increased individualisation are, first, that lessons have been learnt from the operation of the New Deals, which suggest that assisting claimants of non-Jobseeker's Allowance benefits into work requires a more personalised service than hitherto. These client groups are heterogeneous and addressing their barriers to work demands a flexible suite of measures, not a set menu where customers are effectively fitted to the provision available. Second, and a related point, the roll-out of Jobcentre Plus with mandatory 'work-focused interviews' for recipients of non-Jobseeker's Allowance benefits means that advisers increasingly have to provide a service to a wider range of client groups. Third, there is some evidence of policy learning in that lessons about what works in the New Deal for Young People and New Deal 25 Plus have been transferred across the programmes. Fourth, given falling, and low, levels of unemployment the mandatory New Deals are now increasingly focused on groups of people who are further away from the labour market and thus harder to reach. Arguably the government's target of increasing the number of people in employment over the economic cycle requires that a more personalised service is provided as harder-to-reach groups are helped into jobs.

As well as the continuous development of the New Deals, the extension of a more flexible personal adviser model must be seen in the context of ongoing debates about the reform of the public sector. The championing of choice in service provision does seem to herald the next phase in the application of the 'new public sector school of management' to the UK. The underlying reform discourse draws upon the marketisation of public services (see Chapter Two) and in particular the notion of consumer choice. However, the application of choice to employment and benefit services is problematic. For example, in the New Deal for Disabled People, which did seek to give participants a degree of choice in the provider they used, some participants were unaware that they had a choice (Stafford et al, 2004). Where participants did know they had a choice, often they selected a provider on grounds of their proximity and accessibility rather than on the basis of the service provided. Few participants in the New Deal for Disabled People actively investigated what services different providers offered. Choice in activation services does require the delivery of *informed* choice.

Moreover, there are limits to the extent to which a national service covering a wide range of client groups can be 'personalised'. Issues such as 'high' staff turnover in Jobcentre Plus, lack of training in dealing with the hardest to reach, staff not being aware of the full range of provision within a locality and staff finding it difficult to engage in meaningful work-focused discussions with claimants of benefits other than Jobseeker's Allowance (especially those in receipt of incapacity benefits) will constrain the degree to which welfare-to-work services can be tailored to individual claimants.

Predicting the future direction of policy is a precarious activity and prone to error. Nevertheless, it is anticipated that the delivery of programmes will, while unemployment levels remain low, become more personalised in the UK.

Acknowledgements

Thanks are due to Sharon Walker and Nicola Selby at the Centre for Research in Social Policy (CRSP), Loughborough University, UK, who helped to prepare the typescript, and to Laura Adelman who produced Table 7.1.

Notes

[1] In this chapter the provision of 'personalised' services is taken to be synonymous with 'individualised' services, in the sense that services are seen as being tailored to meet the needs of individuals (see Chapter One). However, more recent debates about the reform of public services in the UK have seen the emergence of a wider definition of 'personalised' services, which incorporates the notions of user involvement and co-production. As yet this wider definition has not been applied to employment and benefit services.

[2] The International Labour Office definition of unemployment covers people who: are out of work, want a job, have actively sought work in the previous four weeks and are available to start work within the next fortnight; or are out of work and have accepted a job that they are waiting to start in the next fortnight.

[3] At that time Jobcentre Plus was referred to as the Single Work-Focused Gateway, which was piloted as ONE, before being rolled out nationally as Jobcentre Plus.

References

Arthur, S., Corden, A., Green A., Lewis, J., Loumidis, J., Sainsbury, R., Stafford, B., Thornton, P. and Walker, R. (1999) *New Deal for Disabled People: Early implementation*, DSS Research Report No 106, London: Corporate Document Services.

Atkinson, J. (1999) *New Deal for Young Unemployed People: A summary of progress*, Research and Development Report No ESR13, Sheffield: Employment Service.

Bivand, P. (2000) 'Re-engineered New Deal for 25 Plus', *Working Brief*, 120, www.cesi.org.uk/_newsite2002/publications/wb/w120/html/newdeal25plus.htm (access 27 September 2002).

Blair, T. (2004) *PM speech on reforming the civil service*, 24 February 2004, www.number-10.gov.uk/output/Page5418.asp (access 29 February 2004).

Blunkett, D. (2000) *'On your side': The new welfare state as the engine of prosperity*, London: DfEE.

Bonjour, D., Dorsett, R., Knight, G., Lissenburgh, S., Mukherjee, A., Payne, J., Range, M., Urwin, P. and White, M. (2001) *New Deal for Young People: National survey of participants: Stage 2*, Research and Development Report No ESR67, Sheffield: Employment Service.

Bryson, A., Knight, G. and White, M. (2000) *New Deal for Young People: National survey of participants: Stage 1*, Research and Development Report No ESR44, Sheffield: Employment Service.

Cabinet Office (1999) *Modernising government*, Cm 4310, London: The Stationery Office.

Chatrik, B. and Convery, P. (1999) *The New Deal handbook*, London: Unemployment Unit and Youthaid.

DSS (Department of Social Security) (1998a) *New ambitions for our country: A new contract for welfare*, Cm 3805, London: The Stationery Office.

DSS (1998b) *A new contract for welfare: The gateway to work*, Cm 4102, London: The Stationery Office.

DWP (Department for Work and Pensions) (2005) *The Department for Work and Pensions departmental report 2005*, London: DWP.

Eagle, A. (1999) 'Implementing ONE: government's expectations', Paper presented to the QMW Public Policy Seminar: 'Effectively delivering Welfare to Work ONE – the single work-focused gateway', London: 12 October.

Finch, H. and O'Connor, W. with Millar, J., Hales, J., Shaw, A. and Roth, W. (1999) *The New Deal for Lone Parents: Learning from the prototype areas*, DSS Research Report No 92, Leeds: CDS.

Griffiths, R., Irving, P. and McKenna, K. (2003) *Synthesising the evidence on flexible delivery*, DWP Research Report No 171, Sheffield: DWP.

Hasluck, C. (2000) *The New Deal for the Long Term Unemployed: A summary of progress*, Research and Development Report No ESR46, Sheffield: Employment Service.

Hasluck, C. (2002) *The re-engineered New Deal 25 Plus: A summary of recent evaluation evidence*, WAE Report No 137, Sheffield: Department for Work and Pensions.

HM Treasury (2000a) *Budget 2000: Prudent for a purpose: Working for a stronger and fairer Britain*, HC 346, London: The Stationery Office.

HM Treasury (2000b) *Spending review 2000: Prudent for a purpose: Building opportunity and security for all*, London: The Stationery Office.

HM Treasury (2002a) *Opportunity and security for all: Investing in an enterprising, fairer Britain: New Public Spending Plans 2003-2006*, Cm 5570, London: The Stationery Office.

HM Treasury (2002b) *Budget 2002 financial statement and budget report*, www.hm-treasury.gov.UK/Budget/bud_bud02/budget_re../bud_bud02rechap4.cfm (accessed 24 April 2002).

HM Treasury (2005) *Britain meeting the global challenge: Enterprise, fairness and responsibility, pre-budget report December 2005*, Cm 6701, London: The Stationery Office.

HM Treasury/DWP (Department for Work and Pensions) (2003) *Full employment in every region*, London: The Stationery Office.

Kelleher, J., Youll, P., Nelson, A., Hadjivassiliou, K., Lyons, C. and Hills, J. (2002) *Delivering a work-focused service: Final findings from ONE case studies and staff research*, DWP Research Report No 166, Leeds: CDS.

Legard, R. and Ritchie, J. (1999) *New Deal for Young Unemployed People: National gateway*, Research and Development Report No ESR16, Sheffield: Employment Service.

Legard, R., Ritchie, J., Keegan, J. and Turner, R. (1998) *New Deal for Young Unemployed People: The gateway*, Research and Development Report No ESR8, Sheffield: Employment Service.

Lewis, J., Mitchell, L., Sanderson, T., O'Connor, W. and Clayden, M. (2000) *Lone parents and personal advisers: Roles and relationships*, DSS Research Report No 122, Leeds: CDS.

Loumidis, J., Stafford, B., Youngs, R., Green, A., Arthur, S., Legard, R., Lessof, C., Lewis, J., Walker, R., Corden, A., Sainsbury, R. and Thornton, P. (2001) *New Deal for Disabled People: Evaluation of the personal adviser service*, London: CDS.

Millar, J. (2000) 'Keeping track of welfare reform: The New Deal programmes', Paper presented to the Joseph Rowntree Foundation Seminar: 'Work, Security and the Single Gateway', London, 15 March.

National Statistics (2005) *Labour market statistics November 2005*, London: National Statistics.

Osgood, J., Stone, V. and Thomas, A. (2002) *Delivering a work-focused service: Views and experience of clients*, DWP Research Report No 167, Leeds: CDS.

Secretary of State (1997) 'Harriet Harmon sets out plans to transform delivery of social security', DSS Press Release, 22 July.

Stafford, B. (2003a) 'Beyond lone parents: extending welfare to work to disabled people and the young unemployed', in R. Walker and M. Wiseman (eds) *The welfare we want? The British challenge for American reform*, Bristol: The Policy Press, pp 143-74.

Stafford, B. (2003b) 'Service delivery and the user', in J. Millar (ed) *Understanding social security: Issues for policy and practice*, Bristol: The Policy Press, pp 213-34.

Stafford, B. with Ashworth, K., Davis, A., Hartfree, Y., Hill, K., Kellard, K., Legge, K., McDonald, S., Reyes De-Beaman, S., Aston, J., Atkinson, J., Davis, S., Evans, C., Lewis, J., O'Regan, J., Harries, T., Kazimirski, A., Pires, C., Shaw, A. and Woodward, C. (2004) *New Deal for Disabled People (NDDP): First synthesis report*, DWP Research Report No WAE199, Sheffield: DWP.

Vincent, J., Walker, R., Dobson, B., Stafford, B., Barnes, M. and Bottomley, D. (1998) *Lone parent caseworker pilots evaluation final report*, Centre for Research in Social Policy Working Paper No 263, Loughborough: CRSP.

Wilson, P. (2002) *Evaluation of re-engineered New Deal 25 Plus*, WAE Report No 111, Sheffield: DWP.

Winterbotham, M., Adams, L. and Kuechel, A. (2002) *Evaluation of New Deal for 25 Plus: Qualitative interviews with ES staff, providers, employers and clients*, WAE Report No 127, Sheffield: DWP.

Woodfield, K., Turner, R. and Ritchie, J. (1999) *New Deal for Young People: The pathfinder options*, ES Research and Development Report ES25, Sheffield: Employment Service.

EIGHT

Between universal policy and individualised practice: analysing activation policy in Finland

Elsa Keskitalo

Introduction

During the 1990s, Finland underwent considerable changes in the labour market and the social protection system. These changes brought increased uncertainty and individualisation of risk in the labour market, and a shift towards activation in social protection. Due to economic recession and difficulties in the state economy, cutbacks were introduced throughout the social security system in the early 1990s (Heikkilä and Uusitalo, 1997). These circumstances in part paved the way for the social policy reforms to follow. Even though the economy has recovered thereafter, unemployment has remained high on the political agenda (Kalela et al, 2001).

Since the mid-1990s, the political discourse has started to emphasise the individual responsibilities of unemployed people vis-à-vis structural factors. Increasingly, unemployment was no longer perceived as a consequence of economic development, but as being related to individual job-search activity and labour market attachment. The policy shift this brought about involved a number of activation policy reforms, which intended to make the service system more effective and to redefine benefit conditions. An activation requirement has been attached to the social assistance and the employment benefit systems, and the process of service provision has been reformed to reinforce active job search and individual activation of unemployed people.

In an activation reform introduced in 2001, *Laki kuntouttavasta työtoiminnasta* (Rehabilitative Work Experience Act), an attempt was made to combat long-term unemployment and the risk of social exclusion by means of a comprehensive activation strategy. In justifying the reform, reference was made to dissatisfaction with the quality and effectiveness of services and with the cooperation between administrations and agencies, but also to local variations in the activation efforts. The 2001 reform can be characterised as a *centralised* programme aimed at introducing a *universal* activation strategy, while implementation should simultaneously be directed by an *individual* approach. The core activation instrument is an individual activation plan that is to be developed with all young and long-term unemployed people who fulfil the age and benefit criteria as stipulated in the Act.

This chapter is based on an empirical analysis of the implementation of this reform. We are particularly interested in the intersections of redefining benefit conditions and reforming service structures, and their implications for individuals. The policy context and the development of activation policies in Finland is described and analysed, with specific attention to the 2001 activation reform. We examine the design and the implementation of this reform, and the scope and content of the individual approach it promotes. The specific nature of the programme – a universal policy that aims at individualised activation practices – is analysed. The data are based on a study of the implementation and effectiveness of the reform, carried out at STAKES in 2001-04 (Ala-Kauhaluoma et al, 2004).

Policy context and development

Commitment to activation and investment in individual capacities is not new to the Northern European welfare states (Esping-Andersen, 2002). Over the decades, active labour market policies have been an important part of employment policy – in terms of resources and the number of people covered by training and employment promotion programmes. In Finland active labour market policies were introduced into employment policy in the 1980s. Moreover, activation – as a continuation of a strong work ethic and work requirement – is seen as a fundamental aspect of social security entitlements. In this context, social assistance is a residual form of benefit aimed at promoting self-sufficiency (Drøpping et al, 1999).

The core feature of Nordic social policy is a high degree of universalism: all citizens and residents are entitled to basic social security benefits and services, regardless of their position in the labour market. Income security is based on earnings-related benefits for those with a work history and a flat-rate basic security for all residents. In recent years, the Nordic countries have been especially characterised as service states (Sipilä et al, 1997; see Esping-Andersen, 1999, p 79). Social and healthcare services are financed by taxation and provided, and mostly also supplied, by local authorities. This means that the role of autonomous municipalities in service provision is strong (Kautto et al, 1999). In the Finnish social welfare and service legislation, national standards and principles are generally provided by law, but considerable power for discretion is left to local authorities. Accordingly, the role of professional social welfare staff is crucial in how social rights are implemented and how the individual approach is realised in practice (Rostila, 2001).

In Finland, the qualifying period for earnings-related unemployment benefit (*tyottomyyspaivaraha*) is 10 months in employment. The maximum entitlement period is 500 days. Labour market support (*tyomarkkinatuki*) is unemployment assistance for those who do not qualify for unemployment insurance as a result of a limited work record. Most recipients are young unemployed or long-term unemployed people who have exhausted unemployment benefit entitlements. Labour market support is administered by the employment administration and delivered by the National Insurance Institution, KELA. Whereas labour market support is funded by the state, social assistance (*toimeentulotuki*) is administered and, for the main part, financed by the local municipalities. A typical feature of Finnish social assistance is that the majority of recipients top up other income and benefits with social assistance (Heikkilä et al, 2001). In 2004, the number of social assistance recipients was around 400,000, that is, 7.7% of the population. Most of them were receiving social assistance on a short-term basis (Toimeentulotuki, 2004).

Traditionally, activation of unemployed people has been the responsibility of the state and public employment services in Finland. It involved active labour market policy measures, such as training and work placement, but also the provision of employment services. In this context the right to unemployment benefit was dependent on one's willingness to accept an offer of work or training. In the late 1990s, activation was extended to social assistance recipients and municipal social welfare. Activation underwent several legislative reforms that adopted the individual action plan as an activation instrument. A 1998 reform adopted individual job-seeking plans as a means to activate jobseekers and reform employment service provision (Skog and Räisänen, 1997). At the same time, the idea of individual plans was adopted in the 1998 Social Assistance Act, targeted at recipients who refused an offer of work or training. In 1999, the action plan was adopted in the Integration of Immigrants and Reception of Asylum Seekers Act as a method for promoting the integration of immigrants into society and working life. Finally, in the 2001 activation reform, the individual activation plan was adopted as a basic activation instrument to promote entry into the labour market and social inclusion of young and long-term unemployed people. The subsequent Rehabilitative Work Experience Act is built on an approach to activation aimed at integrating active labour market measures and social services in the general activation plan. Recipients of labour market support and social assistance are activated according to the same rules, in cooperation between public employment services and social welfare offices.

Activation policy as introduced during the last decade has been commonly interpreted as a recommodification of the social welfare developed in the post-war period. Activation includes a range of policies, but they generally signal a stronger emphasis on supply-side-oriented programmes and conditionality of welfare (see Clasen and Van Oorschot, 2002). Besides the policies themselves, the issue as to how vigorously activation requirements are put into practice is obviously an important one. Despite a strong commitment to activation in the Nordic countries, the 1990s were characterised by stringent eligibility criteria and expenditure reductions rather than by strengthening investments in terms of new resources and opportunities for activation (Clasen et al, 2001). It has, nevertheless, been argued that the new activation requirements introduced since the early 1990s has meant more of a policy shift in Denmark and Finland, compared to Sweden and Norway (Hvinden et al, 2001). In this context, the goal of the 2001 activation reform in Finland was to improve the effectiveness of activation by activating simultaneously the service and benefit system and individual unemployed people.

Activation reform in Finland: between paternalism and citizenship

With the 2001 activation reform (the Rehabilitative Work Experience Act), the state clearly took collective responsibility in the promotion of employment and individual capacities. The reform was guided by strategies and instruments determined by policy makers and by a generalised picture of unemployment (see Chapter Two): national policy makers determined the objectives of the reform, the overall structure of activation and the rights and obligations of the participants. The target group, the timing of actions, as well as the forms of cooperation between the authorities are all determined in a relatively detailed way in the Act. However, policy delivery takes place in the interaction between the frontline staff and recipients, emphasising the importance of bottom-up processes in activation (Hill, 1997).

In fact, it was one of the aims of the Rehabilitative Work Experience Act – prepared in 1999 by a broad ministerial working group involving trades union representatives among others (Aktiivinen sosiaalipolitiikka – työryhmän, 1999) – to establish a uniform activation structure for the whole country. This objective needs to be interpreted against the background of numerous local initiatives and projects that were started in the 1990s, and accelerated following European Union membership in 1995. Regional and local activities were highly diversified and the government wanted to improve equality of access in the provision of activation services, while at the same time increasing the responsibility of municipalities in relation to activation.

The reform is a combination of paternalism and social citizenship, both of which are characteristics of the Nordic welfare states (Hvinden, 1999; van Berkel and Hornemann Møller, 2002). The state took responsibility for promoting employment for, and the employability of, long-term unemployed people, while at the same time imposing new obligations and work requirements on recipients as a condition of benefit receipt. Long-term unemployment was categorically perceived as reducing competence among unemployed people, which was used as a further justification for the introduction of activation and rehabilitative activities. This is reflected in the name of the new activation scheme. Within the paternalistic policy framework, an individualised activation approach was adopted: individuals were required to participate in designing their individual activation plans in dialogue with welfare staff.

New conditions for citizenship

In the debates on the Finnish activation reform, and in the regulations regarding the rights and obligations of clients and authorities, the citizenship perspective was important. Parliament had to take into account the new constitutional rights introduced in 1995. An important implication of this was that Parliament discussed whether the new Act was incongruent with the protection of a minimum subsistence level as granted by the Constitution. This led to the decision that in situations where clients refused to participate in activation, social assistance could be reduced but not totally withdrawn. Furthermore, rights and obligations were formulated in detail in the Act in an attempt to ensure the equal treatment and protection of the social rights of recipients as guaranteed by the Constitution (Sakslin and Keskitalo, 2005). In line

with the Nordic tradition in social policy, the Finnish activation reform
was built on universal provisions.

The Rehabilitative Work Experience Act is a universal programme
in the sense that it covers all unemployed residents who fulfil the
conditions as laid down in the Act. Eligibility for activation is
determined by age and benefit criteria. All unemployed people are to
be activated after a certain period of dependency on labour market
support or social assistance. As in many other European activation
programmes, young unemployed people are targeted earlier than older
age groups (see Lødemel and Trickey, 2001). For example, young
unemployed people under the age of 25 have to be activated after
four months of being on social assistance, whereas those over the age
of 25 have to be activated after 12 months. What is new in the reform
is that all the unemployed people targeted are obliged to participate in
drawing up an individual activation plan in an individualised service
process. Entitlement to minimum income benefits is tied to compliance
with behavioural requirements. Participation is controlled by sanctions
and administrative rules for behaviour (see Mead, 1997).

Individualised activation process

In line with the 'European' activation approach, the reform aims at
promoting labour market attachment and at developing human
resources (Theodore and Peck, 2001; also see Chapter Six, this volume),
for example by improving access to training and other active labour
market measures, and by supporting life management of long-term
unemployed people. This is indicated in the individual action plans
that take the form of contractual arrangements between the individual
and the state (Mosley and Sol, 2005), with subsequent measures agreed
between the participants.

The individual action plan should include a step-by-step path towards
employment. The ultimate goal of the activation process is employment.
This is illustrated by the fact that the activation process is terminated
only after the unemployed person has been in employment for 10
months. If work is not an option, active labour market measures, such
as training and various work subsidies, are provided. Rehabilitative
work experience can be used when no other measures are applicable
within three months, and can be supplemented by social, healthcare
and rehabilitation services. More than other measures, rehabilitative
work experience is targeted at combating social exclusion among
long-term unemployed people.

Rehabilitative work experience is a tailor-made work experience scheme provided by municipalities. Placements are provided by the public sector, non-governmental organisations and associations, and related workplaces. Unlike labour market training and other labour market measures, rehabilitative work experience placements cannot take place in the private sector. Participation in rehabilitative work experience is obligatory only for those under the age of 25. This obligation presupposes that no other measure is applicable and that participation in a work experience scheme is agreed upon in the individual activation plan. A financial bonus for participation is paid on top of social assistance or labour market support to increase the attractiveness of the scheme (*Laki kuntouttavasta työtoiminnasta* – Rehabilitation and Work Experience Act).

Integrated approach in activating unemployed people

Traditionally, employment policies and social policies are governed by different ministries and agencies. Basically, activation policies have blurred this traditional division between labour market policy and social protection (Clasen and Van Oorschot, 2002). In Finland, coordination between employment and social welfare agencies has been a particular feature of activation programmes aimed at long-term unemployed people. This also involved the issue of sharing responsibilities and finances between the state (employment administration) and local authorities (the municipalities). The integrated approach to activation (European Foundation for Improvement of Living and Working Conditions, 2002) was justified by the fact that the municipal social welfare office and the local employment office shared a large number of clients.

The Finnish model of integrated activation implies integration of the objectives of employment and social inclusion under the same programme, and close cooperation between local employment offices and municipal social welfare offices. The core instrument in the integrated activation approach is the activation plan that always has to be drawn up through tripartite negotiations, involving an employment officer, a social worker and the client. The integrated model should improve targeting and enhance the effectiveness of activation measures. The rationale underlying this model is that the multidimensional nature of long-term unemployment and exclusion problems calls for an interdisciplinary approach in assessing and tackling these problems: not only employment problems, but wider life management issues and barriers to employment should be dealt with in the activation process. The skills and professions of the employment administration and the social welfare office are mobilised in the activation process (van Berkel and Roche, 2002).

Activation reform in the local context: towards individualised practice

The evaluation study of the reform (Ala-Kauhaluoma et al, 2004) focused both on the attainment of the employment and social inclusion objectives of particular activation processes, and on the implementation process. Outcomes of the activation reform were investigated in 51 out of 448 municipalities; a more detailed study of implementation was conducted in seven of those municipalities. The core question of the evaluation was how participation in the activation plan and the measures agreed in the plan influenced labour market participation, income and well-being. Moreover, the researchers were interested in finding out to what extent the reform was delivered as intended by the Act, and what form activation took in practice. Finally, the experiences of the implementing staff and clients with the reform were investigated. In general, the focus was on the individualised activation process and its implications.

The results of the study showed that, in general, implementation was not a straightforward process from policy making to practice. Implementation started with delays, and varied considerably across the local municipalities and employment offices. The reform was also received with criticism by the local actors. Although local authorities saw combating long-term unemployment and the risk of social exclusion as important goals, the (lack of) means provided by the legislative reform were received with caution: resources to implement the reform were found to be inadequate in relation to the needs. These circumstances implied that the universal policy objectives were not fully achieved. Eligibility had to be defined locally by the street-level organisations and discretion had to be applied in the selection of clients (Lispky, 1980). The staff had to make decisions about which members of the target group would be prioritised in activation. In practice, priority was given to young unemployed people under the age of 25 and those who were expected to benefit from the integrated activation plan process (Ala-Kauhaluoma et al, 2004).

Experiences with the activation plan

Nearly all participants in the activation plan had previously been involved in drawing up a jobseeking plan together with an employment officer. In the two preceding years, only 28% of the participants had not participated in any labour market policy measures. This means that in most cases, drawing up an activation plan implied a renewed activation process. The difference this time was that the activation plan was drawn up in cooperation with the employment officer, the social worker and the unemployed person. Despite previous participation in the jobseeking planning process and activation measures, the majority of the participants responded to it in a positive manner. Shortly after having participated in the formulation of their individual activation plan, as many as 83% of the participants saw it as personally significant. A particular expectation among the participants was that they hoped to gain access to work through the activation plan.

The official policy objectives were reflected in policy practice. Within the integrated activation model, most activation measures included in the plans were derived from the employment administration: jobseeking activities and active labour measures were emphasised. The primary objective was to reintegrate young and long-term unemployed people into the regular labour market and labour market measures. Nevertheless, human resource and social policy-oriented measures were included in a considerable number of activation plans. Approximately 15% of the activation plans included social and healthcare services. In general, it was usual for several measures to be included in the plans as optional choices.

The outcomes of activation were examined six or eight months after the activation plan had been drawn up. The findings show that 50% of those who had been involved in drawing up the activation plan were still unemployed six or eight months later. Of the other 50%, a majority had been placed in various labour market policy measures, in most cases in training, on-the-job training and subsidised work placements. Around 10% of the participants actually started the rehabilitative work experience scheme. According to the findings, participation in the activation plan process did not have any significant impact on employment in the open labour market in the six-month period following the drawing up of the activation plan: only 8% of the participants were employed in the open labour market.

Besides employment, the impact of activation on other goals (such as social well-being, health, quality of life, income and participation in various activities) was examined. If the outcomes of activation were work related, they contributed to economic and other types of well-being among the participants. Social well-being was linked to changes in the individual employment situation, implying that participation in active labour market policy measures and employment in the open labour market is linked to improved well-being. Furthermore, participation in the activation plan facilitated participation in various active measures for those who had been unemployed for longer periods.

While expectations of activation were high when measured just after the activation plan was agreed upon, they started to fall if expectations were not realised. After six months, less than half the participants (46%) considered the activation plan personally useful, compared to 83% just after the individual action plan was drawn up. Basically, the policy was capability friendly in that it aimed at labour market attachment and the development of human resources (Salais, 2003). However, by investing in individual activation and individual employability only, employment targets were not achievable, and this contributed to the lowered expectations among the participants. In the evaluation period, the overall demand for labour limited the opportunities for participants to access the open labour market.

All in all, the drawing up of individualised activation plans worked roughly as anticipated, but the functioning of the labour market and problems with personal qualifications, health and social circumstances of the unemployed people had a negative influence on their level of success. In the short evaluation period, half the participants were placed in various forms of active labour market policy measures and rehabilitative work activities. These might improve their individual capacities and employability in the future, but in order to live up to their promise of being a leg-up to employment, activation policies should include both supply- and demand-driven policy measures. Obviously successful activation policy calls for dynamic labour markets and the availability of entry-level jobs, and this was not the case in this period (Theodore and Peck, 2001).

Implementation of rights and responsibilities

The new activation scheme includes an obligation to participate and act on the measures agreed upon in the individual action plan. Non-compliance could result in sanctions. Sanctions are not a new thing: reducing social assistance has been possible since 1996 if a recipient refused an offer of work or training. A new feature of the Act was the obligation to participate in the drawing up of an individual activation plan and to engage in a process of promoting one's employability and employment. Sanctions are imposed if a client does not participate without an acceptable reason as mentioned in the Act, or if they do not follow the plan as agreed. Although the principle of sanctioning is laid down in the Act, its practical application is decided on an individual basis by the frontline staff.

According to the empirical findings, although the programme was mandatory and recipients were obliged to participate in the activation plan, sanctions were avoided whenever possible. Social workers described how their decisions were based on individual discretion and consideration of the nature of the non-compliance. Accordingly, sanctions were imposed if clients were 'unwilling to do anything'. In this sense, sanctions operated as a 'work test' or 'activity test' for the recipients. The staff emphasised that complying with obligations is a legal duty under the Act that binds both parties. They also stressed an atmosphere of trust and cooperation with their clients in implementation. In practice, only a small minority of the invited recipients refused to participate in the planning process or in the measures agreed upon in it. Correspondingly, sanctions were imposed on a few per cent of the eligible recipients.

The sanctioning policy was slightly different in employment offices that administered labour market support and in social welfare offices that provided social assistance. The differences were related to the relevant legislation: sanctioning rules in labour market support are more categorical, whereas in social assistance individual circumstances and fairness should be taken into account in the decision making on sanctions. Sanctioning social assistance recipients should not endanger the necessary subsistence level guaranteed by the Constitution. Reflections on the importance of compulsion and sanctions differed among staff members. Some viewed sanctions as necessary to promote clients' compliance with duties and to stress the importance of contributing to one's own employment. Others were sceptical about the importance of sanctions and were of the opinion that they were hardly ever helpful in individual cases. A third group saw the threat of sanctions as important to stress the legitimacy of the activation measures.

The unemployed people who were interviewed did not adopt a very negative position towards compulsory participation in the activation plan. They tended to perceive it as 'a rule of the game'. Some wondered why the authorities oblige everyone, when not everyone can be activated due to a lack of resources. Although most people accepted the duty to be active, they admitted that the mandatory nature of the programme gives it a negative label. For a number of the interviewed participants the individual activation plan itself proved to be an important process that helped to break through their long-term unemployment and to find a training place or even a future career. Some of the participants acknowledged that compulsory participation and behavioural requirements had significantly helped them personally. Professional competencies and commitment of the staff were found decisive for the individual process.

Rehabilitative work experience is a tailor-made scheme that provides work experience placements in the public sector and in associations. A positive aspect of the scheme was that placements could be tailored to individual circumstances. It provided an opportunity for participants to become aware of their competencies by actually practising their skills in day-to-day activities. Through participation in work-like activities, clients were able to improve their self-confidence and establish a daily routine. However, working in a work placement without having a regular work contract and thus forming a secondary labour force was considered a negative element. These problems resulted in a number of cancellations and drop-outs. Although rehabilitative work activities were initially aimed at those under the age of 25, most participants were in fact over 25 (and joined the scheme voluntarily). This can be explained by the fact that a larger number of options were available for the young unemployed people compared to older age groups.

Besides contributing to the activation of the unemployed people, what was equally important was that the programme stimulated the authorities to become more active towards unemployed people (see van Berkel and Roche, 2002). Compulsory activation encouraged the service institutions to take their role as activators more seriously. The activation plan contributed positively to the cooperation between authorities and to the overall functioning of the service provision process. Moreover, the integrated activation model provided concrete tools and a route to active labour market policy measures for social assistance recipients, which was an improvement compared to the situation in which the measures were provided solely by the local municipalities (see Torfing, 1999). Thus, the integrated activation plan changed the way the service organisations were operating, something the unemployed people benefited from. Not only had the staff to renew their services for the unemployed people, they also had to reflect on their practices and align them to those of the partners with which they had to cooperate.

Implications of the individualised service: user involvement in activation

Activation or action plans are a form of client contract commonly used to regulate the relations between the individual and the state. Formally, a client contract refers to a document that a recipient signs showing their willingness to cooperate in finding a job (Mosley and Sol, 2005). The contract approach raises many issues and also tensions from a user perspective. Individual client contracts have both symbolic and legal meanings. Symbolically, the contracts refer to the reciprocal nature of relations between the provider and the client inspired by the idea of a negotiation process between two parties. Legally, client contractualism is not in accordance with the basic idea of freedom of contract, but refers to conditions that qualify the individual for the benefit. The contracts can also be understood as a tool for case management, functioning as an appropriate legal instrument to facilitate the relationship between the service system and a recipient (Eichenhofer and Westerveld, 2005). From the user perspective, findings of the Finnish activation reform in relation to achieving a balance between the principle of equality and an individualised contract approach, are important.

The Finnish activation reform largely relies on the individual activation plan as a form of agreement between individual citizens and the authorities. The evaluation study found that, in practice, the contractual process was followed in the sense that all participants signed the activation plan and that it was interpreted as binding when signed. It could, however, be amended if circumstances changed. It functioned more as a working tool to commit participants than as a contract in legal terms. Recipients felt that they had a voice in the process and that they were heard: they were able to inform the staff about their needs and to influence the content of their individual plan. The draft plan was altered if a recipient did not agree with it. The activation plan provided a forum for negotiation about labour market choices and placements and the qualifications required. It aimed to facilitate, but also required, citizens capable of making decisions and expressing their opinions. At the same time, it formed a learning process for both the staff and recipients. Compared to the former service provision process, recipients experienced it as more democratic. One of them formulated it as follows in the evaluation study: 'Now they ask our opinion. The functioning of the employment office has really changed compared with how it was in the past'.

This cannot, however, disguise the power imbalance between staff and recipients. Even though recipients have a say in the process, they cannot opt out without there being consequences, as their livelihood is dependent on social security benefits (Hirschmann, 1970). Signing the activation plan, showing willingness to cooperate and undertaking job-search activities are conditions for benefit entitlements to be effectuated (see Mosley and Sol, 2005). In other words, the whole context of the individualised activation plan is important in determining how individual opinion and voice can be expressed. In the context of conditional benefits, one can question the extent to which clients can turn down offers of employment, and whether passive consent can be interpreted as agreement. Based on the data of the Finnish evaluation study, it was obvious that the activation plan provided a forum for discussion and some form of co-determination and choice for the recipients. As the process of drawing up the activation plan was prescribed by law, it made the working methods of the staff more visible and verifiable, and that should support the user perspective – at least, it is expected to make the service process more transparent.

When activation policies denote a redefinition of rights and duties for the recipients and make benefit receipt in fact conditional on participation in various forms of activation, institutional norms and rules play an important role in guaranteeing social rights and equal treatment of citizens. If they are left merely to discretionary decision making at the delivery end of the policy, there is a risk that clients receive different treatment and, therefore, there is a risk that their social rights are violated. From a citizenship perspective, centralised policies are more predictable than totally individually oriented policies. Accordingly, if social rights are reformulated, as is the case in activation policies, citizens should be aware of the new rules and conditions. This was an important objective set by policy makers in the Finnish reform, and equally found to be of importance by the staff and recipients.

Activation changes the position of clients vis-à-vis service providers. In this context, the introduction of individualised activation plans can, on the one hand, be perceived as a shift from user participation to user involvement (see Chapter Five). The contractual procedure that regulates the process of drawing up activation plans might increase user involvement compared to the former situation that was characterised more by discretionary social work practice. Defined rights and duties create more transparency and predictability than traditional social work practice. Since the activation reform, recipients receive written information about rights and duties in advance and are aware of the process and its consequences. On the other hand, the paternalistic policy framework adopted in the 2001 activation reform can be seen as a limitation from the perspective of users. Involuntary participation and the possibility of sanctions can be viewed as obstacles from the perspective of user involvement.

Yet another relevant question from the perspective of users is whether the individualised activation policy provides 'more' or 'less' compared to the previous policies (Lødemel and Trickey, 2001, pp 10-12). Indicating these options, in the evaluation study social workers interpreted participation in the activation plan process as a positive obligation for clients, which not only provides them with benefits, but also with the means to inclusion (see Rosanvallon, 2000). Recipients tend to understand involuntary participation as a rule of the game, basically intended to provide them with some form of opportunity, despite the negative label attached to the scheme.

Conclusions

Activation policies reveal several obvious contradictions. On the one hand, activation provides individual solutions in the context of structural changes in the labour market: unemployment and, consequently, the risk of exclusion are individualised. On the other hand, individualised and targeted policies are required from an individual perspective as they are expected to provide space for reflexive services that better meet the needs of individual biographies (Beck and Beck-Gernsheim, 2002; see Chapter Four, this volume). As in many other countries, activation in Finland takes place through contractual arrangements between individuals and the government: the individual activation plan. How the individual activation approach works from the perspective of the individual citizen is ultimately an empirical question. The goal of this chapter has been to find answers to this question on the basis of an empirical study of the Finnish 2001 activation reform.

With the reform, the state took collective responsibility in advancing employability and investing in individual capacities. It involved a combination of active labour market policy, rehabilitative activities and social as well as employment services. An outstanding element of the reform was the integrated provision of activation services as a joint effort of employment and social welfare offices. In accordance with the overall activation strategy, the reform represented first and foremost a supply-side approach aimed at promoting individual employability, treating the demand side more or less as given. Although the reform with its individualised activation was received well by frontline staff and recipients, and although it contributed to individual capacities, employment goals were not achievable with this strategy.

The findings of the evaluation study show that clients had practical opportunities to express their opinions and preferences in the formulation of the activation plan, although participation in drawing up the plan itself was compulsory. The experiences with the reform show that it was important to find a balance between rights and duties and their application in the individual activation process. In this process the competency of staff was decisive. The legal norms can support the realisation of citizenship rights and promote equality among clients. However, adequate flexibility and discretion is necessary in the implementation to enable individual preferences and resources to be taken into account.

The Finnish activation reform is a combination of paternalistic and citizenship-based aspirations. Reflecting the strong universal tradition of the Nordic welfare states, the rights and duties of the authorities and citizens were included in detail in the legal regulations, even though this does not take away the fact that new conditions and behavioural requirements were attached to minimum income benefits. In a similar way, although the policy was directed by rather paternalistic assumptions about unemployed people, the policy was justified by a striving for social justice, social equality and protection of social rights: it should protect citizens in changing and increasingly risky labour market conditions. The starting point of the official policy was an individualised approach in drawing up activation plans and a variety of activation pathways in terms of employment and human resources.

The problem with the rehabilitative work activity and the whole programme in general is the paternalistic departure of the policy that gives it a negative label: it reflects the 'new paternalism' (Mead, 1997) in which recipients have to follow certain behavioural rules in order to be entitled to social protection. The problem with the paternalistic approach is that it assumes that policy makers know better than citizens what is good for them. As Lawrence Mead (1997) has admitted, paternalism keeps the citizen in the position of a child in need of surveillance. This contradicts the idea of active citizenship and active participation of citizens that is nevertheless the ultimate goal of activation policies. Activation policies carry several paradoxes; and this is one of them (see Chapter Six, this volume).

References

Aktiivinen sosiaalipolitiikka – työryhmän muistio (Proactive Social Policy – Working Group Memoranda) (1999) *Työryhmämuistioita 20*, Helsinki: Sosiaali- ja terveysministeriö (Ministry of Social Affairs and Health).

Ala-Kauhaluoma, M., Keskitalo, E., Lindqvist, T. and Parpo, A. (2004) *Työttömien aktivointi: Kuntouttava työtoiminta – lain sisältö ja vaikuttavuus* (Activating the unemployed: Rehabilitative work experience – the content and effectiveness of the Act), Research report, Helsinki: STAKES.

Beck, U. and Beck-Gernsheim, E. (2002) *Individualization*, London: Sage Publications.

Clasen, J. and Van Oorschot, W. (2002) 'Work, welfare and citizenship: diversity and variation within European (un)employment policy', in J. G. Andersen, J. Clasen, W. van Oorschot and K. Halvorsen (eds) *Europe's new state of welfare*, Bristol: The Policy Press, pp 233-45.

Clasen, J., Kvist, J. and Van Oorschot, W. (2001) 'Increasing work requirements in unemployment compensation schemes', in M. Kautto, M. Heikkilä, B. Hvinden, S. Marklund and N. Ploug (eds) (2001) *Nordic social policy: Changing welfare states*, London: Routledge, pp 198-231.

Deacon, A. (2002) *Perspectives on welfare*, Buckingham: Open University Press.

Drøpping, J. A., Hvinden, B. and Vik, K. (1999) 'Activation policies in the Nordic countries', in M. Kautto, J. Fritzell, B. Hvinden, J. Kvist and H. Uusitalo (2001) *Nordic welfare states in the European context*, London: Routledge, pp 133-58.

Eichenhofer, E. and Westerveld, M. (2005) 'Contractualism: a legal perspective', in E. Sol and M. Westerveld (eds) *Contractualism in employment services*, The Hague: Kluwer Law International, pp 21-39.

Esping-Andersen, G. (1999) *The social foundations of postindustrial economies*, Oxford: Oxford University Press.

Esping-Andersen, G. (2002) 'Towards the good society, once again?', in G. Esping-Andersen, D. Gallie, A. Hemerijck and J. Myles (eds) *Why we need a new welfare state*, New York: Oxford University Press, pp 1-25.

European Foundation for the Improvement of Living and Working Conditions (2002) *Integrated approaches to active welfare and employment policies*, Luxembourg: Office for Official Publications of the European Communities.

Heikkilä, M. and Uusitalo, H. (eds) (1997) *The cost of cuts: Studies on cutbacks in social security and their effects in the Finland of the 1990s*, Helsinki: STAKES.

Heikkilä, M., Fridberg, T. and Keskitalo, E. (2001) 'Guaranteed minimum income: recent trends and socio-political discussion', in M. Heikkilä and E. Keskitalo (eds) *Social assistance in Europe*, Helsinki: STAKES, pp 13-36.

Hill, M. (1997) *The policy process in the modern state* (3rd edition), London: Prentice Hall.

Hirschmann, A. (1970) *Exit, voice and loyalty: Responses to decline in firms, organisations and states*, London: Harvard University Press.

Hvinden, B. (1999) 'Activation: a Nordic perspective', in European Foundation for the Improvement of Living and Working Conditions, *Linking welfare and work*, Luxembourg: Office for Official Publications of the European Communities, pp 27-42.

Hvinden, B., Heikkilä, M. and Kankare, I. (2001) 'Towards activation? The changing relationship between social protection and employment in Western Europe', in M. Kautto, J. Fritzell, B. Hvinden, J. Kvist and H. Uusitalo (eds) *Nordic social policy*, London: Routledge, pp 168-97.

Kalela, J., Kiander, J., Kivikuru, U., Loikkanen, H. A. and Simpura, J. (eds) (2001) *Down from the heavens, up from the ashes: The Finnish economic crisis of the 1990s in the light of economic and social research*, Government Institute for Economic Research, Helsinki: VATT Publications 27:6.

Kautto, M., Heikkilä, M., Hvinden, B., Marklund, S. and Ploug, N. (1999) 'Introduction: the Nordic welfare states in the 1990s', in M. Kautto, M. Heikkilä, B. Hvinden, S. Marklund and N. Ploug (eds) *Nordic welfare states in the European context*, London: Routledge, pp 1-18.

Lipsky, M. (1980) *Street-level bureaucracy: Dilemmas of the individual in public services*, New York: Russell Sage Foundation.

Lødemel, I. and Trickey, H. (eds) *'An offer you can't refuse': Workfare in an international perspective*, Bristol: The Policy Press.

Mead, L. (1997) *The new paternalism*, Washington, DC: Brookings Institute.

Mosley, H. and Sol, E. (2005) 'Contractualism in employment services: A socio-economic perspective', in E. Sol and M. Westerveld (eds) *Contractualism in employment services*, The Hague: Kluwer Law International, pp 1-20.

Rosanvallon, P. (2000) *The new social question*, Princeton, NJ: Princeton University Press.

Rostila, I. (2001) 'Social work or bureaucracy?', in M. Seltzer, C. Kullberg, S. P. Olesen and I. Rostila (eds) *Listening to the welfare state*, Ashgate: Aldershot, pp 241-60.

Sakslin, M. and Keskitalo, E. (2005) 'Contractualism in Finnish activation policy', in E. Sol and M. Westerveld (eds) *Contractualism in employment services*, The Hague: Kluwer Law International, pp 359-82.

Salais, R. (2003) 'Work and welfare: toward a capability approach', in J. Zeitlin and D. M. Trubek (eds) *Governing work and welfare in a new economy*, Oxford: Oxford University Press, pp 317-44.

Sipilä, J., Andersen, M., Hammarqvist, S.-E., Nordlander, L., Rauhala, P.-L., Thomsen, K. and Nielsen, H.W. (1997) 'A multitude of universal, public services – how and why did four Scandinavian countries get their social care service model?', in J. Sipilä (ed) *Social care services: The key to the Scandinavian welfare model*, Avebury: Aldershot, pp 27-50.

Skog, H. and Räisänen, H. (1997) *Toimivampiin työmarkkinoihin* (Towards a better functioning labour market), Helsinki: Ministry of Labour.

Theodore, N. and Peck, J. (2001) 'Searching for best practice in welfare-to-work: the means, the method and the message', *Policy & Politics*, vol 29, no 1, pp 81-94.

Toimeentulotuki 2004 (Social Assistance 2004) *Statistical Summary 24/2005*, Helsinki: STAKES.

Torfing, J. (1999) 'Workfare with welfare: recent reforms in the Danish welfare state', *Journal of European Social Policy*, vol 1, pp 5-28.

Van Berkel, R. and Hornemann Møller, I. (2002) 'The concept of activation', in R. van Berkel and I. Hornemann Møller (eds) *Active social policies in the EU: Inclusion through participation?*, Bristol: The Policy Press, pp 45-71.

Van Berkel, R. and Roche, M. (2002) 'Activation policies as reflexive social policies', in R. van Berkel and I. Hornemann Møller (eds) *Active social policies in the EU: Inclusion through participation?*, Bristol: The Policy Press, pp 197-224.

NINE

Do we know where we are going? Active policies and individualisation in the Italian context

Vando Borghi

Introduction

The processes of socioeconomic and demographic transformation affecting European countries since the 1970s brought about the need for *active* welfare states and increasingly *individualised* social policies. Although this need seems to be the same in all European countries, embedded in a common social discourse supported by national and transnational institutions and organisations, it leads to different concrete transformations and restructuring of the former welfare systems (Borghi, 2005; Borghi and Van Berkel, forthcoming: 2007).

Looking at the Italian context, one may – even though it is difficult to identify really individually tailored measures and schemes (see below) – observe some easily recognisable (institutional) consequences of the pressures towards the activation and individualisation of policies. The emergence of new forms of governance, indeed, can be linked to the necessity of providing new services and reforming the already existing ones. First, the increasing complexity of emerging social needs implies the integration of different competencies and professional skills in order to address these adequately with – usually – less and less standardised measures. Second, the increasing tendency to externalise, privatise and outsource public services to third sector bodies implies a pluralisation of actors and imposes the need to coordinate public and private agencies through new forms of governance arrangements (Pavolini, 2003). As a consequence, the problem of coordination (horizontally, among the different actors involved in the implementation of the policies; vertically, among the different levels at which the policies are designed and ruled) emerged as the central one (Kazepov and Sabatinelli, 2002).

In order to understand the specific Italian translation of the pressures towards active and individualised policies, we will try to summarise some important features of the country's welfare regime, focusing then on two particular fields of policy and reform – social assistance and labour market services – in which it is possible to see some efforts (and the respective problems) heading in that direction.

The context of welfare policies in the Italian case

The characteristics of the Italian model of welfare and unemployment have been studied for nearly thirty years and have been well known in the international debate since the 1970s (Ferrera, 1996; Trifiletti, 1999; Naldini, 2002; Saraceno, 2002; Ferrera et al, 2003). We can summarise the main characteristics of the Italian welfare system, which developed after the Second World War, as follows:

- *a strong relationship between labour market participation and social protection*: provisions – except health – depend on the claimants' labour market position or on the categories they belong to (for example, single mothers, blue collar workers in large- to medium-sized firms, older people);
- *a strong subsidiarity*: the family plays a major role in cultural (Church), economic (family businesses) and participatory terms; women have low activity rates and heavy care responsibilities in a still strongly gendered division of labour.

However, if we want to understand the Italian welfare system as the sum of all agencies producing welfare and their interactions within this process, this well-known synthetic picture is incomplete; in fact, it can describe other continental European models as well (for example, Germany). In order to understand the Italian specificities, we have to consider some additional features:

- a *strong North–South divide*: the territorial imbalances not only characterise the socioeconomic structure, but also the institutional design of policies (often regionally and locally fragmented). The two taken together bring about high industrialisation in the centre-northern regions, where a diffused small- and medium-sized enterprise-based industrial sector strengthens the occupational basis; in contrast with high unemployment in the southern regions, where widely spread informal work goes hand in hand with a subsistence economy. A high income inequality is a clear consequence;

- *an underdeveloped last safety net (assuring at least a minimum level of assistance)*: fragmented social policies, in particular social assistance schemes, and a strong emphasis on pensions serve to consolidate inequalities in the redistributive system;
- *a weak and passive form of subsidiarity*: the state does not directly support families in order to sustain standards of living and overcome conditions of need, it only supports people already in the labour market. The strong gender division of labour implicit in this form of subsidiarity brings about a very unbalanced distribution of power within households;
- *women and young people as particularly vulnerable groups*: this is especially the case in the South, where unemployment hits women and young people specifically and where their labour market participation is very low. The result is overall difficult conditions, in which female emancipation is unlikely to occur.

This model was reproduced and reinforced within the institutional settings of labour and social policies at least until the second half of the 1980s. The lack of a framework law at a national level left regions and municipalities in a legislative 'vacuum' for more than 20 years. The negative consequences of this situation have deeply structured the consolidation of institutional inequality in Italy (Negri and Saraceno, 1996; Kazepov, 2000).

One main consequence of this complex morphology has been the consolidation of a differentiated system of social citizenship, framed by very different legal contexts within which *citizens* are entitled to different sets of rights, related not so much to their condition of need, but to the specific eligibility rules and to the specific way in which social services are organised in the place where they live.

In synthesis, in Italy social assistance has been characterised up to now by extreme local differentiation and fragmentation (Fargion, 1997; Kazepov, 1998, 2000), in particular in relation to:

- the categorisation of claimants in need (single mothers, minors, older people, and so on);
- the existence of budget constraints: support is provided only if financial resources from regions and city councils are available, partly independent of people's needs. Therefore, entitlement to economic support is subordinated not so much to the condition of need per se, but to the wealth of the municipality;
- the income thresholds for the means test and the equivalence scales for the household's size.

Towards individualisation? Transformations in social assistance and labour market services

Since the end of the 1990s social assistance and labour market regulation and services went through a deep process of reform. As already mentioned, the demand for these reforms, apart from internal socioeconomic reasons, have to be associated with the general pressures towards individualisation and activation. Even if in a desynchronised way, as far as the development of labour market legislation and social policy is concerned, and in a context of persisting fragmentation on a territorial level, new laws, measures and schemes were introduced in different institutional fields, resulting in (a) an increasing weight of the (horizontal and vertical) subsidiarity principle in the social policy area, and (b) a growing recognition of the legislative autonomy of the regions in social assistance issues (Ferioli, 2002). The main effects of these reforms have become immediately visible in terms of:

- new duties and responsibilities for the regions (planning, coordination and defining the general aims of the regional social policies);
- the increasing role of municipalities (defined as the 'directors' of the local system of services;[1]
- a new and wider involvement of private actors (mostly non-profit organisations) in the delivery of services. Besides other elements (demographic and strictly financial reasons), the increasing emphasis (coherently with the more comprehensive move towards the 'service economy'; Borghi, 1998) on social quality (de Leonardis, 2002), on more client-centred services and on citizens' active involvement in designing and realising policies, is at the basis of the restructuring of both welfare and labour market institutions.

Against the background of these general trends, we will particularly take into consideration two areas of change clearly exemplifying these new developments in the Italian picture. On the one hand, the experimentation of *Reddito Minimo di Inserimento* (RMI), in the context of a more general and complex reform of the Italian social assistance system; on the other hand, the reform of the public employment services (PES). Both of them are explicitly oriented at producing a more individual active role in defining strategies, actions and steps for coping with difficult biographical passages and phases.

In October 2000, a national framework law for the realisation of an integrated system of social provisions and services (National Law 328/

2000) was aimed at reorganising the existing fragmentation, which up to that period was institutionalised into often diverging and unequal access criteria to services and welfare provisions at regional and local level. The meaning of this framework law – entitled 'General law for the realisation of an integrated system of social interventions and services'[2] – can be identified along the following lines (Bifulco, 2003):

- the definition of an *essential level of social services* that welfare institutions have to provide all over the country (universalistic aims);
- overcoming the traditional limits of the Italian welfare system (treating recipients of services as passive subjects; fragmentation of service access according to predefined categories), stressing the *aim of the general citizens' well-being;*[3]
- realising the principle of *the integration of services,* in order to overcome both the division into separate category-based compartments of the services and the separation among different sectors of social policies (social assistance, healthcare, education, training, labour);
- involving a *plurality of different social actors* (state, regions, provinces, municipalities, third sector organisations, citizens' associations, local communities), unified by principles of vertical and horizontal subsidiarity in the planning and delivery of social policies.

This regulating framework was the first law in Italy aiming at providing an integrated network of services and assistance, overcoming existing fragmentation and inequality and guaranteeing a universal basis of rights. RMI, on the social assistance side, and reformed labour market services, on the labour market side, can be analysed as (different) instruments for concretely constructing individualised and activating devices of social inclusion in the context of such an integrated and coordinated social protection net.

As far as the introductory experimentation of RMI is concerned, one important aspect should be particularly stressed: its already mentioned universalistic and homogeneous nature, aiming at overcoming different sources of discrimination (between the *deserving* and *undeserving* poor, and due to strong territorial and institutional differentiation) and at strictly integrating a universalistic minimum income support scheme with programmes aimed at social and labour market inclusion. With regard to the individualisation of the policies, the most significant element of the scheme is its contractual device: an individual agreement between local social services and recipients has to be signed, conditioning the access to different levels of economic support to the individual/family situation and to their willingness to participate in individually tailored programmes of socioeconomic integration (education, counselling, professional training, subsidised or formal labour market inclusion, and so on). It has to be emphasised at once that the RMI experimentation, which initially involved 39 Italian municipalities for two years (1998-2000), and was then extended in 2000 for two more years involving an additional 272 municipalities, has been cancelled by the former government.[4] Instead of revising it on the basis of the problems highlighted by the Monitoring Report (IRS et al, 2001), and before its expansion to the whole Italian territory, 'the baby was thrown out with the bath water, mainly for ideological reasons (to get rid of anything done by the former centre-left governments)' (Sacchi and Bastagli, 2005, p 111).

Looking at the reform of labour market services, the specific national starting point has to be underlined. Considering that the traditional and inadequate system of unemployment protection remained substantially untouched, the introduction of elements of individualisation and activation happened in a particular way when comparing it to other countries: without introducing any punitive elements into unemployment schemes, on the one hand, but also continually postponing any sort of expansion and upgrading of benefit and social protection coverage, on the other. The implicit rationale of the process of reform seems to be that 'if anyone has not been doing his job, that is first of all the State, with its strangling regulations and self-reinforcing bureaucracy'; hence, 'the effort – perhaps too optimistic – was to provide an overhaul of the public sector', redefining its tasks, structures and institutional procedures (Fargion, 2003, p 8). Such an effort was effectively needed in order to obtain more individualised labour market services: before the reforms, the PES were almost completely absorbed by mere bureaucratic controls and standardised procedures, reaching no more than 10-15% of the Italian jobseeking population (Paci, 1997).

RMI in the Italian path: introduction and evolution

As was mentioned before, the fundamental innovation of the RMI programme is that it introduces for the first time a measure acting as a non-categorical guaranteed safety net. The RMI is geared to *all* families whose income lies below a certain threshold, calculated according to the family's composition, in line with a uniform scale of equivalence for the entire country, which takes into account the presence of family members who are not self-sufficient (children under the age of 18, disabled and older people) or who have additional difficulties (drug addiction or problems related to immigration, such as language learning, facing practical everyday problems with bureaucracy, public and private services, finding accommodation, resolving formal problems with regularisation, and so on), assigning a higher ranking to them. The sum awarded corresponds to the difference between their actual income and the threshold. During the first wave (1998-2000) of experimentation, 34,700 families were involved, 93% of them living in the South of Italy; at the end of 2000, about 43% of the beneficiaries were involved in programmes of social insertion. However, looking at separate municipalities, the latter percentage ranged between 8% and 92% (in any case, these data tell us very little about the actual nature of programme involvement. Social insertion may involve a really wide variety of interventions, such as public health accompanying measures, preliminary orientation services, training courses and stages, temporary employment, and so on [Kazepov and Sabbatinelli, 2002; Ferrera et al, 2003]). Table 9.1 summarises the main features of the scheme.

One of the key features of the RMI was the emphasis placed on activation measures for recipients. An individually tailored agreement concerning a pathway for social and/or labour market reintegration was signed with every recipient; this is similar to what happens in France under the RMI there, but was something entirely new for Italy. As stated above, it has to be considered that the data in themselves do not tell us the whole, concrete story. Programmes may range from a return to compulsory schooling, to vocational training, to labour market integration, to LSU (Socially Useful Jobs), to psychological support or healthcare, and so on. People of working age who are

Table 9.1: RMI claimants and beneficiary households (1998-2000): beneficiaries involved in insertion programmes (on 31 December 2000)

Region	Claims submitted (number of households)	Accepted/submitted claims (%)	Beneficiaries (number of individuals)	Activated beneficiaries over total beneficiaries (%)
North	2,050	71.5	2,415	64.1
Centre	2,674	66.9	3,406	58.3
South and islands	50,798	62.0	79,997	41.9
Total	55,522	62.6	85,818	43.2
Total without Naples			68,482	28.8

Source: Sacchi and Bastagli (2005, pp 117 and 120)

unemployed and fit for work are expected to be available to attend vocational training courses and to accept any suitable job opportunities offered to them. In order to maintain the right to the benefit, beneficiaries are asked to undertake precise *obligations*, on the basis of a personalised contract. A picture of the variety of interventions that the insertion contract can result in is summarised in Table 9.2.

The combination of economic support and labour market integration under this scheme presupposed (a) the availability of adequate nationwide funding; (b) the existence of a network of local actors – public, private and non-profit – willing to cooperate in the various phases of social and employment projects; and (c) the presence (or the construction) of cognitive and cultural resources in the local administrations and in the street-level bureaucracies preparing them for assuming responsibilities, taking on active roles and empowering initiatives. The RMI should in all cases have acted as a catalyst and multiplier of partnerships, policy agreements and local conventions.

First Monitoring Reports pointed out various effects of the experimentation (IRS et al, 2001; Calza Bini et al, 2003; Sacchi and Bastagli, 2005). On the one hand, there were some positive aspects: leaving behind traditional category-based schemes, that had already showed their inefficacy in fighting social exclusion processes, and the introduction of a homogeneous measure for the entire national territory; enabling some promising capacities of activation, both of individuals (via specific programmes of socioeconomic integration) and of local administrations, even though the latter were faced with constraints in adopting new strategies and new institutional practices. On the other hand, there were negative aspects too, due to the frequent reinterpretation of the RMI scheme through old cognitive and practical ways of doing things. This stripped the agreement between recipients and social services of any *mutual* activation duties and responsibilities,

Table 9.2: Participation of activated beneficiaries in various types of insertion programmes

	Overall (%)	Without Naples (%)
Occupational	14.9	15.9
Public utility	9.6	18.6
Training	11.6	15.4
Schooling	14.5	19.5
Rehabilitation	2.3	4.1
Caring and family support	20.5	12.4
Social integration	24.5	10.1
Other programmes	2.1	4.0
Total	100.0	100.0

Source: Sacchi and Bastagli (2005, p 121)

and reduced the scheme to its mere economic and bureaucratic aspects (and sometimes to its usefulness for maintaining local systems of patronage or social control) (Agodi, 2003; Ferrera et al, 2003; Pennisi and Consoli, 2003). Research of the RMI implementation process shows, in particular, the crucial effect 'of the subjects or institutional agencies that, already before the scheme's implementation, played a key role in determining action and orientation criteria of the scheme recipients' (Agodi, 2003, p 61). It is clear that policy makers undervalued this aspect, and did not request useful indicators for monitoring how institutional mechanisms (at the municipal level) were reproduced/changed in the implementation of RMI.

Addressing in particular the aspects at the centre of this chapter, it has to be pointed out that the evaluations explicitly state that the RMI's beneficiaries (even those actors with stronger social networks and individual capabilities) are 'always, in all the case studies, objects, passive recipients and not active subjects of the social intervention' (Kazepov and Sabatinelli, 2002, p 209).

It is clear that the introduction of such a measure in the Italian context is risky: local municipalities (especially smaller ones) did not always have sufficient institutional and administrative capabilities at their disposal to create conditions of individualised activation and insertion. Moreover, in the more deprived areas of the country, the measure was functionally overloaded, soon becoming 'the only game in town' (Ferrera, 2005). But considering the strong territorial differences and citizenship inequalities, the current poverty situation in Italy and the weak effects of existing policies in reducing social exclusion risks, RMI nevertheless remains a device that should be (re)introduced.

Individualised labour market integration? Institutional change in the Employment Services

One of the forms that the pressures towards more individualised policies and services have taken is the widespread institutional emphasis (hegemonic in the 1990s) on the concept of employability (see Chapter Three, this volume). Improving employability became a trans-sector objective, and works as an 'institutional guideline idea'[5] for several public policy reforms (in Italy these include, apart from labour market regulation, also educational structures, vocational training, and so on). In particular, the first pillar of the European Employment Strategy guidelines stressed that 'within five years the member states should offer every young person within the first six months of unemployment an opportunity for training, retraining, work experience, or participation in an employment scheme; similar opportunities should be provided for adults within the first year' (Goetschy, 1999, p 127). This recommendation was fully received in the directions of reform undertaken in the Italian institutional context at the end of the 1990s. A radical restructuring of the PES was identified as the first step in improving the employability of young and adult (long-term) unemployed people and the precondition for promoting more individualised labour market services (Fargion, 2003). As was mentioned before, individualised labour market services are still very far from constituting the core of daily and normal activities, which still mainly consist of dealing with individual labour market passages (hiring, dismissals, and so on) in a bureaucratic way, and of applying standardised procedures.

From 1996 onwards, decentralisation processes (as part of a more general move towards the increasing insertion of New Public Management principles; Lippi, 2003) have been implemented in different directions, with regard to the institutional framework of labour market regulation, as well as to agreements, bargaining and new territorial employment and development projects (involving national, regional and municipal institutional levels, trades associations, and so on in order to create new job opportunities). This general trend towards decentralisation affected the PES too, resulting in an increasing role of regions, provinces and private actors (Table 9.3).

This process of devolution demanded a heavy organisational passage consisting mainly of (CNEL, 2002; Dau, 2003; Fargion, 2003; Ministero del Lavoro e delle Politiche Sociali, 2003):

- moving personnel from the state bureaucracy to regions and provinces (about 5,485 people, almost 60% of the current employees);
- an extensive formative effort (through training courses, change of responsibilities and offices) in order to deeply change procedures, practices and administrative cultures and to promote the adoption of more orientation and counselling focused on functions;
- trying to set common basic functions to be performed in the new PES, in order to avoid widening of the already existing gap between northern and southern Italy;
- providing interviews with young unemployed people before six months of registration and offering an individually tailored project of labour market reinsertion or training to specific target groups (such as long-term unemployed people and women re-entering the labour market);

Table 9.3: Distribution of tasks before and after the reform

(a) Before the reform (1996)

Ministry of Labour	• Political guidelines. • Planning and coordination of labour policies. • Government management of employment offices.
Regions (21)	• School counselling. • Vocational training.

(b) After the reform (2001)

Ministry of Labour	• General political and administrative guidelines. • SIL (Informative Labour System): planning, management and development.
Regions (21)	• Planning. • School counselling. • Vocational training. • Coordination of actions aimed to match labour supply and demand.
Provinces (103)	PES: information and counselling (for jobseeking and firms); supply–demand matching coordination; management; information supply to SIL.
Private sector	• Job placement services' agencies. • Agencies providing services (counselling and skills' evaluation for jobseekers) to PES.

Source: Our elaboration of Dau (2003, p 99)

- applying a general new regulation on the treatment of unemployed people, largely depending on a reform of existing benefit schemes. As the latter reform is still pending, many aspects of the PES reform itself could consequently not be implemented.

Another important point of the reform was the redefinition of the juridical status of unemployment: in order to be classified as unemployed, beyond being 'without a job' and 'immediately willing' to be employed (within 15 days), jobseekers have to undertake 'active job searching, according to ways agreed with the proper services'.[6] Non-compliance with the agreements with PES by the unemployed person or the non-acceptance of a 'proper job offer'[7] must be sanctioned with the loss of unemployment status.

Some structural and functional data about PES can give us a more precise picture of the current situation (Table 9.4). Employees in PES number about 10,000. About 60% of them are working in the southern PES centres (219 centres, out of a total of 527). Most PES agencies are small (up to nine employees) or medium-sized (between 10 and 15 employees); but in the South of Italy 15% of the centres have more than 21 employees.

Table 9.4: Resources and workload of PES

Region	Employees		Persons registered at the employment centres/PES employees	Job-searching persons/PES employees
	Number	%		
1 North West	1,055	10.9	423	289
2 North East	1,419	14.6	185	123
3 Centre	1,445	14.9	459	223
4 Centre–north[a]	3,919	40.4	350	205
5 South	5,792	59.6	426	243
Total	9,711	100.0	411	228

[a] Centre–north: 1 + 2 + 3.

Source: Our elaboration of Ministero del Lavoro e delle Politiche Sociali (2003)

As can be concluded from these data, the reform process is still far from realising its objectives. In a context influenced by a slowing economic cycle (private employment agencies show reduced activity as well), a comparison between the first six months of 2001 and 2002 reveals an evident drop in the services offered by public agencies to jobseekers: adding persons registered and not registered with PES, about 113,000 individuals were contacted in the first six months of 2002, compared to 157,000 during the first six months of 2001. In addition, this figure is significantly lower than the number of contacts and offers realised by private actors and/or private employment agencies (about 318,000 in the same six months) (Ministero del Lavoro e delle Politiche Sociali, 2003).

The current trend of increasing labour market flexibilisation adds to the necessity of a well-functioning PES. Contrary to what seems to be happening at the moment, PES should be empowered, since – as confirmed also in recent research (Reyneri, 2005) – people with more labour market insertion difficulties and with weaker alternative job-search strategies (women, older unemployed people, and so on) tend to address mainly public services. This empowerment is called for also by considering the increased and enlarged set of activities, compared to the past, that PES agencies have to cope with. The current undersized resources and endowments of the PES need to be emphasised: looking at PES employees only (about 15,000 at the end of 2001), their number should be increased (assuming labour force as a reference) to 23,000 (to reach Spanish or Dutch levels) or to 57,000 (to reach German or Swedish levels) (Biagioli et al, 2004, p 308; Reyneri, 2005).

Discussion: which individualisation? Perspectives and challenges in the Italian context of social policies

Studying the Italian case in the context of the international transformations of welfare states (Gray, 2002) demands first of all that we think about the institutional meanings of these processes of change. We can interpret the processes discussed earlier as a country-specific version of an international *isomorphic* move. In other words, organisational and institutional reforms taking place with the aim of making welfare states more active emerge as the results of common sources and pressures of institutionalisation, even if their concrete effects are different inter- and intra-nationally. Following the neo-institutional perspective on isomorphism (DiMaggio and Powell, 1991), three main dimensions of these pressures can be identified:

- direct pressures, caused by the *need for political and institutional legitimisation* (coercive isomorphism). Under this category we can classify the effects and impact of the recommendations of supranational organisations – summarised in what has been called the 'Washington consensus' (Dezalay and Garth, 1998) – resulting in a combination of significant cuts in welfare payments and services, on the one hand, and a growing adoption of workfare or activation policies, on the other. Although a field of conflicting interpretations and practices (Van Berkel and Hornemann Møller, 2002), the workfare model *is* nevertheless playing an attractive and hegemonic role internationally in restructuring relationships between work and social policies. As Peck wrote (2001, pp 3, 10), whether they adopt or resist it, national states are commonly pushed to position themselves vis-à-vis the very simple formula of 'enforcing work while residualising welfare';
- indirect pressures, coming from the need to respond to several sources of *uncertainty* (mimetic isomorphism). These are uncertainties generated by different societal transformation processes that encourage institutional and organisational imitation: when aims are ambiguous or symbolic uncertainty is predominant, researching and adopting an external model that is considered socially legitimate and successful often constitutes a practically viable and economically advantageous path (DiMaggio and Powell, 1991);
- institutional changes resulting from drives towards the *harmonisation of competencies and practices*: cognitive schemes, cultural patterns, routines and administrative procedures (normative isomorphism). These are generated by two different social sources of

institutionalisation. On the one hand, currently enlarging European and international 'epistemic communities' (Bertozzi and Bonoli, 2002) – shared vocabularies, visions, key words, conceptual instruments, and so on – strongly contribute to restricting the range of alternative agendas of institutionalisation. On the other hand, 'private power' (international economic elites guiding the most influencing organisations and institutes of international economic and financial governance; Leys, 2001; Pizzorno, 2001; Farnsworth, 2004) and transnational corporations themselves (looked upon as successful institutional models; Boltanski and Chiapello, 1999; Ferrarese, 2000; Chiapello and Fairclough, 2002) contribute as well to drive social discourses and to set institutional logics and semantics.

On the basis of the key sets of relationships distinguished by Clarke and Newman (1997), we can summarise the results of these common pressures as shown in Table 9.5.

Looking more specifically at the reforms and the experiences summarised earlier, some general points can be raised about their capacity of providing more individually tailored policies.

First, in general, it can be easily recognised that *individualised measures and schemes still remain very far from being actually implemented*. Both the PES reorganisation case (delay in providing some important services; still lacking the take-off of the integrated information system of labour [SIL]; persisting ambiguities concerning the role of PES in general and towards subjects more at risk of labour market exclusion in particular) and the RMI implementation case (widespread difficulties in building reciprocal [clients–services] and effective activation; frequent reductionist reinterpretation and implementation of RMI as a mere economic, bureaucratic device; cognitive, cultural and material weakness of many local administrations for effectively dealing with such an organisationally demanding scheme) show that much work remains to be done.

Second, the results of policies and measures aiming at the activation of welfare recipients appear to be very much influenced by *socioeconomic structural conditions*. Entry or exit from social assistance schemes is often associated with socioeconomic cycles rather than with the generosity of social assistance schemes or, for that matter, with the (in)adequacy of activation programmes and their implementation. Moreover, the emphasis on individualisation and activation of welfare recipients tends to hide structural socioeconomic causes of social exclusion, resulting in further stigmatisation of people remaining excluded (see Standing, 2002). This is particularly true for the Italian move towards more

Table 9.5: The impact of active welfare state reforms on key sets of relationships: general and Italian trends compared

Key sets of relationships	General trends	Italy-specific trends
National/central state versus local state	A clear increase in the role and responsibilities of local welfare states vis-à-vis the central state leading (potentially) to stronger intermunicipal differences	Uncertain future of national legislation and fragmentation of available resources
State/market/civil society	Increasing involvement of non-state actors in the provision of (active) welfare services; move towards privatisation	'Plurality of actors' approach, including crucial role of non-profit third sector organisations
Recipients and providers	*Activation of citizens as an important aim of social policy interventions; individualisation and contractualisation of services*	In the 1990s, cautious steps towards more universalism in (fragmented) income support schemes in the context of fragmented availability of (a broader array of) activation services; currently: no intention of the Berlusconi government to develop nationwide social safety net, returning to pre-Law 328/2000 situation of territorial disparity

Source: Borghi and Van Berkel (forthcoming: 2007)

individually tailored measures, strongly marked by the persisting territorial fragmentation affecting policy implementation. Mainly taking the form of a strengthening of the North–South socioeconomic divide (although not only: the diversity of regional welfare systems in general is currently increasing[8]), this territorial fragmentation tends to move in the opposite direction to the universalistic principles introduced by Law 328/2000 on social assistance. The results of the reform's implementation reveal significant territorial differences (in a general context, as described earlier) with regard to the capacity to innovate street-level bureaucracies' routines and to offer a qualitatively higher level of services.

Once again, in Italy the status of citizenship appears to be an empty envelope, covering different concrete rights according to the territorial collocation of each specific citizen. The ambiguities of the concepts of individualisation and of policy user involvement (see Chapters Four and Five, this volume; Borghi and Van Berkel, forthcoming: 2007) have to be recalled here. Many of the difficulties of policy implementation mentioned here also stem from the impossibility of solving socioeconomic structural problems at the individual (biographical) level (for example, the difficulties of planning and realising individually tailored projects of social and labour market insertion in regions historically affected by structural mass unemployment and a lack of economic activities). In this perspective, the individualisation of policies has to be considered carefully, always taking into account the opportunities of institutional innovation and individual empowerment it opens up, on the one hand, but also the risks of personalisation and moralisation of situations of social injustice, on the other.

Third, apart from the necessity to broaden the analytical perspective from an almost exclusive focus on individuals and policy design to a more (locally) contextualised set of different dimensions and processes, we need to reflect on the *practical meaning* (Brodkin, 2000) of activation itself. Contrary to what appears to be the widespread dominant thinking, two elements have to be underlined. First, the quality of activation programmes and processes as an important variable in the successfulness of these programmes. One aspect of this concerns the perspective that is adopted in the interpretation and evaluation of individual cases and situations. As Bonvin and Farvaque argue (Chapter Three, this volume), an interpretative framework based on individual 'shortcomings' and a 'backward-looking' type of responsibility does not take effectively into account social complexity. Instead, a focus on competencies and capabilities and a type of responsibility that is 'forward-looking' is advocated, in order to avoid the risk of frustrating or perverse effects. This latter orientation asks for higher levels of attention to the quality of activation services and to the ways in which, and the conditions under which, social workers deliver services. Second, the (methodological) lessons given by projects of urban re-qualification (for example, Urban European Union projects) and deliberative democracy should be seriously considered (Bonvin and Thelen, 2003; Fisher, 2003). In these projects, activation and participation are stressed as well. However, they avoid a reductively narrow focus on individual behaviour, and approach activation with a more intersubjective meaning, in which many different aspects of social life (employment, communication, social relations, cultural life, quality of urban spaces, and so on) are treated in an integrated way, recognising the autonomous logic of each aspect in itself and overcoming any simplistic equation between activation and labour market integration. These experiences clearly showed, moreover, the importance of seriously taking into account the 'capability for voice' (Bonvin and Thelen, 2003) as a fundamental element of every concrete process of activation.

A fourth aspect emerges when we interpret the research on social policy governance in terms of an analysis of the "public' sphere more broadly' (Daly, 2003, p 119). An important element – more evident when the Italian situation is viewed in comparison to the international situation – concerns the still very *weak coordination of labour and welfare policies*. Particularly at the local administrative level, the routines and practices of the two public policy areas often remain reciprocally separated. This represents a problem generally affecting the institutional and administrative treatment of social issues in the Italian welfare system. However, the current enlarging plurality of actors involved in social policies as well as their localisation increase, for various reasons, the urgency of (vertical and horizontal) coordination of actions and actors and make weak improvements in policy arrangements more visible. More generally, looking at this issue from the perspective of the experience presented earlier, it can be said that we are witnessing a trend in which *public (welfare) institutions appear to be weakened* or *confirmed in their weak concrete capability* – due to the diminishing role, in terms of competencies and authoritativeness, attributed to them in many fields and to the extremely ambiguous and unclear relationships between different institutional levels (municipal, regional and national).

A fifth issue concerns the *difference between information and social learning*. Many observers of activation policies and programmes claim that having no or little information about welfare recipients is a major issue that should be tackled. In our view, this argument should be developed one step further if we fully want to grasp the processes of public sphere building: social learning emerges only when knowledge is socially recognised and included as part of the (local) public debate, as a resource for local strategies to cope with social problems (Cohen, 2001). As various experiences and research projects show, conditions in which choices remain open, in which particular attention is dedicated to building contexts of open discussion about different options and strategies, and in which there is an effective involvement of the different actors of the local system (capability for voice), favour the transformation of information into social learning. When, on the contrary, information is appropriated as part of private 'competitive advantage' or is fragmented within the realms of separate administrative offices, a social learning process is less probable. In the Italian case, spaces of knowledge and discussion about policies tend to remain separated from spaces of decision (which measure, how long applied, and so on). This threatens to transform activation processes into bureaucratic routines rather than into an act of co-responsibility. When social problems are treated as 'private affairs' (for instance, through the voucher device; Bifulco and Vitale, 2006), or when they are reduced to bureaucratic access (or not) to a temporary, merely economic benefit, no social learning processes are generated, and social issues remain confined within strictly technical and private – in any case, depoliticised – boundaries, without entering the collective reflexivity expressed in the public sphere (Fraser, 1990).

Finally, returning to the implementation process of social policies, the issues we have discussed point out the need for *a shift in the monitoring focus* from the characteristics of the scheme participants to the institutional and administrative (social policy) decision-making processes. This is necessary in order to evaluate more precisely the actual workings of the 'decisional tree' of the street-level welfare measures and their (structural, cultural, cognitive and political) capacity/ incapacity to produce activation, mutual (institutional and individual) responsibility, and so on. In other words, for a better understanding of (social) policy we need to restructure our 'informational bases of judgement in justice' including capabilities and institutional factors of conversion (Chapter Three, this volume; Bonvin and Favarque, 2004; Borghi and Van Berkel, forthcoming: 2007). It is a very demanding, but necessary, task of self-observing complex systems that public institutions have to undertake, if they really want to deal with the increasing complexity of social policy governance.

Notes

[1] This is an area of conflict between central and local governments. Regions and municipalities are denouncing a large gap between growing peripheral duties and persisting strong centralisation of economic resources.

[2] This picture is currently complicated by the statements of some important representatives of Berlusconi's government, who state that Law 328/2000 has to be abandoned and argue in favour of a more 'federalist interpretation' of these (and other) policy issues. In their view, institutional reforms consist in giving more and more autonomy to the regions in defining the welfare system (with regards to instruments, institutional arrangements, role of non-profit organisations, targets covered by social policy measures, role of citizens and families, and so on) and in trying to overcome the universalistic general aim of that law. This is already resulting in an increase of differences concerning the concrete meaning of having a right to health, education, social assistance, child and elderly care, and so on.

[3] In this respect, the law stresses four priorities: empowering and sustaining family responsibilities; strengthening minors' rights; strengthening measures against social exclusion; and sustaining persons who are not self-sufficient through domiciliary services.

[4] The decision to cancel the RMI scheme at the national level has already resulted in increasing territorial and policy differentiation. For example, after central government abolished the national scheme, one important northern region (Emilia Romagna) reintroduced the measure in its regional welfare system (December 2003); and one southern region (Campania) approved the introduction at the regional level of a Citizenship Basic Income (different from RMI because it is an individual measure, not conditioned by any agreement and targeted at people who have been residents of the region for at least 60 months).

[5] When social problems and needs are addressed, it is important, in our perspective, to stress and study 'how institutions think' (Douglas, 1986; Rothstein, 1998), that is, how institutions classify and structure the premises of the public discussion and treatment of these problems. Social issues do not exist independently from the ways policies treat them (practically and symbolically), and policies should be analysed not as technical answers to exogenous problems, but as themselves part of the problems addressed (Fraser, 1990; De Leonardis, 2003).

[6] Legislative Decree n. 297, 19 December 2002.

[7] The meaning of 'proper job offer' is not clearly specified, and some conversations with local employment services' civil servants confirmed that this is an issue open to discretionary and situated interpretation.

[8] For instance, the decision of the former government to stop RMI implementation contributed to policy fragmentation: some regions have no income integration measures at all, others reintroduced an RMI scheme similar to the one previously experimented with, and others again introduced a Citizenship Basic Income.

References

Agodi, M. C. (2003) 'Procedimenti amministrativi e professioni sociali nel mutamento delle politiche di sostegno ai redditi', *Quaderni di Sociologia*, no 31, pp 45-65.

Bertozzi, F. and Bonoli, G. (2002) 'Verso una convergenza delle politiche nazionali per l'occupazione? La costruzione di un modello europeo attraverso il metodo di coordinamento aperto', *Rivista italiana di politiche pubbliche*, no 3, pp 31-57.

Biagioli, M., Reyneri, E. and Seravalli, G. (2004) 'Flessibilità del mercato del lavoro e coesione sociale', *Stato e Mercato*, no 71, pp 277-314.

Bifulco, L. (2003) 'La riforma italiana dell'assistenza: il disegno e le linee di implementazione', in L. Bifulco (ed) *Il genius loci del welfare: Strutture e processi della qualità sociale*, Rome: Officina, pp 29-43.

Bifulco, L. and Vitale, T. (2006) 'Contracting for welfare services in Italy', *Journal of Social Policy*, vol 35, no 3, pp 495-513.

Boltanski, L. and Chiapello, E. (1999) *Le nouvel esprit du capitalism*, Paris: Seuil.

Bonvin, J.-M. and Farvaque, N. (2004) 'What informational basis for assessing job-seekers? Capabilities vs. preferences', Paper presented to the workshop: 'Capabilities and Happiness', Cambridge, 18-19 March.

Bonvin, J.-M. and Thelen, L. (2003) 'Deliberative democracy and capabilities: the impact and significance of capability for voice', Paper presented to the 3rd conference on the capability approach: 'From Sustainable Development to Sustainable Freedom', Pavia 7-9 September.

Borghi, V. (1998) *Il lavoro tra economia e società*, Milan: Angeli.

Borghi, V. (2005) 'Il lavoro dell'attivazione: lo statuto sociale del legame tra welfare e lavoro nelle politiche di attivazione', in L. Bifulco (ed) *Le politiche sociali: Prospettive emergenti*, Rome: Carocci, pp 39-60.

Borghi, V. and Van Berkel, R. (forthcoming: 2007) 'New modes of governance in Italy and the Netherlands: the case of activation policies', *Public Administration*.

Brodkin, E. Z. (2000) 'Investigating policy's 'practical' meaning: street-level research on welfare policy', Working paper project on the Public Economy of Work, University of Chicago, IL.

Calza Bini, P., Nicolaus, O. and Turcio, S. (eds) (2003) *Reddito minimo di inserimento: Che fare?*, Rome: Donzelli/Irpps.

Chiapello, E. and Fairclough, N. (2002) 'Understanding the new management ideology: a transdisciplinary contribution from critical discourse analysis and new sociology of capitalism', *Discourse & Society*, no 2, pp 185-208.

Clarke, J. and Newman, J. (1997) *The managerial state*, London: Sage Publications.

CNEL (Consiglio Nazionale dell'Economica e del Lavoro (2002) *Rapporto sul mercato del lavoro 1991-1997*, Rome: CNEL.

Cohen, S. (2001) *States of denial: Knowing about atrocities and suffering*, Cambridge: Polity Press.

Daly, M. (2003) 'Governance and social policy', *Journal of Social Policy*, vol 32, no 1, pp 113-28.

Dau, M. (2003) 'Italy: opening the circuits', in OECD, *Managing decentralization: A new role for labour market policy*, Paris: OECD, pp 97-102.

De Leonardis, O. (2002) *Social market, social quality and the quality of social institutions*, in W. Beck, L. van der Maesen, F. Thomese and A. Walker (eds) *Social quality: A vision for Europe*, The Hague: Kluwer Law International, pp 178-204.

De Leonardis, O. (2003) 'Un approccio istituzionale ai processi di esclusione sociale', Unpublished paper.

Dezalay, Y. and Garth, B. (1998) 'Le 'Washington consensus'', *Actes de la recherché in sciences sociales*, vol 121, no 2, pp 3-22.

DiMaggio, P. and Powell, W. (1991) 'The 'iron cage' revisited: institutional isomorphism and collective rationality in organizational fields', in W. Powell and P. DiMaggio (eds) *The neoinstitutionalism in organizational analysis*, Chicago, IL: University of Chicago Press, pp 63-82.

Douglas, M. (1986) *How institutions think*, Syracuse, NY: Syracuse University Press.

Fargion, V. (1997) *Geografia della cittadinanza sociale in Italia*, Bologna: Il Mulino.

Fargion, V. (2003) 'The European Employment Strategy and the Italian case', Paper presented at the ESPAnet conference: 'Changing European societies: The Role for Social Policy', Copenhagen, 13-15 November.

Farnsworth, K. (2004) *Corporate power and social policy in a global economy*, Bristol: The Policy Press.

Ferioli, E. (2002) 'Verso welfare locali', *Animazione sociale*, October, pp 11-19.

Ferrarese, M.R. (2000) *Le istituzioni della globalizzazione*, Bologna: Il Mulino.

Ferrera, M. (1996) 'The 'southern model' of welfare in social Europe', *Journal of European Social Policy*, vol 6, no 1, pp 17-38.

Ferrera, M. (2005) 'Welfare states and social safety nets in Southern Europe: an introduction', in M. Ferrera (ed) *Welfare state reform in Southern Europe*, London/New York: Routledge, pp 1-31.

Ferrera, M., Matsaganis, M., Capucha, L. and Moreno, L. (2003) 'Esiste una rete sociale di sicurezza sociale in Sud Europa? Le politiche contro la povertà in Grecia, Italia, Portogallo e Spagna', *Rivista italiana di politiche sociali*, no 1, pp 39-63.

Fisher, F. (2003) *Framing public policy: Discursive politics and deliberative practices*, Oxford: Oxford University Press.

Fraser, N. (1990) 'Talking about needs: interpretive contexts as political conflicts in welfare-state societies', in C. Sustein (ed) *Feminism and political theory*, Chicago, IL: Chicago University Press, pp 159-81.

Goetschy, J. (1999) 'The European Employment Strategy: genesis and development', *European Journal of Industrial Democracy*, vol 5, no 2, pp 117-37.

Gray, A. (2002) 'European perspectives on welfare reform', *European Societies*, vol 4, no 4, pp 359-80.

IRS (Istitutu per la Ricerca Sociale), Fondazione Zancan and CLES (Centro di Ricerche e Studi sui Problemi del Lavoro, dell'Economia e dello Sviluppo (2001) *Valutazione della sperimentazione del Reddito Minimo di Inserimento*, Rome: Presidenza del Consiglio dei Ministri.

Kazepov, Y. (1998) 'Urban poverty and local policies against social exclusion in Italy: the North-South divide', in H. J. Andress (ed) *Empirical poverty research in a comparative perspective*, Aldershot: Ashgate, pp 391-442.

Kazepov, Y. (2000) 'Italia, Europa: il Rmi tra sperimentazione e generalizzazione', *Prospettive sociali e sanitarie*, vol 20/22, pp 44-7.

Kazepov,Y. and Sabbatinelli, S. (2002) 'Il caso italiano', *Assistenza sociale*, no 2, pp 187–214.

Leys, C. (2001) *Market-driven politics: Neoliberal democracy and the public interest*, London/New York: Verso.

Lippi, A. (2003) "As voluntary choice or as a legal obligation': assessing New Public Management policy in Italy', in H. Wollman (ed) *Evaluation in public-sector reform*, Cheltenham: Edward Elgar, pp 140–68.

Ministero del Lavoro e delle Politiche Sociali (2003) *Monitoraggio delle politiche occupazionali e del lavoro*, Rome, www.welfare.gov.it

Naldini, M. (2002) 'Le politiche sociali e la famiglia nei paesi mediterranei: Prospettive di analisicomparata', *Stato e mercato*, no 64, pp 73–99.

Negri, N. and Saraceno, C. (1996) *Le politiche contro la povertà in Italia*, Bologna: Il Mulino.

Paci, M. (1997) 'Le politiche attive del lavoro', *Assistenza sociale*, no 3, pp 81–94.

Pavolini, E. (2003) *Le nuove politiche sociali*, Bologna: Il Mulino.

Peck, J. (2001) *Workfare states*, New York: Guilford Press.

Pennisi, C. and Consoli, T. (2003) 'Mediazione giuridica e politiche negli interventi a sostegno del reddito in Sicilia', *Quaderni di Sociologia*, no 31, pp 27–43.

Pizzorno, A. (2001) 'Natura della disuguaglianza, potere politico e potere privato nella società in via di globalizzazione', *Stato e mercato*, no 2, pp 201–36.

Reyneri, E. (2005) 'Quando le organizzazioni sono chiamate a far fronte al fallimento del mercato e delle reti sociali: il caso dei servizi per l'impiego', *Sociologia del lavoro*, no 100, pp 125–40.

Rothstein, B. (1998) *Just institutions matter: The moral and political logic of the universal welfare state*, Cambridge: Cambridge University Press.

Sacchi, S. and Bastagli, F. (2005) 'Italy – striving uphill but stopping halfway: the troubled journey of the experimental minimum insertion income', in M. Ferrera (ed) *Welfare state reform in Southern Europe*, London/New York: Routledge, pp 85–140.

Saraceno, C. (ed) (2002) *Social assistance dynamics in Europe: National and local poverty regimes*, Bristol: The Policy Press.

Standing, G. (2002) *Beyond the new paternalism: Basic security as equality*, London: Verso.

Trifiletti, R. (1999) 'Southern European welfare regimes and the worsening position of women', *Journal of European Social Policy*, vol 9, no 1, pp 49–64.

Van Berkel, R. and Hornemann Møller, I. (eds) (2002) *Active social policies in the EU: Inclusion through participation?*, Bristol: The Policy Press.

TEN

The individual approach in activation policy in the Czech Republic[1]

Tomáš Sirovátka

Introduction

The 'Active Welfare State' concept (Giddens, 1998) has become the guiding principle of the welfare state's paradigmatic change, with 'activation goals' permeating ever deeper through all its domains. The change is explicit particularly in the European Employment Strategy (EES), although the meaning of 'activation' may be understood differently (see Chapter Two, this volume). The above-mentioned paradigmatic change within the welfare state is, however, not as yet reflected in the post-communist countries, where more converse tendencies can be seen. On the one hand, the social changes under way in these countries include 'activation' of citizens and generate the need for activation strategies within the welfare state. On the other hand, the unfavourable economic conditions and inadequate capacity of public institutions often make the implementation of the objectives and measures difficult. The strategy of market transformation implicitly contains, among other things, citizen education towards individual responsibility, even by means of economic incentives. It also implies the need to cultivate citizens' human capital as a precondition for their future productivity. At the same time, transformation means new social risks that must be absorbed, which in turn necessitates new expenditure (see Offe, 1996).

Considering these circumstances, risk-absorption efforts have so far centred primarily on redistributive and compensatory tools.[2] 'Activation' measures – particularly active labour market policies – have been lagging far behind the EU countries (see Cazes and Nešporová, 2003), primarily owing to insufficient resources and staff capacity necessary for their effective implementation. However, compensatory strategies do not seem effective in the fight against new social risks. Public expenditure has increased, employment has declined and unemployment is high in the post-communist countries of central Europe, often accompanied by increasing threats of poverty and social exclusion. Such a situation then forces political representations into taking unpopular short-term steps (such as curtailing social benefits, particularly unemployment benefits, tightening conditions of early retirement and adopting other public finance reforms); as well as long-term measures aiming at paradigmatic change according to the principles of activation – in line with the EES guidelines. At the same time, activation strategies in post-communist countries are likely to assume specific forms depending on their respective ideological discourses and notions of activation strategy, as well as their specific institutional environments and processes of implementation.[3]

This chapter aims to evaluate the activation strategies applied in the Czech Republic's labour market. First, it explores the role of the individual approach within activation policies. Second, it examines the implementation of individualised activation strategy in the Czech Republic in the form of Individual Action Plans (IAPs) implemented by employment offices. It analyses the extent to which the plans' implementation is influenced by the specific notion and discourses of activation strategies, and by the specific institutional conditions of implementation. This analysis is based on case studies carried out at five local employment offices that run the IAP programme.

Activation strategies and the role of the individual approach

Activation strategies belong among the central pillars of the welfare state reform that is now under way. Their prime aim is to integrate the highest possible number of people fit for work into the system of paid employment throughout their whole life.[4] In order to achieve this goal, a suitable combination of public policy, social policy and employment policy measures is applied.

Available literature on activation strategies identifies two fundamental approaches to the goal of activation, although these have a variety of names. They are a *workfare approach* versus *insertion approach* (Morel, 1998, cited in Lødemel and Trickey, 2001, a *workfare approach* versus *'Nordic' productivism* (Esping-Andersen, 1999), a *defensive approach* versus *offensive approach* (Torfing, 1999, cited in Lødemel and Trickey, 2001), a *workfare model* versus *social inclusion model* (Nicaise, 2002), a *paternalist optimist's approach* – *'enforced participation'* versus an *activation optimist's approach* – '*inclusion through participation*' (Van Berkel and Hornemann Møller, 2002), or an *employability approach* versus *capability approach* (Bonvin and Farvaque, Chapter Three, this volume). Their basic features can be summarised as shown in Table 10.1.

Both approaches differ in the policy discourse, in the objectives and principles of activation, and in the definition of the role and status of clients. They also differ in the understanding of the importance, the nature and the application of an individual approach towards clients. Bonvin and Farvaque (Chapter Three, this volume) highlight the *employability approach* which focuses on the employment objective, insisting solely on individual responsibility and individual employability, associated with a culture of blame; and the *capability approach* which is focused on the client's choice of decent job opportunities, on collective responsibility and the client's ability/possibility to behave responsibly.[5]

In the case of the employability approach or 'enforced participation', based on a 'top-down' approach, clients are perceived as objects of intervention and there is not much room for their active involvement in activation – they are primarily expected to accept the conditions of activation imposed on them and to comply with those conditions. Selected measures depend above all on the capacity of institutions: this approach is built on the assumption of rational choice (based mainly on economic incentives) and works with a model of activation that can be applied regardless of the specific characteristics of the unemployed person and their individual needs. Individualisation is only applied in determining individual activation commitments and evaluating whether they have been met by the clients. Such an individual approach is instrumental in its nature (see Table 10.2).

Conversely, the capability approach relies on individualised and complex programmes that encourage motivation, self-confidence, knowledge, skills, experience, and so on, and are based on an individual approach grounded in precise identification of clients' needs and capacities, as well as in communication and the active participation of clients. Measures are tailored to clients' individual needs thanks to their involvement in the policy-making process. 'Radicalised individualisation' (Chapter Four, this volume) or 'activation through participation' (Van Berkel and Hornemann Møller, 2002) represent a bottom-up approach, where clients' rights are cherished and clients become active participants in the measures (subjects of activation). Setting individualised objectives of activation and suggesting and applying individualised measures plays a central role.

Analyses of the nature and implementation of individual approaches within activation strategies in the Czech Republic will proceed from

Table 10.1: Two modes of activation (level of objectives and principles)

Core features	Workfare – employability approach	Social inclusion – capability approach
1 Causes of unemployment and poverty	• Individual failure, poor work ethic • Lack of skills • Simple causes	• Interplay of structural and cultural factors (labour market segmentation etc) • Multiple causes
2 Locus of responsibility	• Individual – citizen	• Collectivity, society, state
3 Policy discourse	• Dependency, incentives • Welfare expenditure cuts • Obligations, individual responsibility	• Social exclusion, social inclusion • Social cohesion • 'Reflexive activation'
4 Objectives of activation	• Labour market attachment • Labour force flexibility • Employability	• Social inclusion • Capabilities (resources and abilities) • Job quality
5 Agents in charge	Professionals/experts	Clients and professionals/experts
6 Objects of activation	Clients	Clients and institutions
7 Status of clients	Subordinated, have duties, exposed to financial, administrative and legislative pressures	Partnership, reciprocity, they possess both rights and obligations
8 Target groups	Long-term welfare state clients – social welfare recipients, weakest groups	Universal coverage and preferential treatment of the most disadvantaged
9 Principles of activation strategies	Work first, enforcement, making work pay	Balanced measures – income, training, work, empowerment

Table 10.2 : Two modes of activation (level of instruments and implementation)

Approach to 'individualisation'	Workfare – employability approach	Social inclusion – capability approach
1 Role of individual approach	Formal, instrumental	Substantial
2 Form of implementation / Attention to clients' needs	Stereotypical, formalised, limited individualisation	Fully individualised, not necessarily formalised, centred around clients' needs
3 Typical individualisation strategies	• Selective access, categorical in nature, provides incentives (positive and negative sanctions) for categories of clients • Monitoring of individual clients	Universal access, individual in nature, provides resources, abilities and empowerment
4 Choice for clients	• Very limited or non-existent • Weak activation rights	• Broad range of choices • Strong activation rights
5 Institutional setting	• Public Employment Services dominate • Marginal role of other parties	More balanced involvement of Public Employment Services, non-governmental organisations, private agencies
6 Role of implementation agencies	Executive tools	Autonomous parties

the above typology of activation strategies and the corresponding types of individual approach, without us expecting the typology to fully correspond to reality.

Individual approach within activation strategies in the Czech Republic

The discourse: unemployment and welfare dependency

The nature of market transformation consists of recommodification: in the privatisation of ownership and the re-establishment of market relations, including the exchange of work for wages – and thus in activation of people within the labour market. This is no longer realised by means of 'enforced employment' or the obligation to work (applied under the command economy), but through individual interest and economic incentives. It can be interpreted as a labour market–cash nexus where economic incentives motivate individuals to assume personal responsibility and engage in the labour market. It is therefore no wonder that from the very outset of the transformation, great attention was devoted to the question of work incentives in the formal labour market in post-communist countries. In addition to this, there was a range of other reasons: incentives are not sufficient in the new environment, given the low wages (especially in the secondary labour market[6]), relatively easily accessible opportunities in the informal economy, failure of the public administration to effectively eliminate the grey economy, and given other factors – especially deep-rooted 'cultural' habits and reliance on the state inherited from communist times – are considered important.

The growth in unemployment, particularly long-term unemployment,[7] along with the booming grey economy led to the formulation of a hypothesis – commonly shared in the professional public services discourse – about a relatively significant proportion of 'artificial unemployment'.[8] This hypothesis continues to be echoed by the mass media and shared by the general public. In mid-1999, when unemployment amounted to 8%-9%, 54% of respondents in the Czech Republic agreed that unemployed people often or very often misused unemployment benefits. Also, 54% stated that unemployed people often or very often had illegal jobs; 49% said that unemployed people were often or very often passive in searching for a job (Sirovátka, 2002, p 338).[9] Public employment offices, as well as non-governmental organisations (NGOs) and sometimes private agencies, often worked with so-called 'hard-to-place' or 'disadvantaged' groups of unemployed people. This fact, however, did not substantially influence the discourse as it was assumed that these 'deserving' subgroups represented just a small and specific fraction of unemployed people, distinctive from those considered to be passive or abusing benefits while working illegally.

Two groups must, however, be distinguished within artificial unemployment: on the one hand, unemployed people who are active in the grey economy; while on the other hand, 'passive' unemployed people who prefer to live on welfare benefits. Even though we lack enough facts and figures to support the hypothesis about the significance of the grey economy in post-communist countries, everyday experience presents numerous arguments.[10] The hypothesis about 'passivity' on the part of unemployed people is – be it true or not – supported by the fact that the replacement ratio of the aggregate of available social benefits (apart from unemployment benefits, these are social assistance and other income-tested benefits) in the Czech Republic is relatively high: for example, the replacement ratio for a two-parent household with two children and a long-term unemployed member (the second spouse is assumed to be inactive with no earnings in a one-earner couple), when compared to one person's earnings of about two thirds of the average wage, was in 2001 96% and in 2002 still 91%. For lone parents, it was about 80%, which is better than in Germany, France, the UK or the Netherlands and comparable, for instance, with the situation in Sweden or Austria (OECD, 2004).

The institutional framework

Given the above circumstances, the discussion about the need for activation centres around the issue of artificial unemployment. It shows, however, that although artificial unemployment has been identified as a problem by public employment services (PES) and social department personnel, staff shortages at employment offices and in social assistance administration together with inadequate professional skills of the staff represent a major stumbling block to its elimination. The 2004 Employment Act states that unemployed persons who reject a suitable job[11] or fail to cooperate with the employment office may be struck off the register.[12] Persons subjected to such a penalty strike-off represented about 10% of people leaving employment offices' registers in the years 2002-04. While the figure may appear high, it is far from reaching the estimated number of 'passively' unemployed people. Typically, unemployed people who are suspected of participating in the grey economy are subjected to specific pressures and procedures performed by employment office staff: for example, they are invited for interviews more often, at times when they are assumed to be working. The workload of 300-500 clients per member of staff who has direct contact with clients makes individual assistance in job search, as well as evaluation of job-search efforts problematic, not to mention the lack of coordination among the institutions' operations. Given the increase in unemployment and in the number of welfare state clients, the relative staff capacity of these institutions has been on the decline. Given these circumstances, activation of clients was pursued through intensifying job-search evaluations, tightening legislation that defines entitlement to benefits and reducing the benefits replacement ratio. In 1998, unemployment benefits were reduced from 60% to 50% and from 50% to 40% of the individual's previous wage (during the first three months and the following three months of unemployment, respectively). The subsistence minimum was valorised to reflect the growth in prices (with a delay), still lagging behind the growth in wages. Entitlement to unemployment benefits was restricted by imposing the requirement of a six-month period of uninterrupted employment on persons who had already been in receipt of benefits in the previous period. In 2003, the Minister of Labour and Social Affairs proposed to exclude school graduates from entitlement to unemployment benefits. This proposal was rejected by the government but was included in the new Employment Act in 2004. On the other hand, the replacement rate was increased in the second three months of unemployment (to 45%) in order to meet the standards of the European Union (EU) Social Charter.

Individual and group counselling has also been intensified at employment offices, within the limitations of the staff capacity of PES. All employment offices run Information and Counselling Centres that offer vocational and job-search counselling to young people. In addition, almost all offices have set up Job Clubs headed by highly qualified personnel (typically psychologists). Special activation programmes targeted at young people and based on a highly individualised approach are available throughout different parts of the country.[13] Generally speaking, services for young people predominate in the sector, although Job Clubs for long-term unemployed adults also exist. Given the limited staff capacity, working with young people appears to be easier and to have a greater impact. Nonetheless, even these activities are still rather limited in scope – in comparison with unemployment figures.

Between late 1996 and late 1999, registered unemployment increased from 3.5% to 9.4% and continued to grow further – to 10.3% at the end of 2003 (and remained the same throughout 2004). Long-term unemployment increased from 20% to 40% of total registered unemployment (and to 50% according to Labour Force Surveys) over the same period. These figures rank the Czech Republic among the countries with the highest proportion of long-term unemployment in Europe. The problem of benefit 'dependency' became acute when around 75% of households registered as repeated social assistance benefits recipients turned out to be unemployed. In 2002, the average duration of claiming social assistance benefits reached 18 months (Sirovátka and Trbola, 2003).

Nonetheless, activation efforts have so far centred largely around defensive strategies based on sanctions and on motivation through restricting entitlements to benefits. 'Offensive' activation strategies based on the individual approach and on active labour market policy programmes are also being applied, but only in a rather limited scope. Counselling capacities of PES, as well as active labour market policy funds, are finite. In response to a threefold rise in unemployment, the Czech Republic did increase active labour market policy expenditure between 1997 and 1999, but still did not reach the standard common in the EU countries – the expenditure comes to less than 0.2% of GDP, which is twice or even four times less than in countries with a comparable unemployment rate.[14] Social insurance contributions allocated to the unemployment fund are three times higher than the expenditure on unemployment, as the difference is used by the government to cover the deficient pension fund. Within the framework of the public finance reform in 2003, the government decided to permanently lower the social insurance allocation to labour market policies from 3.6% to 1.6% of the payroll, in favour of the pension fund. This certainly signals that the government does not intend to significantly increase expenditures on offensive activation strategies in the future.

Discourse on activation and adopted measures: reforms

Due to the dominating discourse of artificial unemployment hidden in the grey economy, the discourse on activation policies emphasised primarily the necessity of shifts from collective towards individual commitments and rights conditioned by duties (see Chapter Two, this volume), where the labour force has to be taught to adapt itself to the flexible labour market, and where welfare clients are expected to meet requirements imposed by public employment officers. Such a shift is not surprising as it corresponds to the overall welfare state paradigmatic change in post-communist countries identified as early as in the first half of the 1990s and consisting of the 'individualisation of the social'. It was noticeable in many areas, particularly in the field of individual–collective responsibilities (for example, Ferge, 1997). The discourse on the privatisation of public services (Chapter Two, this volume), associated with activation policies, was also important in this overall paradigmatic shift. According to Ferge (1997), privatisation, which was at the core of the economic and social transformation, affected the public sector more intensively than in many old EU countries.

In connection with preparations for membership of the EU, the Czech Republic accepted a National Employment Action Plan in 1999. With increasing long-term unemployment and the forthcoming accession to the EU, the shortage of adequate individualised activation measures was gaining momentum. From 2002, National Action Plans openly stated that the PES administration did not have sufficient resources to meet the EES Guideline 1 (prevention and activation). Nevertheless, in the interest of meeting Guideline 1 the decision was made to intensify counselling for unemployed people and extend employment services with the aim of reducing the growth in long-term unemployment. Considering the need for activation, this approach appeared to be a convenient and 'inexpensive' instrument for eliminating passivity and benefits dependency or abuse.

Following the example of many European countries, this goal was realised through IAPs. The new Employment Act of October 2004 has introduced several measures considered to be suitable activation tools at the individual level, which aim mainly at increasing the administrative pressures on unemployed people and screening their job-search activities:

- a decision was made to introduce IAPs at all employment offices and extend them *universally* to all unemployed people under the age of 25, and later (beginning in 2006) additionally to unemployed people over the age of 25;
- refusal to participate in labour market training or a temporary job (including subsidised jobs) and non-compliance with IAP commitments may result in sanctioning unemployed people (with respect to benefit entitlements);
- school leavers are no longer entitled to unemployment benefits unless they fulfil the employment record condition (that is, 12 months within the last three years);
- a stricter assessment of job search and a stricter definition of a 'suitable job' may be applied (for example, PES are entitled to examine the

health status of unemployed people with their own medical authorities; family circumstances are no longer taken into account, and so on).

At the same time, quasi-markets have continuously been developing in the field of activation. Since the early 1990s, the existence of private job mediation agencies was allowed. Also, PES are allowed to outsource labour market training, motivation programmes and individual profiling to private subjects, which has in fact become common practice. In addition to that the new Employment Act from 2004 allowed job agencies not only to mediate jobs but also to contract employees and subcontract them to other employers in the form of temporary work in order to further flexibilise the labour market (following the Dutch example). The already mentioned restricted budgets of PES, however, represent a barrier to the development of such activities carried out by private parties. They do not reinforce the position of the clients and their choice either. This is due to the fact that it is not the clients who are in control of the finances. Instead, it is the PES who are responsible for outsourcing 'suitable services' for their clients, based upon a professional discretionary decision.

In summary, the above measures and institutional changes do not represent a substantial welfare state paradigmatic shift: rather they aim to improve the instruments in line with the objective 'to educate the citizens to their individual responsibility'.

Implementation of IAPs

Before their implementation in 2004, IAPs were piloted at 15 selected employment offices (out of 77 employment offices in the country) during 2002 and 2003. Five employment offices launched a programme called 'First Opportunity' for unemployed people under 25 years of age, five of them piloted a programme called 'New Start' for unemployed people over 25 years of age and another five launched both programmes in parallel. The following observations are based on case studies of IAP implementation at selected employment offices.[15] In this chapter, we focus on the implementation of IAPs in order to identify the adopted approach, and the role of the individual treatment of clients.

Employment offices remained the sole agency responsible for IAP implementation and making decisions about the implementation process during the pilot stage in 2003. Although they were completely responsible for the 'case management', they previously outsourced specific activities such as individual profiling, motivation courses, occasional group counselling and job clubs, and labour market training to private agencies or NGOs. Therefore the influence of these private and non-governmental parties on the implementation of IAPs was not negligible as the individual work of these parties with the unemployed person was often more intensive than PES involvement itself.

Setting IAP objectives

When formulating the concrete objectives of IAPs, employment offices primarily accentuated better orientation, as well as increased responsibility, independence and proactivity in job search (by way of illustration, one of the employment offices suggested entitling IAPs 'Responsibility, Independence, Proactivity'). In addition, employment offices expressed the intention, and set themselves the goal, to intensify and perfect their own performance: by improving communication both with the unemployed person and with employers in the process of job mediation. They acknowledged the importance of keeping the client informed, applying an individual approach, respecting the client's potential to work, and cooperating with the client in setting a time plan. Moreover, all employment offices stressed the goal to intensify their own initiative in searching for vacancies and winning over employers' cooperation by being more responsive to their needs. Last, but not least, they embraced the goal to better target the active labour market policy instruments and to better coordinate mediating and counselling programmes.

The prevailing approach to the programme appeared to be in agreement with the strategy of the employability approach – in line with the prevailing public discourse of the context of activation. Nevertheless, later, during the implementation of IAPs, employment offices apparently worked with a broader cluster of goals that to some extent corresponded more with the strategy of the capability approach. The complexity of the task in the realisation of the accepted goals seems to have been recognised precisely in the process of implementation by means of pilot programmes.

The target group and selection of participants

Despite all organisational precautions, employment offices encountered difficulties due to their own capacity limitations during the programme's realisation (see below) – in that the number of applicants per mediator-counsellor usually ranged between 250 and 500, or even more in some places.[16] During the application of IAPs to the selected cohort of unemployed people, time problems were therefore commonplace. In addition, at employment offices with a large clientele, appointments with clients who were not enrolled in the project were often postponed.

Owing to the limited staff, IAP implementation was based on the principle of voluntary participation in the programme. The original intention and also a set goal was to invite all applicants to participate in IAPs. However, employment offices in locations with high unemployment, where this goal was beyond the capacity of available staff, immediately deviated from the model. The selection of participants was initially based on the assessment of individual cases, which, however, did not avoid some degree of classifying the applicants on the basis of stereotypical views – as generally described by Lipsky (1980). The programme thus targeted those applicants who were assessed as having a bleak outlook in the labour market, but at the same time as people with a sufficient degree of motivation to secure effective cooperation. In other words, employment offices did not include those applicants in the experiment who were deemed sufficiently active and motivated and whose needs lay – in the mediator-counsellor's opinion – in merely gaining information from the employment office (that is, these clients were expected to be able to find a job by themselves). Second, applicants whose life situation was deemed too complicated and who seemed to need intervention initially by other institutions were not admitted to the programme either. From the point of view of employment offices, it was unrealistic to expect these applicants to accept a job in the near future. Applicants who were deemed 'hard to place' by the mediator-counsellors due to lacking social adaptability constituted another excluded group. Although some employment offices extended their invitation to the programme to these applicants, it was precisely this group of unemployed people who often by themselves refused to participate. Gradually, other employment offices arrived at similar selection criteria.

Consequently, a typical group enrolled in the project were applicants who were insufficiently oriented, inadequately active and with accumulated disadvantages in the labour market. Some were highly motivated, some less than others, but none of them was expected to significantly hinder cooperation. 'Self-selection' of the applicants together with the selection criteria applied by employment offices resulted in meeting the requirement of participants' motivation to cooperate.

All in all, an estimated 15% of applicants from the cohort of potential participants – that is, of the specific category of the unemployed people to which IAPs were addressed (either young people below 25 years of age or long-term unemployed people registered with the employment office within a given time period) – signed the IAPs. At the employment office located in a high unemployment region, only about 6% fell in the category of persons under 25 years of age and 1%-2% in the category over 25 years of age. At the employment office in a location with below-average unemployment, it was almost 30%. Even these numbers of participants exhausted the employment offices' capacities more or less to the limit. The decisive factor responsible for the great variation in 'participation rates' was the personnel capacities rather than financial resources of the employment offices. This is due to the fact that, in the Czech Republic, employment offices in high unemployment areas (and with prevailing long-term unemployment) are allocated more financial support for active labour market policy measures (and therefore the proportion of participants to the total number of unemployed people is often higher than in lower unemployment areas), while there are strict limitations on staff numbers. Hence, job mediator-counsellors, who undertook the role of case managers, in high unemployment areas find themselves more overloaded. The same is true of those who organise/implement active labour market policy measures.

Institutional conditions thus imposed strict limitations on the number of participants in the programme and necessitated the selection of participants on the basis of an estimation of efficacy: that is, according to their individual 'need' for participation, along with their estimated success in the programme. On the one hand, the principles of universal accessibility of the programme and unemployed people's 'right' to the service were broken. While on the other hand, given the lack of institutional capacities, the application of selectivity made it possible to realise individual work. This represents an important prerequisite for targeting the programme at clients' needs during implementation. Nonetheless, the principle of the individual approach was only exercised to some extent: individual work was often hindered by a shortage of time, and therefore cooperation became formal. This shows that, in the course of implementing the programme, goals are being refined and redefined, depending on institutional conditions of implementation.

Activation and institutional learning

On the one hand, the pilot project of individual activation produced a heavy burden on the participating institutions. On the other hand, it greatly contributed to the processes of 'learning' and 'internal reorganisation' of their operation, resulting in the broadening of opportunities for individual work.

At some employment offices, a basic step was to separate registration work (including administration of financial support in unemployment) from mediation and counselling. Personnel for the counselling section (IAPs) were selected accordingly. This facilitated an overall improvement in efficiency in individual work with clients. At some employment offices, such a separation of competencies led to an increase in the workload of individual mediator-counsellors (to 300-500 applicants), but at the same time enabled them to better focus on counselling. Their overall workload thus did not increase.

Other measures included the use of teamwork in securing an individual approach to IAPs, as well as the application of an effective combination of individual and group counselling. Teamwork was important in several respects during implementation: it enabled the exchange of information, the design of effective procedures, the unification of methodology and joint management of difficult cases. It also made it possible to introduce supervision of IAPs' quality and to improve coordination of activities and cooperation with other departments within the employment office. At some employment offices, new forms of teamwork were systematically elaborated and formalised: 'organisational teams' (in charge of coordination) and 'methodological teams' (in charge of refining operational procedures and controlling quality) were formed.

The interconnection between different aspects of individual counselling – including diagnostic methods and group activities that focus on spreading information, counselling and motivation – was proven to belong among key factors enhancing the effectiveness of activities related to IAPs.

It follows that the introduction of IAPs brought about a substantive change in the organisation of work in registration, mediation and counselling. It certainly contributed to the improvement of the quality of counselling, as well as to the introduction of supervision and unification of methodology. It also significantly enhanced the role of diagnostics, group counselling, motivation and requalification programmes. The formalisation of the process of working with clients resulted – despite the fact that the selection of participants in the programme was obviously guided by stereotypical views of clients – in the deepening of the individual approach towards clients, both at the stage of selection and in the provision of services.

The role and concept of the individual approach

The merit of the individual approach stems primarily from its capacity to take account of clients' needs, in the range of options it opens and in the room it creates for employing clients' individual capacities. Even though no standards of the programme's quality and no criteria for monitoring quality had initially been set, the process of implementation made employment offices realise that the successful accomplishment of the set goals lay in improving the intensity and quality of the individual work rather than in the formal signing of an IAP.

It seems that it was precisely the awareness of staff shortages that kept returning employment offices' attention towards seeking ways of how to best utilise the available capacity, and towards constantly evaluating whether their activities and services were meaningful and of a quality corresponding with the needs of clients, as well as the need for activation. In addition, they seem to have been taking into account whether the full potential of each client was being realised.

The demands placed on mediatior-counsellors, in terms of their professional skills and other general qualities, have tightened: particularly their skills in dealing with clients, their communication skills and their ability to realise individual and groupwork, as well as analyse and process information. The intensified focus on individual clients necessitated a more precise specification of their needs so that a better targeting of mediation was guaranteed. It was necessary to increasingly intensify the searching for ever more suitable jobs, targeted at the needs of both the client and the employer. It was also essential to have at least a few vacancies available (to be offered to the client) at all times – otherwise the client might lose interest in the IAP. At the same time, it became necessary to motivate the employers to cooperate and actively inform the employment office about available vacancies. This can be done by securing unfailing communication and by giving more careful thought to selecting potential employees. The mediator-counsellors had to deepen their knowledge of the labour market and improve their skills in gathering and processing information.[17]

It is hardly surprising that the initial objectives were not always met by employment offices. In the case of many clients – particularly those who were classified as lacking in motivation and in a willingness to cooperate – the elaborated and signed IAPs seemed rather flat and formal: 'there was hardly anything to write down' (said one of the mediator–counsellors). Dealing with more difficult cases was beyond the capacity as well as the professional abilities of the mediator–counsellors. According to the employment office staff themselves, it would be desirable to refer such clients to a specialised mediator–counsellor. Such a service was, however, either not available at all or lacking the necessary capacity. To some extent, employment offices handled the situation by introducing various forms of supervision, consultation and unification of methodological procedures.

Objectively speaking, some IAPs do seem to be rather formal. This can be attributed to the lack of capacity for individual work with the client and the low professional skills that do not always suffice for managing difficult cases. This can be illustrated by the very contents of the IAPs: they describe fairly routine procedures of job search that usually take place in any case and do not deviate from standard practice. On the other hand, the principle of individualisation, in the sense of responsiveness to the needs of clients, won much greater support than it had previously: this is reflected in a more careful approach to compiling case histories and elaborating applicants' individual profiles than is applied today, as well as in a greater initiative in searching for suitable vacancies and offering these vacancies to specifically selected individuals.

The role of the client and freedom of choice

Since employment offices lacked necessary staff at the time of launching the programme, the clients were given the possibility to choose whether or not to participate in IAPs. Those who accepted the proposal secured themselves a broader range of services and better exercised their right to assistance in finding employment. These clients were involved in a closer dialogue with the institution, as they took part in drafting the IAP and in evaluating its meaningfulness. Nevertheless, many clients were omitted in the early phase of inviting applicants – on the basis of the decision-making discretion and professional judgement of the providers of services. As soon as individual work in the form of IAPs was initiated, another problem emerged: how to proceed in the case of clients who were not successful in finding a job during the IAP programme. It is precisely in such cases that more intensive counselling and/or a carefully chosen form of support – through active labour market policy instruments – should be applied. The reality is, however, that the required scope of such measures is not available, despite the fact that many of the clients would welcome the possibility of labour market training or other interventions.

Some employment offices manage the situation by placing unsuccessful IAP clients in Job Clubs, with the aim of maintaining their level of initiative and motivation. It must also be noted that, in implementing active labour market policy instruments, all employment offices apply a set of criteria that include giving preference to long-term unemployed people. Nevertheless, neither the opportunities for participation in activation measures nor the professional counselling capacities are sufficient. In this respect, the clients' freedom of choice remains as limited as before. This fact, however, was not considered of major importance during the experiment, as the main objective was believed to be 'activation' through the *employability approach* (applied on a finite circle of selected clients), and not a 'choice for everyone'. Nonetheless, it is now clear that upon completion of the IAP programme, 30%-40% of participants remain on the register, without it being possible to offer them a job vacancy, an active labour market policy programme or other services. Employment offices are therefore beginning to recognise this 'limitation of choice' to be a problem – since it weakens clients' motivation. They are also beginning to acknowledge that if no jobs are available during and after the IAP period, other opportunities for labour market participation are a necessary condition for keeping the clients motivated.

Conclusions

Activation policies in the Czech Republic are not as yet very elaborate. There is no doubt that employment offices do apply the individual approach, but they do so only on a relatively small scale. This is a result of the given implementation conditions – particularly the staff shortages in public administration institutions – but also the prevailing activation discourse that strongly focuses on individual responsibility and endorses the *employability approach* of *enforced participation*. A limited focus on individualisation is another feature of the situation. The given approach is largely a legacy of the past. Nevertheless, different instruments are applied today – instead of legal sanctions and the obligation set by law to have a paid job, economic incentives are used. This approach follows from today's reality of high long-term unemployment, partially mixed with artificial unemployment combined either with illegal work or a preference for social benefits. The existing employability approach of enforced participation is, nevertheless, inconsistent: the implementation circumstances (insufficient administrative capacity and professional skills) do not make it possible to subject the clients' job-search activity to a thorough and efficient evaluation.

With respect to the application of this model of activation, a major role is played by the existing notion of activation objectives, as well as by practical implementation conditions that are characterised by a shortage of relevant staff and their poor professional skills, and by a limited range of activation opportunities. Owing to these factors, the individual approach is sometimes reduced to a mere formal framework to satisfy the set operational scheme. The limited opportunities for participation in active labour market policy measures make it impossible to provide participants in IAPs with guarantees of activation fulfilling their individual needs. Similarly, the staff capacity of PES does not make it possible to consistently encourage the participants to assume responsibility and meet their obligations.

The specific implementation conditions also modify the model in other respects. First, they necessitate a reduction in the number of participants: the need to make good use of the insufficient institutional capacities leads to a preferential exclusion of those potential participants who are lacking in a willingness to cooperate. Yet it is precisely these persons who should be targeted within the strategy of enforced participation in the first place, considering the objective of 'motivation towards greater responsibility'. The strategy of selection is not aligned with the set objectives. In order to keep control over their work with clients, employment offices preferred to accept participants who were likely to cooperate, but who did show certain disadvantages that made it worthwhile to try to diagnose their needs and seek solutions. This means a further diversion from the employability/enforced participation approach: in order to be able to manage these clients' situation, PES must individualise their approach, both towards the clients and towards employers. They must also undergo the process of 'institutional learning' and internal reorganisation, including cooperation with external (private) agencies and even NGOs (the latter typically in the case of disabled unemployed persons). It is precisely this involvement of private agencies and NGOs that helps to reinforce individualisation and shift the objectives of activation.

These, at the very least partial, alterations of the model that take place in the course of implementation also justify the application of the *capability approach* of the *inclusive participation* model. The freedom of choice available to both potential and actual participants in the programme is, nonetheless, insufficient (only a small number of participants can enrol in the programme and only a few programme graduates are provided with further support if the improvement of the job-search process by itself proves insufficient in managing their situation).

In summary, the definition of objectives as well as the implementation conditions of activation strategies in the Czech Republic correspond with the *employability approach* of *enforced participation*. On the other hand, the application of specific forms of activation, inspired by examples from the EU countries (such as the IAP) and adopted within a process of learning, leads – under imperfect implementation conditions – to a modification of the initial approach. This approach is being modified towards greater individualisation and towards incorporation of more inclusive aspects of individualisation strategies, with emphasis on the clients' capabilities. If we go back to Tables 10.1 and 10.2, we can conclude that, in some respects, the practice of IAPs shows a combination of both models, although the employability approach of enforced participation clearly prevails. When looking at Table 10.1, we first see that the selection procedure at least allows for clients' own initiative (rows 5, 7 and 8). Second, in Table 10.2 we can see that the form of implementation makes it possible to pay somewhat higher attention to the clients' needs (rows 2 and 3) and to involve a range of parties/agencies (row 5), which can gradually gain more autonomy (row 6).

The complex interaction among activation objectives (as defined both in the national context and at the EU level), among the adopted forms of the individualised activation strategy and, finally, among the institutional conditions that guide the realisation of objectives and forms of activation, generates a number of unintentional consequences for the final shape of interventions. Although the objectives of activation are defined in terms of the employability approach, inadequate conditions of implementation (the availability of staff, and the scope of available jobs and active labour market policy measures) do not make it possible to apply this approach consistently. At the same time, new forms of individualised work with clients are emerging (individual profiling, motivation programmes, and so on). Also, some degree of choice given to clients regarding their participation in activation programmes can be seen, as well as participation of private and non-governmental parties in the process of activation. These factors create favourable conditions for 'institutional learning' and for the adoption of a more individualised and inclusive capability approach. At least at this stage of implementation, 'awareness' of good practice, as well as examples of its practical application, can be observed. These elements of the capability approach may be considered to be unintended consequences of implementation conditions rather than intended objectives and a conscious aim of the activation approach. Once they emerge and are recognised, they may, however, influence desirable shifts in objectives, through the continuous process of bottom-up policy formation. Considering that the use of individual approaches within activation strategies is only within its early stages in the Czech Republic, a dynamic development can be expected, particularly if the implementation conditions are improved.

Notes

[1] This study was written with the support of the Ministry of Education of the Czech Republic (MSM 0021622408 *Social Reproduction and Social Integration*).

[2] During the 1990s, the growing unemployment rate was fought by pursuing the strategy of exclusion from the labour market (Offe, 1996): for example, encouraging early retirement and possibly prolonging parental leave, along with introducing social assistance benefits and benefits that partially compensate for income devalued by growing inflation and housing costs.

[3] For example, poor performance of public administration in the new member states is a subject of strong criticism by the European Commission.

[4] Even though other forms of activation, such as voluntary work and education, are also important (Van Berkel and Roche, 2002).

[5] More traditionally, Nicaise (1995) divided approaches towards active labour market policy measures into two groups: those focusing on single causes and disadvantages (for example on insufficient professional skills) that are usually standardised, and those focusing on multiple causes and disadvantages that are far more individualised.

[6] Typically, unskilled, low-skilled or semi-skilled occupations in general constitute this secondary segment. Following 1989, primary labour markets shrank substantially due to economic restructuring. At the same time, some categories of workers remain locked in the secondary labour market irrespective of their human capital, on the grounds of their social ascriptive attributes: typically women with small children, people with disabilities, school leavers or older workers, or Roma.

[7] In 2003 and 2004, long-term unemployment represented 40% of registered unemployment (and over a half of total unemployment according to the Labour Force Survey) in the Czech Republic.

[8] Common estimates by employment office personnel are a third of the total of unemployed people.

[9] The 'Effects of Social Policy Transformation' research, quota sample, n = 1,319, School of Social Studies, Masaryk University.

[10] Possibly the best estimate is based on Gutman's monetary method. which was used by Fassmann (2003, p 70). who estimated 6.1% in 1992, 11.7% in 1996, 18.1% in 1998, 19.7% in 2000 and 15.9% in 2002.

[11] A job requiring lower qualifications and providing a lower wage can be classified as a suitable job. However, unemployed persons' health and family situation (that is, care commitments) are taken into consideration.

[12] The law allows for a substantial decision-making leeway – for example, upon failing to attend an appointment without excusing oneself.

[13] For example, the Bridge project, designed according to a British model, that involves individual diagnostics, counselling, employment training and subsidised employment with follow-up career guidance.

[14] In 2002, it was 0.17% of GDP, half that of Britain, three times less than that of Hungary and four to six times less than that of Spain, Finland or Germany.

[15] This analysis is based on findings from five employment offices, of which three worked with both target groups, one with the group under 25 years of age and one with the group over 25 years of age.

[16] Most experts from employment offices estimate that for the contact with clients to be sufficiently frequent and, primarily, of desirable quality – in order to make IAPs meaningful – the workload has to be reduced to 150-200 clients per mediator-counsellor. This would allow for at least two 20-30 minute appointments per month with each applicant. This, however, was not the operational reality of employment offices.

[17] These increased demands also brought about increased requirements of personnel management: the selection, training and remuneration of mediator-counsellors. However, such requirements are hard to meet: Czech employment services lack a system of professional training of staff. Remuneration is considered inadequate by the management of employment offices and the staff capacity in counselling and mediation is believed to be the biggest weakness of PES (in our survey from 2003, 350 key managers from all employment offices in the country marked staff capacities in major services for clients with the average grade of 3.5 on a scale from 1 [completely adequate] to 5 [completely inadequate], and the possibility to sufficiently remunerate personnel for quality performance with the average grade of 4.3).

References

Cazes, S. and Nešporová, A. (2003) *Labour markets in transition: Balancing flexibility and security in Central and Eastern Europe*, Geneva: ILO.

Esping-Andersen, G. (1999) *Social foundations of post-industrial economies*, Oxford: Oxford University Press.

Fassmann, M. (2003) *Stínová ekonomika II*, Prague: CMKOS and Sondy.

Ferge, Z. (1997) 'The changed welfare paradigm: the individualization of the social', *Social Policy and Administration*, vol 31, no 1, pp 20-44.

Giddens, A. (1998) *The Third Way: The renewal of social democracy*, Cambridge: Polity Press.

Lipsky, M. (1980) *Street-level bureaucracy: Dilemmas of the individual in public services*, New York: Russel Sage Foundation.

Lødemel, I. and Trickey, H. (eds) (2001) *'An offer you can't refuse': Workfare in international perspective*, Bristol: The Policy Press.

Morel, S. (1998) 'American workfare versus French insertion policies in application of Common's theoretical framework', Paper presented to the Annual Research Conference of the Association for Public Policy and Management, New York, 29-31 October.

Nicaise, I. (2002) 'The active welfare state: The response to social exclusion', Vives lecture, 23 April, Bruges.

OECD (Organisation for Economic Co-operation and Development) (2004) *Benefits and wages: OECD indicators*, Paris: OECD.

Offe, C. (1995) *Disorganised capitalism*, Cambridge: Polity Press.

Offe, C. (1996) *Modernity and the state: East, West*, Cambridge: Polity Press.

Sirovátka, T. (2002) 'Opinions of Czechs about the welfare state', *Czech Sociological Review*, vol 38, no 3, pp 327-44.

Sirovátka, T. and Trbola, R. (2003) *Příjemci dávek sociální péče z titulu sociální potřebnosti, Výzkumná zpráva*, Prague: Výzkumný ústav práce a sociálních věcí.

Torfing, J. (1999) 'Workfare with Welfare: recent reforms in the Danish welfare state', *Journal of European Social Policy*, vol 9, no 1, pp 5-28.

Van Berkel, R. and Hornemann Møller, I. (2002) 'The concept of activation', in R. van Berkel and I. Hornemann Møller (eds) *Active social policies in the EU: Inclusion through participation?*, Bristol: The Policy Press, pp 15-44.

Van Berkel, R. and Roche, M. (2002) 'Activation policies as reflexive social policies', in R. van Berkel and I. Hornemann Møller (eds) *Active social policies in the EU: Inclusion through participation?*, Bristol: The Policy Press, pp 197-224.

ELEVEN

Rushing towards employability-centred activation: the 'Hartz reforms' in Germany

Dirk Jacobi and Katrin Mohr

Introduction

A common feature of reform processes and discourse throughout Europe since the mid-1990s has been the shift from 'passive' towards 'active' policies for unemployed people. While in some countries the move towards activation implies the introduction of a comprehensive framework of active labour market policy, others have long-standing traditions in this respect. Germany belongs to the latter group, having a tradition of providing unemployed people with benefits, as well as offering measures to enhance individual employment prospects.[1] However, an individual-oriented approach to active labour market policy has meant different things at different times in history. As part and parcel of a wider strategy of Keynesian economic policy making, the Labour Promotion Act (*Arbeitsfoerderungsgesetz/AFG*) introduced in Germany in 1969, which regulated both the provision of Unemployment Benefits and active measures,[2] was geared to foster labour market mobility and to adapt the professional skills of workers to structural changes in the economy. Its main instruments were counselling, placement, vocational training and qualification. These instruments were aimed not only at unemployed people, but also at those who were threatened with unemployment or who wanted to work their way up the ladder within the employment structure. They were therefore not only meant to bring people back into the workforce, but also to safeguard occupational upward mobility. Unemployment was generally perceived as a structural problem – one that was best overcome by equipping unemployed people with qualifications and skills.

Today's policies of activation look profoundly different. Embedded within a supply-side-oriented paradigm of economic policy making, activation now seeks to insert unemployed people in areas of employment that do not necessarily correspond to their prior qualifications and status (Heinelt, 2003, p 125). Unemployment is no longer looked at as primarily a structural problem, but as a lack of individual employability. The relationship between the state and unemployed people is now guided by the idea of a reciprocal social contract (Chapter Two, this volume) in which obligations on the part of unemployed people to (re)gain employability are to be matched by obligations on the part of the state to provide effective support in helping unemployed people (re)integrate into the labour market.

In this chapter, we will describe the basic principles that underlie this new approach to activation in Germany, paying specific attention to the individualised measures and services that form an important part of the philosophy of a 'new social contract'. In doing so, we will first give a brief overview of the structure and characteristics of unemployment compensation and active labour market policy, as well as the developments that have prepared the stage for recent reforms. We will then outline the first steps taken by the Red–Green government towards an individualised approach to activation, before portraying what have come to be called the 'Hartz reforms', a series of laws that have profoundly changed the German system of unemployment compensation and placed an individualised approach to activation centre-stage. Finally, we lay bare the meaning of individualisation in the German approach to activation, and discuss the overall course of the reforms as well as their implications for an individualised approach to activation.

Unemployment compensation and active labour market policy: the status quo ante

Until the end of 2004, Germany had a three-tiered system of unemployment compensation. Unemployment Benefit (*Arbeitslosengeld*) formed the first tier. It was generally granted for between one and three years, depending on age and contribution record, and the amount paid out to a recipient was related to prior income.[4] The programme was financed by social insurance contributions and administered by the Federal Employment Agency (FEA) (*Bundesagentur fuer Arbeit*). The second tier, Unemployment Assistance (*Arbeitslosenhilfe*), was also administered by the FEA and was similarly dependent on prior income.[5] However, this programme was financed by general tax revenues, was means tested and could be received for an unlimited period of time. Those unemployed who were not covered by either Unemployment Benefit or Unemployment Assistance were supported by the municipally administered system of social assistance (*Sozialhilfe*). Responsibility for long-term unemployed people was thus split between two different bureaucracies and federal levels. Social assistance provided a minimal benefit that was based on need and assessed in terms of the specific living situation of the individual claimant and their family. To tailor benefits to individual needs, standard allowance rates were supplemented by several discretionary additional and special payments.

Responsibility for and administration of active labour market policy for recipients of contribution-based Unemployment Benefits (*Arbeitslosengeld* and *Arbeitslosenhilfe*) rested with the FEA and its regional and local branches. The branches provided a wide repertory of measures and services, from counselling and placement via vocational training and qualification to placements in intermediary labour markets to wage subsidies. These measures and services adhered to a common federal standard but were carried out at the local level, a system which inherently led to some variation in implementation and approach to the individual claimant.

Since until 2005 the municipalities were responsible for unemployed people who were not entitled to contribution-based benefits, they engaged in active labour market policies of their own, and in the 1990s municipal programmes gained in importance. This development took place against a background where mass unemployment as well as cutbacks in the first and second tiers of unemployment compensation had left the municipalities with the administrative and financial responsibility for an increasing share of unemployed people – a process that has been termed the 'municipalisation of unemployment' (Hanesch, 1997).[6] As a consequence, municipalities started to engage in active labour market policies in the late 1980s (see Lamping and Schridde, 1999; Grell et al, 2002) using the instruments the Federal Social Assistance Law (*Bundessozialhilfegesetz/BSHG*) provided for this purpose.[7] Guided by the principle of 'helping people to help themselves' (*Hilfe zur Selbsthilfe*), activation had always been an aspect of social assistance, and was generally more restrictive or even repressive than active labour market policy in the area of unemployment insurance, which was primarily based on rights and focused on (re)integration and rehabilitation (Hanesch et al, 2001, p 131). Although implementation measures varied greatly from municipality to municipality, they had two things in common: to deter people from applying for social assistance in the first place, and to divert recipients into regular employment in the intermediary labour market. Through participation in programmes like these, social assistance recipients could accrue entitlements to insurance-based Unemployment Benefits. In other words, this roundabout system allowed municipalities to permanently shift fiscal responsibility for unemployed social assistance recipients to the FEA, and with rising caseloads and fiscal pressures, this 'shift-yard' (*Verschiebebahnhof*) came into wide use from the late 1980s onwards. These attempts among different tiers of the protection system to shift administrative responsibility for unemployed people to the other system led to a growing political consensus in the 1990s – that the coexistence of unemployment insurance and assistance on the one hand and social assistance on the other was a highly problematic constellation.

The consequences of German reunification and the massive upheaval in the labour market in the former German Democratic Republic (GDR) after 1990[8] formed another important source of discontent within the traditional system of labour market policy. In a climate of national euphoria and high hopes of a quick recovery of the East German economy, the political decision was taken to finance unemployment compensation and active labour market policy in East Germany from insurance funds rather than through general taxation. The premise that it would only be necessary to compensate for a massive loss of employment for a short time led decision makers to begin using the instruments of active labour market policy to an unprecedented extent. Their decisions in turn led to huge deficits at the FEA, and threatened to destabilise the institutional foundations of the system itself (see Heinelt, 1994, p 193). Despite massive extension of active labour market programmes, unemployment in East Germany remained high, causing increasing political dissatisfaction with the traditional instruments of active labour market policy (see Heinelt, 2003, p 140). The Social Democrats and trades unions, which until then had generally remained sympathetic towards active labour market policy, became convinced that the isolated use of measures was no longer an adequate response for coping with the multiple employment barriers faced by long-term unemployed people, and began demanding a more across-the-board approach. After a short period of extensive use of active labour market policy in the early 1990s, the Conservative government, which was generally critical of the state intervening in employment issues, backed away and resumed its hands-off course from the 1980s.

With regard to specific policies, this trend was most clearly reflected by the integration of the 1969 Labour Promotion Act (*AFG*) into the overall Social Policy Code. In the Social Policy Code III (*Sozialgesetzbuch/SGB III*), lawmakers dropped aims of achieving full employment with the help of state intervention and of permanently enhancing the employment structure, and instead began stressing the 'special responsibility of employers and employees' in employment matters. Several modifications were also made as a response to the disappointment with the traditional instruments of labour market policy (Grell et al, 2002, pp 8-10; Heinelt, 2003, pp 134-5); wage subsidies were extended, for example, while the budget for the more conventional – and expensive – training and job creation programmes was scaled back.

Developments in active labour market policy in the 1990s were accompanied by successive reforms of the benefit system. Although these reforms were incremental, their cumulative effect was the source of significant change in the social rights of unemployed people. The new laws tightened conditions for eligibility, reduced benefit levels for Unemployment Benefit and Unemployment Assistance, and several times suspended the regular adjustment of social assistance levels. Starting in the mid-1990s, lawmakers also extended a recipient's obligations to actively seek work and accept work offers and placement in activation programmes, as well as reinforcing sanctions in cases of non-compliance, both in the social assistance programme and in the insurance-based Unemployment Benefit system (see Heinelt, 1994, p 201; Mohr, 2004, pp 299-302).

Moving towards an individualised approach to activation under the Red–Green government

The 1990s thus saw both blows to the institutional foundations of active labour market policy and the first steps towards reform, but reforms of active labour market policy only began to intensify after the Red–Green government took power in 1998. During its first term in office, the new ruling coalition set out to take an activating approach. However, the movement towards activation only really began to gain momentum after a scandal involving the FEA in 2002 (see below) led to the appointment of the 'Hartz Commission', a body which eventually delivered the blueprint for a major overhaul of the unemployment compensation system and active labour market policy.

As in many other European countries, Social Democrats in Germany in the 1990s sought to reformulate social-democratic thinking by drawing on British debates about a 'Third Way' (Giddens, 1998). In Germany, this debate revolved around the concept of an 'activating state' (*aktivierender Staat*), an idea which became an important intellectual keystone for the successive reforms implemented by the Red–Green government after the 1998 elections.[9] The concept of the activating state – one which is supposed to promote and enable an active citizenry rather than 'just handing out benefits', thereby contributing to the 'passivity' of its citizens – played a double role in Gerhard Schroeder's strategy when he first ran for Chancellor in 1998. It was not only meant to play an important role in the fight against unemployment, but also to address the morality of an envisaged new voter clientele that was being called the 'new middle'.

A central element of the concept of the activating state is reforming public administration as a prerequisite for the activation of citizens.[10] The proponents of an activating state generally want to accomplish institutional activation by 'relieving' the state through a transfer of the production of services to 'society'; in other words to private firms, third sector organisations and the clients of the welfare state themselves (von Bandemer et al, 1995, p 53). Even though it proposes many fundamental changes, however, this concept does not aim for an overall privatisation of state activity. Its proponents still want the production of services to be guaranteed and controlled by the state.

Another important component of the concept of the activating state is the call for self-responsibility. In the German context, however, this does not mean individualisation. Instead it implies the 'familialisation' of responsibilities, a concept that reflects the long-standing principle of subsidiarity in social policy, which stresses the role of the family as both a shield against life's misfortunes and as a unit for providing benefits. Yet while the concept of the activating state does take up the neo-liberal call for self-responsibility, unlike the neo-liberal approach it also stresses the role of the state in creating active, self-responsible citizens. This rationale, however, is far from new. In Germany, it has a long-standing tradition in the area of social assistance, where the concept of 'helping people to help themselves' has always played a central role. With the concept of an activating welfare state, however, the principle was to become a universal one in providing welfare to unemployed people.

The activation of citizens by the state was meant to be accomplished not just by enabling them, but also by imposing 'activating duties' (Hombach, 1998, 1999). In Germany, a 'new balance' of rights and duties imported from British debates about the Third Way and expressed in the formula *Foerdern und Fordern* (support and challenge) became the key principle of the new approach to labour market policy (Hombach, 1999, p 44). All these elements of the activating state – the call for self-responsibility, the enabling of citizens and the implementation of 'activating duties' – call for measures that are able to address the specific situation and to mobilise the personal resources of the individual.

Although highly disputed within the Social Democratic Party itself, the concept of the activating state was nevertheless very successful in bringing about a far-reaching consensus across party boundaries.[11] Even so, the first years of the Red–Green government policy saw little activity in the field of labour market policy. This was partly due to the shift of policy responsibility to the tripartite negotiating arena of the *Bündnis für Arbeit* (Alliance for Jobs), which after being suspended by the Conservative government had been revived by the Red–Green coalition as a tool for developing reform proposals to bring down unemployment in consensus with social partners. While the 'Benchmarking Group' of the Alliance for Jobs, a council of scientists set up to provide expertise for the negotiating partners, strongly supported the concept of an activating state and pleaded for the expansion of the low-wage sector (Fels et al, 2001), trades unions and employer organisations were unable to come to agreements on far-reaching changes (Blancke and Schmid, 2003, p 224). With regard to individualised activation in active labour market policy, the most significant reform at the time was the introduction of a special programme for young people called *Jugend mit Perspektive/JUMP* (youth with perspectives), which was set up with the consent of the parties in the Alliance for Jobs. The programme aimed to integrate young unemployed and young people who had not been able to find an apprenticeship in the dual training system, and it included the introduction of an *Eingliederungsvereinbarung* (insertion agreement) that was similar to the Individual Action Plans implemented in many other countries.[12]

In 2001, when the number of people out of work started to rise again, public opinion forced the government to take a stronger stance on the issue of cutting unemployment (Blancke and Schmid, 2003, p 255f). In September 2001, it passed the *Job-AQTIV-Gesetz*[13] (see BMWA, 2002; Trube, 2002). One of the central aims of this reform was to improve the FEA's job placement services by tailoring them to better match the individual needs of the unemployed client. To achieve this, the law called for individual assessments of the unemployed person's profile, needs and aspirations, and required all clients of the FEA to consent to an insertion agreement. Although not a major reform in terms of extent or financial volume, the Act still represented a decisive step towards a more individualised approach to active labour market policy.

Before long, however, the significance of the reform was overshadowed by other events. In January of 2002, the month the *Job-AQTIV-Gesetz* came into effect, what came to be called the 'placement scandal' threw open a window of opportunity for more far-reaching reforms when the federal audit division (*Bundesrechnungshof*) published a report concluding that local FEAs had manipulated statistics and greatly overstated quotas of successful placements. Under heavy pressure, and with federal elections coming closer, the Red–Green government reacted immediately. Within a month it announced several changes related to the placement service of the FEA. The government also set up a commission aimed at developing proposals for the reform of the FEA. The commission's report, *Moderne Dienstleistungen am Arbeitsmarkt* (Modern Services for the Labour Market) was published in August 2002, just one month before the federal elections. The report not only suggested a major reorganisation of the FEA, but also proposed extensive reforms of both active labour market policy and the system of unemployment compensation (Kommission Moderne Dienstleistungen am Arbeitsmarkt, 2002).

The Hartz Commission report explicitly argued in favour of broadly adopting an individualised approach to activation. The report's self-proclaimed 'guiding principle' of *Eigenaktivitaet ausloesen – Sicherheit einloesen* (release self-activity – redeem security) is a reformulation of the principle to 'support and challenge' (Kommission Moderne Dienstleistungen am Arbeitsmarkt, 2002, p 45). Its starting point was not an unemployed person's established entitlements, but their individual integration effort, which it said had to be promoted by the FEA. The report also stressed that the integration process needed to be managed and guided by the unemployed person themselves. This idea is reflected in the call for the FEA to adopt a new, more customer-oriented approach in order to be more responsive to the needs of unemployed people. In direct contrast to the suggestions for a more service-driven approach to clients, however, the report also recommended increasing efforts to modify and control the behaviour of unemployed people through the use of insertion agreements and a differentiated set of sanctions (Kommission Moderne Dienstleistungen am Arbeitsmarkt, 2002, p 49).

Translating the Commission's proposals into public policy became one of the central reform projects of the Red–Green government's second term in office when it was included as part of a more extensive reform package known as 'Agenda 2010', a plan that also envisioned changes to other systems such as social security and labour market regulations. In 2002 and 2003, four Acts – colloquially named the 'Hartz Acts' – were passed that successively came into effect in the period from 2003 to 2006. The following section will attempt to address the most important features of these reforms as well as their implications for an individualised approach to activation.

Individualised activation and the Hartz reforms

The Hartz reforms contain a wide array of changes that fall into three primary areas of reform activity: the entitlement structure, the instruments of active labour market policy and the organisational and administrative infrastructure for activation.

Entitlement structure

Three important changes that the reforms set in motion involve entitlement. The first and most fundamental has to do with the *Fourth Act on the Modernisation of Labour Market Services* (Deutscher Bundestag, 2003), which merged the systems of unemployment compensation for long-term unemployed people into a single system called Unemployment Benefit II (*Arbeitslosengeld II*). The new benefit scheme came into effect in January 2005, and is administered by the newly formed Jobcentres. In most cases, these are jointly run by local branches of the FEA and the municipalities under the aegis of the FEA.

The new benefit serves unemployed people and their families who are either ineligible for the insurance-based Unemployment Benefit I or who have exhausted their entitlement.[14] It provides a flat-rate, strictly means-tested benefit at the level of traditional social assistance, and is financed out of the general federal budget.[15] The nominal amount of the benefit is slightly higher than the personal allowances paid out by social assistance in the past, because most of the additional and exceptional payments that used to be granted on a discretionary, individualised basis have now been standardised and integrated into the new benefit on a lump-sum basis. Those who apply for the new benefit after having exhausted their entitlement to Unemployment Benefits also receive a supplement that decreases over time, aimed at cushioning the transition from the insurance-based to the means-tested benefit.

In addition to this major change in benefit structure, the duration of payments of insurance benefits for older unemployed people (over the age of 55) was reduced from a maximum of 32 months to

18 months. Those under the age of 55 generally only receive it for one year. In combination with the abolition of Unemployment Assistance this change, which came into effect in February 2006, effectively means that even older unemployed people with long contribution records now find themselves relegated to the residual system of *Arbeitslosengeld II* after a relatively short period of time.

Finally, the Hartz Acts introduced and tightened work-related benefit criteria. One facet that has been implemented is that employees who lose their jobs must now announce their unemployed status to the local FEA immediately after receiving notice of termination (instead of when unemployment has come into effect). The burden of proof for the acceptability of job offers was also reversed[16] and the criteria defining availability for work were recast, giving administrators more power to challenge unemployed people in their jobseeking behaviour. Germany used to have a graded definition of what kind of job offer unemployed persons who received insurance-based benefits had to accept in terms of salary, with the level of benefits as a minimum floor.[17] Under the new system, every job an unemployed person is 'able' to do is considered to be acceptable – even when remuneration is below bargained wage scales and local going rates. This restrictive definition, which was standard in the old social assistance scheme, became a feature of the new benefit system.

The new system also allows harsher sanctions compared to the old regulations of unemployment insurance, especially for younger unemployed people. While adult recipients are now subject to a 30% reduction of their benefit if they refuse to accept a job or training offer, recipients below the age of 25 can be disqualified for three months for the same refusal. In cases of this nature, the disqualified young person receives only housing benefits and in-kind provisions.[18] Sanctions have also become more differentiated, allowing the administration to respond more flexibly to individual circumstances and (mis)behaviour.[19]

These changes to the entitlement structure have several implications for an individualised approach to activation. Combining Unemployment Assistance and social assistance into a new strictly means-tested scheme, with benefit levels at the level of traditional social assistance, means that the goal of maintaining income status and living standards for unemployed people by intervening through social policy – until now a dominant and defining characteristic of the German welfare state (Esping-Andersen, 1990) – no longer applies to long-term unemployed people. Reducing the maximum duration of Unemployment Benefits and abolishing Unemployment Assistance shifts the responsibility for long-term unemployment from the collective social insurance towards a means-tested, minimal provision. The Hartz reforms thus clearly reflect the third, neo-liberal discourse on the individualisation of activation policies identified in Chapter Two, this volume.[20]

The new rules for assessing entitlement further exacerbate this trend towards individualising life risks. While the old Unemployment Assistance was paid on an individual basis, with income from a claimant's partner disregarded up to the level of the tax-free level of subsistence, an applicant's eligibility for the new benefit is now assessed based on household income according to strict criteria for testing means. This reorganisation of the entitlement structure shifts a great deal of responsibility for long-term unemployment to families, and has effectively led to the de-individualisation of entitlement. Although this development clearly runs counter to the general trend of benefit individualisation in terms of how it affects the erosion of the traditional family (see Chapter Two, this volume), it is in line with the principle of subsidiarity that has always been a prominent feature of the German welfare state (Jacobi, 2006).

The reforms also strongly reflect elements of the fourth discourse on individualisation – the discussion of rights and duties in the context of a new social contract. The overriding goal and principle of the new Social Policy Code II, which lays down the rules for the new Unemployment Benefit II, is the obligation to attempt to (re)gain employment and become independent of public support. The new obligations and sanctions that have been introduced reflect an image of unemployment as a problem that is primarily caused by a lack of individual motivation and effort, and they reveal a new 'distrusting welfare state'.

Instruments of active labour market policy

Elements of a reflexive approach to activation that originates in the situation and needs of unemployed individuals (Valkenburg's fifth discourse on individualised activation: see Chapter Two, this volume) played prominent roles in the rhetoric that accompanied the introduction of new instruments and approaches to active labour market policy. In practice, however, they were overridden by other imperatives.

In Germany, as in many other countries, an assessment of the personal profile and needs of the unemployed person and an individual activation plan form the core of the individualised approach to activation. The activation plan itself is called an 'insertion agreement'

market and seek to (re)integrate unemployed people into some kind of job, even a contingent one, other routes to integration have been marginalised or only approved as second-best solutions. Traditional instruments of qualification and work in the secondary labour market, for example, have played only a sideline role in the new design of active labour market policy. Payments for qualification courses are only granted when the 'success quota' is over 70% (when 70% of the participants gain employment after taking part in the programme). Job creation schemes in intermediary labour markets are largely confined to regions with especially high unemployment, mainly in Eastern Germany. Even so, the intermediary labour market will not disappear completely. In order to fulfil the 'activation quota' – the proportion of unemployed claimants taking part in some kind of integration measures – of 23% of unemployed people (52% for young unemployed people), the government initially aimed to provide about 600,000 'work opportunities' (*Arbeitsgelegenheiten*). Modelled on the benefit top-up option of activation in social assistance,[24] over a quarter of a million of these work opportunities had been created by September 2005. Yet despite the evidence that these measures do not offer much in the way of prospects for integration, they now represent the most frequently used instrument for attempting to achieve it (Schmachtenberg, 2005, p 12). The new toolkit of active labour market policy thus combines a hotchpotch of instruments that aim at fast integration into the labour market irrespective of quality and sustainability of employment with a lean version of the secondary labour market earmarked as such by remuneration, working conditions and lack of social security. Qualification and training, in contrast, play only a subordinate role in the new framework of active labour market policy.

Administrative reforms

Beginning in the late 1990s, the government initiated pilot cooperation projects between local FEA and social assistance offices to function as gateways for specific target groups, especially for young people (Bertelsmann-Stiftung and Bundesanstalt für Arbeit, 2003). The Hartz reforms have now generalised this approach by establishing jobcentres. These new one-stop agencies coordinate all of the services pertaining to benefit payment and activation for the recipients of Unemployment Benefit II (Schmid, 2003), and are intended to become the infrastructural backbone of the reformed framework of active labour market policy, enabling support 'from a single source' (*Hilfe aus einer*

Hand) and facilitating the development of integrated strategies for activation. Implementing the new structures, however, went on at a very hectic pace, in spite of the fact that the process involved merging two administrative bodies that differed widely in their procedures, bureaucratic cultures and personnel qualifications. Unlike in Britain, for example, where jobcentres were successively rolled out nationwide over five years, the *Dritte Gesetz für moderne Dienstleistungen am Arbeitsmarkt* (Third Act for Modern Services in the Labour Market), passed in December 2003, scheduled only a year to prepare for the extensive administrative restructuring. The bulk of the administrative reforms were consequently carried out in tandem with the introduction of the new system of employment compensation in January 2005, which led to delayed benefit payments and a temporary disregard of both placement and activation for the first half of that year. Even where administrative restructuring is now complete, the principle of 'support from a single source' does not apply to all services and benefits. Wage supplements for low-income families and special housing allowances, for example, are still supervised by separate administrations (Jacobi, 2006).

The majority of the new jobcentres are run jointly by the FEA and the municipalities, but a few are administered solely by the municipalities. This administrative inconsistency can be traced back to a compromise agreed between the Red–Green government and the opposition in the second chamber of Parliament. When the laws were passed creating the Hartz reforms, the Conservatives had a majority there. As the president of the FEA, Frank-Juergen Weise has repeatedly stressed,[25] however, joint governance of the jobcentres *auf gleicher Augenhöhe* (on a par with each other) by the local branches of the FEA and the municipalities has proven 'difficult to administer'. As a consequence, the administrative structure was changed again in August 2005 to strengthen the role of the municipalities and limit the responsibility of the FEA to supervision and control of delivery of services and benefit payments. It is still unclear whether the new governance structure will be able to solve the present problems. Until now, its only obvious result is that administrative responsibilities have been in a constant state of flux for more than a year now.

Along with the administrative restructuring, new instruments to govern the jobcentres have also been introduced. While we cannot yet assess the effects that benchmarking, controlling and the FEA's still-pending target agreement with the local jobcentres will have on the capacity of the administration to support individualised activation, one of the new instruments for governance has already come under heavy fire. The *Aussteuerungsbetrag* is a compensation payment made by the FEA to the federal government for every unemployed person who moves from the list of those receiving the insurance-based Unemployment Benefit (*Arbeitslosengeld I*) to the list of those receiving the benefit for long-term unemployed people (*Arbeitslosengeld II*). The justification for the compensation payment is that the federal government pays for *Arbeitslosengeld II*, not the FEA. But having to make the payment also induces the FEA to concentrate active labour market policy on short-term unemployed people and those with low employment barriers, and to only focus on measures that have a chance to 'succeed' before unemployed people lose their entitlement to insurance-based Unemployment Benefit (Allmendinger, 2005).

Although there has been a lot of emphasis – in word if not in deed – placed on individual user involvement in the recent reforms, introducing and reforming collective user involvement has not been part of the political agenda (Chapter Five, this volume). The long-standing tradition in Germany of joint representation and participation of social partners in the administration of labour market services remains anchored in place.[26] The only new body the reforms introduced that involves collective user participation is the *Ombudsrat*, a committee appointed to help oversee the implementation of the Hartz reforms. However, this committee was dissolved in July 2006, and its reports and recommendations are not based solely on the appeals and petitions of unemployed people.

Another element of institutional activation that has to be mentioned when discussing individualised activation is the introduction of 'placement vouchers' (*Vermittlungsgutscheine*). These vouchers, granted as entitlements, enable unemployed people to commission a private agency to help them find work. A pilot project until the end of 2006, this instrument was introduced to generate competition in the field of placement services and as a means of challenging the FEA's performance. Preliminary evaluations have shown, however, that only a small fraction of unemployed people have actually received vouchers, and that among these few even fewer were able to use them to successfully find employment.[27] There are also indications that fraud and creaming effects could be undermining the programme (Dann et al, 2005, p 5).

Discussion

The Hartz reforms represent a major restructure of the system of unemployment compensation and active labour market policy in

Germany. The administrative framework of labour market policy is undergoing a broad process of reorganisation. The government has introduced new instruments of active labour market policy and implemented major changes to the entitlement structure of Unemployment Benefits. Taken as a whole, the reforms have fundamentally redefined the role of the state in active labour market policy and profoundly changed its overall approach to active policies. A political window of opportunity enabled far-reaching changes in 2002, but they have been driven by fairly long-term developments that both prepared the stage for recent reforms and influenced their course.

The reforms are shot through with different definitions of individualisation that in some areas are in concordance, but in others stand in direct conflict. While there has been a lot of talk about creating a reciprocal, client-oriented approach that will empower citizens to take charge of their own lives and develop individual capabilities, discussions have also contained a strong neo-liberal element that seeks to reduce the role of the state and transfer responsibility to individuals and families – regardless of their capacity for self-help. While the approach to active labour market policy is now individualised and the administration necessary to support such an approach has been reformed, entitlement to the new benefit has become effectively de-individualised – strengthening the principle of subsidiarity. Finally, a strong moral element focused on rights and duties now pervades the discussion, placing demands on unemployed people to be actively involved in adapting to changing circumstances. This attitude threatens to override the reflexive approach to individualised activation, because the reciprocal relationship between the administration and the client that has been postulated in theory is in practice dominated by a structural asymmetry of power between the two parties. In addition, user involvement plays nothing more than a marginal role in the new approach to activation, and there are no specific procedures of appeal in place for unemployed people to challenge the administration to fulfil their part of the 'contract'.

Another point of tension between the reflexive approach to individualised activation and the implications of the reforms arises from their overall course. As we have shown, the dominating aim of activation within the context of the Hartz reforms is to foster the quick integration of unemployed people into the primary labour market – an approach that has been called the 'Work First' or 'labour market attachment' variant of activation (see Peck and Theodore, 2000; Hanesch et al, 2001). Rather than enhancing qualifications and increasing personal chances and opportunities, such an approach instead stresses financial pressures and legal obligations for unemployed people, as well as labour market and fiscal imperatives. It views employment in the primary labour market as the most promising route to integration, and either refuses to acknowledge other paths or looks on them as inferior solutions. In terms of priorities, enhancing skills has given way to expanding the low-wage sector and channelling unemployed people into contingent employment. In Chapter Three, this volume, this approach was described as 'employability-centred', as opposed to a 'capability approach' to activation. The latter addresses the living situation of the individual as well as the economic, social and political contexts, and supports the development of capabilities while aiming first and foremost at enhancing an individual's freedom to act.

However, seen within the context of an employability-centred strategy of activation like that currently prevalent in Germany, individualisation has become less a means for adapting active labour market policy to the special needs of the individual, and more a tool for mobilising the allegedly unused resources and capacities of the individual for labour market integration. Individualised measures are now being evaluated in terms of how much they contribute to reducing the unemployment rate and claimant caseloads, along with how they affect flexibility in labour markets, rather than in terms of how they affect the development of an unemployed person's capabilities and ability to improve their social circumstances. While instruments and procedures like 'case management' have been introduced to focus on those with high employment barriers, even these prioritised aims are in danger of concentrating on those in that category with the fewest employment barriers. This danger is further exacerbated by institutional mechanisms such as the *Aussteuerungsbetrag*, which provides a strong incentive to concentrate activation on short-term unemployed people. With the German labour market characterised by both high unemployment and stark divisions between employed and unemployed people, and coupled with meagre chances for the unqualified to improve their lot, there is a particular danger that society could begin to demand too much from those out of work. A final point is that an activation approach focused on employability also tends to increase competition between low-paid workers, thus eroding standards in the low-wage labour market instead of offering unemployed people the chance to boost their standard of living and giving them a perspective of upward mobility. This is especially true for tight labour markets, where activation policies can do little to increase demand for labour power.

Above and beyond this tension, an individualised approach to activation largely hinges on the institutional capacities and resources necessary to carry out a customised strategy. In other words, it relies on successful 'institutional activation'. Providing sufficient support through appropriate resources of personnel and efficient administrative processes is the first step towards ensuring that we do not make impossible demands of unemployed people. The opposite is true in Germany at the moment, as the reforms that were carried out so rapidly left very little time for implementation and administrative restructuring. Administrative governance structures have been in constant flux for more than a year now. It is also questionable whether the hurried (re)training of administrative staff will provide a sound basis for high-quality activation services. In addition to the implementation problems, the new government coalition between the Christian Democrats and Social Democrats that came to power in October 2005 is now pressing the FEA to reduce costs even more, further endangering an individualised approach to high-quality activation.[28] In our view, the present policy environment leaves a lot to be desired when it comes to developing a reflexive and capability, oriented approach to individualised activation. That can only come from an approach that first looks at the needs, competencies and aspirations of the unemployed individual, and then follows a variety of routes to integrate and develop strategies that are really able to help those without work – especially those who need help most.

Notes

[1] This is also the case in the Scandinavian countries (see Chapter Eight, this volume).

[2] In 1996, the *AFG* was reformed and renamed the *Sozialgesetzbuch III* (Social Policy Code III).

[3] Named after Dr Peter Hartz, the head of the 'Commission on the Modernisation of Labour Market Services', as well as chief executive officer and personnel manager at Volkswagen.

[4] Unemployed people with dependent children receive 67%, others receive 60%, of their prior net income.

[5] Here, an unemployed person with children receives 57%, a person without dependants receives 53%, of prior net income.

[6] In the years before the Hartz reforms, about 40% of all claims for social assistance were caused by registered unemployment (Reissert, 2006). Unemployed claimants of social assistance either did not have a contribution record (and were therefore not entitled to insurance-based benefits) or their insurance-based benefit was so low that it had to be topped up by additional social assistance payments.

[7] Recipients could be either placed in regular jobs in the intermediary labour market (the so-called *Entgeltvariante*) or in work opportunities where they continued to receive social assistance and were paid a small wage in addition to the benefit (the so-called *Mehraufwandsentschädigungsvariante*).

[8] In the process of economic transformation, almost four million jobs were lost and unemployment rates in Eastern Germany reached record levels of 20% (Reissert, 2006).

[9] Most explicitly stated in Bodo Hombach's *Aufbruch: Die Politik der Neuen Mitte*. Hombach was Gerhard Schroeder's counsellor and a minister in the first Red–Green government (Hombach, 1998). For a discussion of the concept of the activating state, see Evers (2000).

[10] The 'activation' of the administrative body has also been labelled 'institutional activation' (Van Berkel and Roche, 2002).

[11] With the exception of the marginalised former communist party, the PDS.

[12] For example, the British Jobseeker's Agreement (see Chapter Seven, this volume). For a theoretical perspective on these instruments, see Chapter Four.

[13] AQTIV stands for Activation, Qualification, Training, Investment and 'Vermitteln' (placement).

[14] The head of the entitlement unit (*Bedarfsgemeinschaft*), which is not the individual but the family, receives *Arbeitslosengeld II*, and their dependants *Sozialgeld*. Those not available for work remain the responsibility of the municipally administered system of social assistance.

[15] For the first adult in the household, the personal allowance is €345. Partners receive 90%, children under 14 years 60% and children

between 14 and 18 years and young adults under 25 years 80% of this amount. Adequate housing costs are also provided.

[16] Whereas formerly the FEA had to prove that a claimant had entered unemployment 'voluntarily' or consciously subverted termination of their unemployment spell in cases of conflict, the burden of proof now lies with unemployed people.

[17] Before this rule, which had been in place since 1997, acceptability was still defined in relation to a person's level of qualification.

[18] In cases where several breaches have occurred, however, adults' sanctions can also accumulate to a severe or complete loss of benefits.

[19] As it was felt that sanctions where still not tough enough, the new government has recently passed a law that will make them even more restrictive from 2007 onwards.

[20] The trend towards an individualisation of life risks is also a dominant feature of the major pension reform instituted in 2001. The level of benefits paid by the public pay-as-you-go pension insurance will be successively and significantly reduced in the coming years, while new subsidies for private pensions have been introduced.

[21] By September 2005, targets for the proportion of staff to clients had been reached (Schmachtenberg, 2005). Evidence on the 'job guarantee' for young unemployed people, however, was not yet available.

[22] It was originally hoped that the PSA could help realise great success in labour market integration. First evaluations, however, show that these hopes are unlikely to be fulfilled (Jahn and Windsheimer, 2004). The new CDU/CSU and SPD coalition has therefore decided to no longer force every jobcentre to have or hire a PSA (CDU/CSU and SPD, 2005).

[23] The special rules for fixed-term contracts for older workers have, however, recently been legally challenged on grounds of discrimination by the European Court of Justice and have to be revised.

[24] These jobs are scheduled for six to nine months and pay a remuneration of €1–€2 per hour on top of benefits. They are meant to be 'additional', not to replace jobs in the regular labour market.

Controlling 'additionality' is difficult, however, and the first signs of substitution for regular employment are evident, especially in the care and crafts sector.

[25] See interview in the German newspaper *Die Zeit*, 1 January 2005.

[26] However, this is a collective and not an individual form of participation, and it is questionable whether trades unions (with the bulk of their constituencies employed) and the employer organisations are able to represent the interests of unemployed people.

[27] One of the evaluation studies found that 6% of entitled unemployed people had received a voucher, and that of these 7% were successful in finding permanent employment (ie employment for more than six months)with the help of the voucher (Hagemann et al, 2004). Another evaluation study found that 2.5% to 7% of unemployed people had received a voucher, and that of these 7.3% found employment with its help (Dann et al, 2005).

[28] Under the coalition agreement, retrenchment in active labour market policy and a rise in value added taxes are to allow for a reduction of insurance contributions from 6.5% to 4.5% (CDU/CSU and SPD, 2005).

References

Allmendinger, J. (2005) 'Weg mit den Strafzöllen', *Frankfurter Allgemeine Zeitung*, no 196, 24 August, p 35.

Bertelsmann-Stiftung and Bundesanstalt für Arbeit (2003) *Job Center: Die lokalen Zentren für Integration in Beschäftigung*, Dokumentation der Fachtagung in Berlin, 7 March, www.bik-online.de/download/ Dokumentation.pdf (accessed 21 September 2004).

Blancke, S. and Schmid, J. (2003) 'Bilanz der Bundesregierung Schröder in der Arbeitsmarktpolitik 1998-2002: Ansätze zu einer doppelten Wende', in C. Egle, T. Ostheim and R. Zohlnhöfer (eds) *Das rot-grüne Projekt: Eine Bilanz der Regierung Schröder 1998-2002*, Wiesbaden: Westdeutscher Verlag, pp 215-38.

BMWA (Bundesministerium für Wirtschaft und Arbeit) (2002) 'Wesentliche Inhalte des Job-Aqtiv-Gesetzes', www.bmwa.bund.de (accessed 24 November 2003).

Bundesagentur für Arbeit (2005) 'Fachkonzept 'Beschäftigungsorientiertes Fallmanagement im SGB II'', Nürnberg. www.arbeitsagentur.de/zentraler-content/A01-Allgemein-Info/ A015-Oeffentlichkeitsarbeit/Publikation/pdf/HEGA-04-2005-kozept-Fallmanagement-Anll.pdf

CDU (Christian Demokratische Union)/CSU (Christlich-Soziale Union) and SPD (Sozial demokratische Partei Deutschland) (2005) 'Gemeinsam für Deutschland – mit Mut und Menschlichkeit: Koalitionsvertrag', www.spd.de (accessed 15 November 2005).

Dann, S., Heinze, A., Hujer, R., Klee, G., Pfeiffer, F., Rosemann, M., Sörgel, W., Spermann, A., Wiedemann, E., Winterhagen, H. and Zeiss, C. (2005) 'Vermittlungsgutscheine auf dem Prüfstand', *IAB Kurzbericht*, no 5, pp 1-8.

Deutscher Bundestag (2002a) *Erstes Gesetz für moderne Dienstleistungen am Arbeitsmarkt*, Bundestags-Drucksache 15/0025.

Deutscher Bundestag (2002b) *Zweites Gesetz für Moderne Dienstleistungen am Arbeitsmarkt*, Bundestags-Drucksache 15/0026.

Deutscher Bundestag (2003) *Viertes Gesetz für moderne Dienstleistungen am Arbeitsmarkt*, Bundestags-Drucksache 15/1638.

Esping-Andersen, G. (1990) *The three worlds of welfare capitalism*, Princeton, NJ: Princeton University Press.

Evers, A. (2000) 'Aktivierender Staat', in E. Mezger and K. W. West (eds) *Aktivierender Staat und Politisches Handeln*, Marburg: Schüren, pp 13-29.

Fels, G., Heinze, R., Pfarr, H., Schmid, G. and Streeck, W. (2001) *Aktivierung der Arbeitsmarktpolitik: Thesen der Benchmarking-Gruppe*, Berlin: Bechmarking-Gruppe des Bündnis für Arbeit.

Giddens, A. (1998) *The Third Way: The renewal of social democracy*, Cambridge: Polity Press.

Grell, B., Sambale, J. and Eick, V. (2002) 'Workfare zwischen Arbeitsmarkt- und Lebensstilregulierung: Beschäftigungsorientierte Sozialpolitik im Deutsch-amerikanischen Vergleich', *PROKLA*, vol 32, no 4, pp 1-23.

Hagemann, S., Sörgel, W. and Wiedemann, E. (2004) 'Vermittlungsgutscheine nach §421g SGB III: Zwischenergebnisse aus der Begleitforschung zur Vermittlung', *IAB Forschungsbericht*, no 1, pp 1-38.

Hanesch, W. (1997) 'Konzeption, Krise und Optionen der Sozialen Stadt', in W. Hanesch (ed) *Überlebt die Soziale Stadt? Konzeption, Krise und Perspektiven kommunaler Sozialstaatlichkeit*, Opladen: Leske and Budrich, pp 21-56.

Hanesch, W., Stelzer-Orthofer, C. and Balzter, N. (2001) 'Activation policies in minimum income schemes', in M. Heikkilä and E. Keskitalo (eds) *Social assistance in Europe*, Helsinki: STAKES, pp 122-52.

Heinelt, H. (1994) 'Arbeitsmarktpolitik nach der Vereinigung: Überforderung und Substanzverlust des Beitragsfinanzierungsprinzips', in T. Olk and B. Riedmüller (eds) *Grenzen des Sozialversicherungsstaates*, Opladen: Westdeutscher Verlag, pp 191-205.

Heinelt, H. (2003) 'Arbeitsmarktpolitik – von 'versorgenden' wohlfahrtsstaatlichen Interventionen zur 'aktivierenden' Beschäftigungsförderung', in A. Gohr and M. Seeleib-Kaiser (eds) *Sozial- und Wirtschaftspolitik unter Rot-Grün*, Opladen: Westdeutscher Verlag, pp 125-45.

Hombach, B. (1998) *Aufbruch: Die Politik der Neuen Mitte*, Düsseldorf: Econ Verlag.

Hombach, B. (1999) 'Die Balance von Rechten und Pflichten sichern: Der Aktivierende Sozialstaat – Das neue Leitbild', *Soziale Sicherheit*, vol 48, no 2, pp 41-4.

Jacobi, D. (2006) 'Rot-Grüne Grundsicherungspolitik und die Herausforderungen des Grundeinkommens für den Deutschen Sozialstaat', in M. Füllsack (ed) *Globale Soziale Sicherheit. Grundeinkommen: Weltweit?*, Berlin: Avinus Verlag, pp 129-50.

Jahn, E. J. and Windsheimer, A. (2004) 'Personal-Service-Agenturen: Teil II: Erste Erfolge zeichnen sich ab', *IAB Kurzbericht*, no 1, pp 1-6.

Kommission Moderne Dienstleistungen am Arbeitsmarkt (2002) *Moderne Dienstleistungen am Arbeitsmarkt: Bericht der Kommission*, Berlin: Bundesministerium für Arbeit und Sozialordnung.

Lamping, W. and Schridde, H. (1999) 'Konturen neuer Sozialstaatlichkeit: Sozialhilfe zwischen Kontinuität und Wandel', *Zeitschrift für Fürsorgewesen*, no 4, pp 74-100.

Mohr, K. (2004) 'Pfadabhängige Restrukturierung oder Konvergenz? Reformen in der Arbeitslosensicherung und der Sozialhilfe in Großbritannien und Deutschland', *Zeitschrift für Sozialreform*, vol 50, no 3, pp 283-312.

Peck, J. and Theodore, N. (2000) ''Work First': workfare and the regulation of contingent labour markets', *Cambridge Journal of Economics*, vol 24, no 1, pp 119-38.

Reissert, B. (2006) 'Germany: a late reformer', in J. Clasen, M. Ferrera and M. Rhodes (eds) *Welfare states and the challenge of unemployment*, London/New York: Routledge.

Schmachtenberg, R. (2005) 'Aktuelle Entwicklungen der Umsetzung des SGB II', Paper presented at the conference of the Evangelische Akademie Loccum: 'Arbeitsmarktpolitik im Argen?', 24-26 October.

Schmid, G. (2003) 'Moderne Dienstleistungen am Arbeitsmarkt: Strategie und Vorschläge der Hartz-Kommission', *Aus Politik und Zeitgeschichte*, no 6-7, pp 3-6.

Trube, A. (2002) 'Entwicklungslinien in der Arbeitsmarkt- und Sozialhilfepolitik. Trends und Gegenvorschläge', *Arbeit und Sozialpolitik*, no 1-2, pp 18-25.

Van Berkel, R. and Roche, M. (2002) 'Activation policies as reflexive social policies', in R. van Berkel and I. Hornemann Møller (eds) *Active social policies in the European Union*, Bristol: The Policy Press, pp 197-225.

Von Bandemer, S., Blanke, B., Hilbert, J. and Schmid, J. (1995) 'Staatsaufgaben – Von der 'Schleichenden Privatisierung' zum 'Aktivierenden Staat'', in F. Behrens, R. G. Heinze, J. Hilbert, S. Stöbe and E. M. Walsken (eds) *Den Staat neu denken: Reformperspektiven für die Landesverwaltungen*, Berlin: Edition Sigma, pp 41-60.

Conclusion

TWELVE

Individualised activation services in the EU

Rik van Berkel

Introduction

In the preceding chapters attention has been paid to the rise of individualised approaches in activation, adopting a theoretical as well as an empirical point of view. As all authors have argued, the trend towards individualised service provision is not a merely 'technical' or 'methodical' issue regarding the way in which services should be delivered. Instead, it is embedded in, and part of, processes aimed at reforming social policies and their governance; which, in their turn, are taking place in order to cope with broader economic, cultural, demographic and social developments. In other words, discussing individualised activation services unavoidably raises questions regarding the necessity, feasibility and desirability of the welfare state transformations of which they are an integral part. This is one of the reasons why the individualisation of activation services is a controversial issue, certainly so among social scientists – and also among the authors who contributed to this volume. It was not the objective of this book to resolve these controversies. Instead, we set ourselves some less ambitious tasks. First, the controversies partly stem from the various interpretations of the concept of 'individualisation' that lie at the basis of individualised service provision. Debates about individualised activation services raise many questions that are often formulated in an either/or form: is individualised activation an instrument to erode universal and decent welfare, or is it an intervention strategy needed to adequately support a very heterogeneous target group? Is it a disciplinary tool to enable case managers to enforce (work) obligations upon their clients, or an alternative to traditional 'one-size-fits-all' services that were designed to service an 'average client' that may exist in statistics but not in real life? Is individualised activation a device to worm information out of individual clients or an attempt to put them in charge of, and involve them actively in, their activation process? Rather than giving answers to these questions, the theoretical chapters in Part One tried to contribute to understanding the background of these controversies, to unravel the discourses on individualisation and to analyse different strands of thinking about individualised service provision. Second, the book wanted to gain insight into the state of the art of individualised activation by exploring policies and practices in various European Union (EU) member states. For this purpose, a group of countries was selected that represents the diversity of welfare states in the EU; in addition, specific attention was paid to an analysis of the EU discourse and policy initiatives (Part Two).

In this concluding chapter, we shall return to some of the issues that were discussed in Chapters One and Two. First, we will return to the concept of individualisation underlying the development of individualised service provision in the context of activation. Second, our starting point that the introduction of individualised activation services has to be analysed against the background of both public sector and social policy reforms is held up against the light: to what degree are the 'new governance' and 'active welfare state' discourses and transformations reflected in the concrete manifestations of individualised activation services in the national case studies? Third, we raise the question as to what degree our case studies show evidence that processes of service implementation and delivery have an important impact on what individualised service provision means in practice. We conclude this chapter with some suggestions for future research.

The concept of individualisation

As has been illustrated throughout this book and was explicitly argued by Valkenburg in Chapter Two, a variety of concepts or discourses of individualisation needs to be distinguished in order to adequately understand debates on, policy proposals aimed at and practices of the individualised provision of activation services, which are usually based on a mix of these concepts. Valkenburg distinguished five discourses of individualisation in the context of social policies:

(1) Social policy interventions should be aimed at individuals, not at families or households.
(2) Social services should be de-standardised, differentiated, flexibilised and adapted to individual circumstances.
(3) Individual service users enter (quasi-)markets of competing service providers as individual customers or consumers.

(4) Social entitlements are granted on an individual basis, contingent upon the individual's conduct, responsibilities and compliance with obligations.

(5) Service users are seen as reflexive, competent citizens and services should support them in realising their individual life projects, and individuals should be put in charge of the service provision process.

The first individualisation discourse is most relevant in the context of reforms of income protection schemes aimed at 'activating' welfare states. Nevertheless, it is not completely absent in the context of activation services. For example, in many countries we see how more and more groups of people dependent on public income provision are subjected to activation and, as a further step, to obligatory activation: lone parents and single mothers, older unemployed people, people in a highly vulnerable position (due to poverty, social isolation/exclusion, homelessness, addiction) and disabled people. In a more narrow sense, this discourse of individualisation is reflected in reforms that oblige both partners in two-parent households dependent on means-tested income protection schemes to participate in activation.

The second individualisation discourse is clearly present in the case studies discussed in this book. Processes of de-standardisation and flexibilisation of activation services can partly be understood as lessons learned from earlier experiences with standard programmes aimed at fixed target groups. As activation programmes had to deal with increasingly heterogeneous target groups, it became clear that standard programmes aimed at broadly defined categories hampered effective activation, as they did not take into account characteristics of the individual. The need to take individual characteristics into account asks for programmes that can be adapted to the individual (that is, that are flexible), and for a not too rigid target group approach. Nowadays, several countries make use of profiling procedures to map the individual circumstances and characteristics of clients. The UK New Deal programmes are an example of activation programmes that reveal a clear trend towards flexibilisation and individualisation. Personal advisers have more room nowadays to develop activation trajectories that they consider adequate given the needs and circumstances of individuals; and although the New Deal programmes are still aimed at specific target groups, there is more room for variation in the activation of individual clients. The Finnish, German and UK cases show that the need for flexibilisation and individualisation is often especially experienced where activating the hardest to employ is concerned. The most vulnerable people often do not manage to enter 'mainstream' activation programmes, or drop out of them. In these cases, tailor-made interventions are considered necessary to make activation successful. Although in a completely different context, the Italian *Reddito Minimo di Inserimento* (RMI) experiments were based on similar insights: individualised, flexible and differentiated services are necessary to help the poorest and the most socially excluded – an important target group of the experiments.

The third discourse puts individualisation in the context of the introduction of markets or quasi-markets for the provision of public social services. By now, several EU countries have introduced market mechanisms in the provision of activation, involving both profit and not-for-profit actors in service provision. The UK, Germany, Italy, the Netherlands and Denmark are examples, whereas other countries, such as Finland, have not taken the path of marketisation and hold on to the bureaucratic-professional model of service provision. Separating purchasers and providers of services, and creating competition among providers is supposed to promote more effectiveness and efficiency, higher quality and lower prices, and increased responsiveness, among other reasons because it renders options of choice and exit to purchasers. However, in most cases where market mechanisms have been implemented, there exists not only a split between purchasers and providers, but also between purchasers and users. That is, benefit or employment agencies buy activation services 'on behalf of' their clients, the actual users of activation services. In these circumstances, service users do not enter the market of activation services as customers who select their own services and service provider: they have little or no choice, control or purchasing power (Wright 2006); which is one of the reasons why these markets are characterised as quasi-markets. But there are some exceptions. In Germany, clients can make use of placement vouchers to buy services on the market (see Chapter Eleven; also see Bruttel, 2005). In the Netherlands, the so-called Individual Reintegration Agreement gives clients (mainly the insured) opportunities to develop their own reintegration trajectories and to select the service provider they prefer. Outside the EU, there is the Ticket to Work in the US for people with disabilities. As Jacobi and Mohr in Chapter Eleven wrote, the results of the German placement voucher in terms of job-finding are not univocally positive. More fundamentally, one may criticise the 'consumerist' approach underlying these kinds of instruments (see, for example, du Gay, 2005). Nevertheless, evaluations of the Dutch Individual Reintegration Agreement revealed that clients – irrespective of the outcomes of activation – do value having voice and choice in their own activation process.

The fourth discourse has had a very clear impact on the nature of the individualised provision of activation services. It is often accompanied by a process of 'contractualisation' of relationships between unemployed people and the state or, more specifically, benefit or social assistance agencies. Contractualisation has taken place in all countries discussed in this book, formalised in the form of Individual Action Plans that clients enter into with their personal adviser. In most countries, the contractualisation tendency is related to attempts to make activation more tailor-made, and is simultaneously embedded in a process of increasing the obligations of unemployed people as well as the conditionality of income support: the contract contains a 'tailor-made' definition of the responsibilities and obligations of the individual and facilitates the surveillance of their attitudes and behaviour and, subsequently, the evaluation of social security claims (Chapter Three). The Italian RMI experiments were an exception in the sense that they were strongly embedded in a discourse on combating poverty and social exclusion, on preventing fragmentation and on promoting universal access to services; far more than in a discourse of strengthening obligations and individual responsibilities. This does not mean that the other countries can be put in one and the same category. For example, Germany and the Czech Republic seem to be much tougher on unemployed people than Finland, a country which is quite sensitive to issues such as rebalancing rights and duties, equality of treatment and coping with the tensions between universalism and particularism (Hoggett, 2005). At the same time, we should distinguish policy rhetoric from policy practice: rhetorical toughness does not always imply a tough treatment in practice. We will return to this issue later in this chapter. What needs to be emphasised here is that the issue of contractualisation of relationships between clients and the state is highly controversial (see Sol and Westerveld, 2005). In the UK, Finland and Germany, for example, clients are obliged to enter a 'negotiation process' with a personal adviser unless they are willing to accept sanctions – which for many is not a realistic option, of course. Clients, on their part, are far less powerful in enforcing agencies to make them an activation offer, or to provide the service that agencies have agreed to provide. Once they have entered the 'negotiation process', much depends on the attitude of the personal adviser and the resources with which, and the conditions under which, they work. Refusing an activation offer may be interpreted as a lack of willingness on the part of the client who may be sanctioned, also in cases where the quality of the offer is evidently low. Clients have few institutionalised resources at their disposal to ensure that an activation offer is made to them that fits their needs and circumstances: in most countries, this is limited to a right to appeal or complain when they disagree with activation plans. In Finland, a formal procedure concerning the process of developing activation plans has to protect individuals from becoming too dependent on local discretion. During the negotiation process itself, the main 'weapon' that the individual client disposes of is that personal advisers depend on their information and cooperation in order for activation to be effective. Because of this lack of 'checks and balances' in the activation process, Freedland and King (2005) – in a critical analysis of the UK Jobseeker's Agreement – argue that client contracts may tend towards 'illiberal contractualism'. In their opinion, the justification of the decisions made and the sanctions imposed by personal advisers is a critical issue here (see also Chapter Three, this volume): when non-compliant behaviour of the client is automatically interpreted and dealt with as an offence against contractual agreements rather than a response to an inadequate intervention of the adviser, contractualism runs the risk of resulting in authoritarianism.

Here, we enter the realm of the fifth discourse of individualisation. As Valkenburg argued in Chapter Two, a core issue in the context of activation and specifically of this discourse concerns the question: who is in charge? This directly relates to the issue of user involvement developed in Chapter Five. In this chapter, we came across various informal or more institutionalised forms of user involvement in which users are:

- providers of information: in the terminology of Chapter Five, this involves the most modest form of user involvement ('user participation') where the user is an informant;
- partners in activation: personal advisers can decide to stimulate user involvement in order to establish relationships of trust, to increase the reliability of information, to enhance the motivation of clients and to strengthen their cooperation. In these situations, user involvement in activation results from a kind of professional pragmatism, rather than from an institutionalisation of resources enabling clients to exercise choice or voice in their activation process;
- customers or co-producers of activation: as was discussed earlier in this chapter, several instruments may be used that institutionalise forms of user choice or user voice.

In the context of the fifth discourse on individualisation, user involvement goes beyond the forms of user involvement mentioned above: it argues that the user should be the director of their own activation process. In other words, the client is put in charge: they are involved in defining the problems that activation should solve and the objectives it should realise, as well as in selecting the means through which this should be accomplished. Even though traces of this discourse are present in policy rhetoric ('empowering the user vis-à-vis service providers', 'taking the individual as a starting point in service provision', and so on), activation practices reveal that, in most cases, the client is not in charge in this sense. For example, the client is not involved in problem definition (unemployment, lack of employability), nor in deciding on the objectives of activation (paid work, benefit independence) – which, of course, does not imply that they always disagree with 'imposed' problem definitions or activation objectives.

Summarising, it is evident that the second and fourth discourses on individualisation have had an important impact on the trend towards individualised service provision in the context of activation. Flexibilising programmes and making offers tailor-made is seen as a prerequisite for effective activation; individualised activation plans and contractualisation are important instruments in what is referred to as 'rebalancing rights and obligations'. The impact of the third and fifth individualisation discourses is less considerable, although present. The liberalisation in the provision of activation services through the introduction of service markets and competition between service providers has, with some exceptions, not led to a widespread increase of a consumerist approach to activation, even though the notion of the user as consumer is often referred to – in a rather instrumentalist way – in debates on how to make service providers more responsive, how to promote competition between service providers and how to establish a market of social services. The core concern of the fifth discourse – putting the user in charge of their activation – is far from realised, even though it crops up regularly, if only for pragmatic reasons: user involvement as an instrument to make activation more effective, and to make providers of activation more inclined to provide services that clients need and want.

Individualisation at the interface of social policy and public sector reforms

As was argued in the introductory chapter, the process of individualisation in the provision of activation services takes place at the interface of social policy and public sector reforms. On the one hand, these reforms influence what individualised service provision actually means in specific activation programmes. On the other, the objective to individualise service provision has an impact on policy and governance reforms.

In terms of the social policy context, the introduction of activation policies and the gradual individualisation of activation services is one of the main characteristics of the transformation of EU welfare states from 'passive' to 'active' welfare states. They clearly reflect the threefold evolution in processes of dealing with unemployment as described by Bonvin and Farvaque (Chapter Three):

- a shift from financially compensating towards activating the unemployed, making the first conditional upon the latter;
- a process of targeting policy interventions at individuals rather than broad categories or target groups, accompanied by a partial privatisation of the responsibility for unemployment and dealing with it;
- a territorialisation of social policies, where regional and local actors gain autonomy in policy making and service delivery.

In the debates on welfare state convergence or divergence, this transformation process is often cited as evidence of processes of convergence. As was argued in Chapter Six, the 'active welfare state' is strongly endorsed at the level of EU discourse, guidelines and policy objectives. In addition, it meets wide support in the member states where Social-Democratic, Conservative, Liberal and Green political parties subscribe to its general principles – although they may disagree when it comes to the elaboration of these principles into concrete reforms. The individualisation of activation is part of this process of convergence and is being implemented EU-wide. The second and fourth individualisation discourses (see former section) play an important role: individualisation is considered necessary to cope with processes of differentiation of the target groups of activation, and to define individual responsibilities and obligations, and monitor the individual's behaviour.

Nevertheless, the EU welfare states 'deal' with the transformation of their social policies in nationally specific ways, dependent on welfare state traditions and cultures, political and policy preferences, the nature and urgency of social problems, and so on. National conditions and contexts are also relevant where the introduction of individualised service provision is concerned. Some examples may illustrate this.

First, it is generally recognised that the development of active welfare states is accompanied by a shift from universality to selectivity (Gilbert, 2002). Individualising policy interventions may be an instrument in accomplishing this shift, as was elaborated in the former section. However, not all countries have walked on the path of straightforward selectivity. Finland has made efforts to preserve and even strengthen universality by embedding individualised activation in a framework of universal rights of the unemployed person and of uniform procedures in order to promote equal treatment. The Italian RMI experiments – similar to the situation in France and the Spanish '*Comunidades Autónomas*' – combined the introduction of individualised service provision with measures aimed at creating a national, more universalistic income safety net, in order to reduce differences in the treatment of different groups and to counter significant regional inequalities and fragmentation regarding access to, and level of, welfare support (Chapter Nine; also see Moreno, 2003). Thus, the Italian reforms were not part of a strategy of making welfare state arrangements more selective. Instead, they were aimed at strengthening social citizenship rights and promoting a situation in which access to social provisions is dependent on need rather than on regionally or locally available resources.

Second, national traditions and conditions also influence the strategies that countries adopt in making welfare states more active. Some countries commenced welfare state reforms relatively early, which enabled a more gradual or incremental reform strategy involving experiments, policy learning and 'evidence-based' policy reforms. 'Late reformers' experienced a much higher urgency for reforms, and saw themselves confronted with the necessity to introduce drastic changes in a relatively short period of time. Of the countries discussed in this book, Germany is a clear example of the latter. Corporatist welfare states have a welfare state regime notorious for the difficulties they experience (for a variety of reasons, including characteristics of the institutional context – the strong role of civil society and social partners – policy preferences – the subsidiarity principle – and policy priorities – the traditionally low female labour market participation; for example, see Zeitlin and Trubek, 2003) in introducing fundamental reforms aimed at making welfare state arrangements more activating. The extensive and drastic reform package that Germany introduced with the Hartz reforms – which, according to Jacobi and Mohr (Chapter Eleven), may affect the very fundamentals of the corporatist German welfare state – now has to be implemented at an unprecedented speed, which is likely to cause significant implementation problems. As things look now, this contributed to the introduction of a relatively tough version of individualised service provision: involving a worsening of benefits for large groups, strict obligations and a Work First approach in activation. Transformation processes involved even more radical changes for the peoples of the Eastern European countries, as Sirovátka illustrated in Chapter Ten. The introduction of market economies in these countries implied a completely new approach to issues related to employment and unemployment. Besides that, the implementation of individualised activation programmes requires building the institutional capacity to do so effectively, which is a crucial issue in Czech individualised activation. We will return to this in the next section.

A third factor influencing the characteristics of individual approaches in activation concerns the nature, the size and the composition of the groups of unemployed people at whom social policies are targeted. Active labour market policies in Finland and Germany, for example, were traditionally targeted at the insured, who are, generally speaking, relatively close to the labour market. For these groups of unemployed people, standardised services are often considered adequate. This changed when the focus of activation was directed at social assistance recipients, partly as a consequence of a process that in Chapter Eleven was called 'the municipalisation of unemployment': a growing number of unemployed people dependent on locally administered (and sometimes locally financed) social assistance schemes as a consequence of, among others, increasing long-term unemployment and changes in social insurance schemes. Generally speaking, social assistance recipients involve a harder-to-employ group of people for whom more tailor-made and individualised services are considered necessary. Interestingly, in Finland Individual Action Plans were initially developed as a disciplinary tool: the first group of people at whom they were targeted were social assistance recipients who refused work or training offers. In the UK, a favourable development of the labour market and employment created a situation in which providers of activation services were confronted with a 'residual' group of hard-to-place unemployed people, which increased the need for personalised and flexible activation services. In the Czech Republic, the nature of unemployment and the characteristics attributed to the group of unemployed people influenced the process of service individualisation in a different way. As Sirovátka described in Chapter Ten, the concept of 'artificial unemployment' is crucial in this context. Public opinion on unemployment and unemployed people contributed to a tough version of individualised activation: a majority of the Czech people believe that misuse of benefits and participation in informal jobs is widespread among unemployed people, and many think that unemployed people are not actively looking for jobs.

Finally, developments in social policies in a broader sense are of course important in determining the conditions under which individualised activation takes place. All countries discussed in this book have introduced policy reforms that influence what happens – or can happen – during the provision of individualised activation. For example, Chapter Ten discussed how the Czech Republic has introduced a stricter definition of what is considered to be a 'suitable job', and how family circumstances are no longer taken into account in determining what is expected of unemployed people. The chapter on Germany also mentions several policy reforms that affect the context in which individualised activation takes place: for example, a redefinition of criteria for being available for work, new criteria used in determining what jobs are considered acceptable, an increasing emphasis in activation on quick job placements and less room for education or participation in secondary labour market jobs. Evidently, these types of policy reforms reduce clients' room for manoeuvre, and increase the room for personal advisers to impose activation interventions upon clients.

Besides these social policy reforms, the national case studies in Part Two point to reforms of public governance – including the administration of social security arrangements and the provision of employment and activation services – as important factors determining the actual practice of individualised activation. The contractualisation of relationships between service providers, benefit agencies and clients that was discussed in the former section is one aspect of these reforms. Besides this, several other aspects of these reforms can be distinguished.

Most countries witness processes of decentralisation in various social policy areas, including activation policies. Promoting opportunities for individualised and tailor-made service provision is an important argument in favour of decentralisation: increasing the opportunities for local or regional authorities to adapt policies to individual and local circumstances is considered necessary to realise individual approaches in activation. At the same time, the ways in which decentralisation takes place, particularly the nature of national, general regulations and frameworks as well as the (re)distribution of resources, have an important impact on the local conditions for delivering individualised activation services – and, thus, for their content. Italy is an extreme example here: the absence of adequate national regulation and redistributive mechanisms creates a situation in which local social policies are strongly dependent on the resources available locally, rather than on the needs of the local populations, thus producing significant territorial fragmentation. Finland is a completely opposite example. Even though local differentiation exists in the Finnish context as well, Chapter Eight described how Finnish government introduced national legislation in order to promote equality and reduce unintended local differences. Besides the countries discussed in this volume, the Dutch case is an interesting case, positioned somewhere in between these two extremes. In 2004, a new Social Assistance Act devolved autonomy in making and delivering activation policies to the municipalities, in order to enable them to develop tailor-made solutions to local unemployment problems. At the same time, financial responsibility for social assistance expenditure was devolved as well, creating a strong incentive for municipalities to reduce social assistance dependency. Whether this 'mode of decentralisation' will indeed promote the provision of activation services tailored to the needs of unemployed people and local labour markets, remains to be seen (see Van Berkel, 2006).

In various countries, public governance reforms are accompanied by the introduction of market mechanisms, competition between service providers and liberalisation: the UK, Germany and the Czech Republic. Perhaps surprisingly, the UK has taken a quite moderate approach in involving private parties in the provision of activation services. Although one might expect that liberal welfare states reveal the strongest inclination to involve the market in service provision, in the EU the Netherlands has introduced the most radical liberalisation of providing activation services. Finland belongs to the countries where this form of the new governance of activation services has had little impact so far: there, the provision of services largely remains a responsibility of national and local state institutions. According to the proponents of the introduction of market mechanisms in the provision of public services, it is *supposed* to make service provision more efficient and effective, and service providers more responsive, more inclined to offer services that meet the needs of customers, and so on (see Le Grand, 1991). In other words, it should contribute to more individualised, tailor-made services. In addition, the introduction of market mechanisms is often embedded in explicit discourses on competent and emancipated citizens who reject the paternalism of bureaucratic professionals and supply-oriented service providers, and want voice and choice. This is clearly the case in the 'Modernising Governance' agenda in the UK, but also in Germany and Italy. However, the impact of market mechanisms on individualised service provision is anything but unequivocal. As we discussed in the former section, policy makers are very hesitant to render voice and choice to citizens where the provision of activation services is concerned, and voucher systems or other instruments to increase people's voice and choice are scarce: citizens are considered not sufficiently competent or capable, increasing their voice and choice would involve 'moral hazard' problems, and citizens might be inclined to 'misuse' their voice and choice. As we saw in Chapter Seven, the concept of choice is central in the UK debate on the modernisation of governance, but mainly in the areas of education and health, and far less prominent in the area of activation (see also Wright, 2006). A similar story could be told about the Netherlands, where choice and voice for users are more widespread in other policy areas (for example, care and health) than in activation. Introducing market mechanisms is often seen as a manifestation of the dominance of neo-liberalist thinking in reforming the welfare state. Seen from the perspective of the position of citizens in the market of activation services, however, the qualification 'quasi-liberalism' would be more appropriate. In addition, it is by no means self-evident that the creation of competition in the provision of activation will result in more tailor-made services. As the Dutch case shows, this does not simply depend on the existence of competition per se, but on the broader context in which competition is embedded, including the role of purchasers, that may have other priorities than purchasing individualised services, or may simply lack the knowledge about their clients to buy appropriate tailor-made activation (see also Van Berkel and Van der Aa, 2005).

Summarising, the social policy and public governance reforms and the way in which these reforms affect individualised service provision, seem to reveal that the notion of an 'active' and 'responsible' citizen contains a paradox indeed, as was concluded in Chapter Six. On the one hand this discourse explicitly refers to an active and autonomous subject, which could be used as an argument in favour of strengthening the position of users vis-à-vis service providers by institutionalising instruments that give the user choice and voice. On the other hand it implicitly (and sometimes explicitly) mistrusts the motives of this very subject, which is considered as a legitimisation for subjecting them to the supervision, control and sanctioning practices of delivering agencies. In Valkenburg's words: in the area of activation, the need to protect the state against its citizens seems to be experienced as more urgent than the need to protect citizens against the state.

The process of implementation and delivery

By now, activation has received considerable attention from social policy scholars. Activation policies and programmes have been investigated and compared, effects of activation have been measured and, more recently, research of the organisational and institutional context in which the administration, implementation and delivery of activation takes place has been carried out. Much less attention is paid, however, to the process of 'producing' activation services: what actually goes on in the organisations and institutions that are responsible for service provision, involving both the primary process of adviser–client interactions in which services are produced or delivered (see Chapter Four), and the secondary process, that is, the management of these organisations and institutions. As several studies have shown (see Chapter One), this is a serious lack in activation research: the quality of management and of service 'production' and delivery processes is a crucial factor in making activation succeed. This is especially so in a context of decentralisation, and of increasing discretionary room for service providers and professional workers.

The national case studies that were analysed in Part Two of this book clearly show that characteristics of the service provision process and the conditions under which it takes place may have serious implications for how (individualised) activation looks in practice. We will discuss several aspects of this.

First, the implementation of individualised activation services requires the 'institutional capacity' to do so, in terms of staff, skills and qualifications, institutional infrastructure, institutional cooperation, and so on. The Czech case, where the introduction of activation programmes lagged far behind in comparison with many other EU countries, clearly illustrates the importance of institutional capacity (as does the Italian case), as well as the potential consequences of a lack of it. Sirovátka's chapter showed that the lack of sufficient and adequate institutional capacity necessary for the implementation of activation services may force national governments to adopt activation strategies focusing on making social security less attractive (reducing benefit levels, sanctioning) and on increased supervision of job-search behaviour, rather than on introducing activation programmes. Italy is another example. Here, national government relies strongly on the involvement of third sector organisations in the provision of services. In the Italian context, this may strengthen processes of clientelism in service provision. This process of including certain groups of people and excluding others, of selectivity and creaming, is, as we will see below, a recurrent theme when attention is directed at the actual process of service delivery.

Second, the transformation from passive to active welfare states and the introduction of new modes of governance has immersed the organisations involved in service provision and delivery in an almost permanent process of sweeping reorganisations and system change. Examples of the latter are the introduction of new forms of cooperation between municipalities and employment services (as in Finland), a redistribution of tasks among institutional agencies (for example, Germany), the creation of new one-stop shops (the German 'Client Centre of the Future' [*Kundenzentrum der Zukunft*] and the Dutch 'Centre for Work and Income'), or a full merger of institutions (the British 'Jobcentre Plus'). These developments in the context of their work will have an impact on professionals and their managers (in terms of work motivation, content of work, job security, required skills, and so on), which will no doubt also affect the work with clients.

Third, professional routines and institutional cultures of the agencies involved in activation are core targets of social policy and governance reforms. Through these reforms, policy makers want to implement a paradigm shift in social policies and in the functioning of public institutions, which requires that workers in the delivering institutions break away from traditional working methods and develop new professional routines, attitudes and methods, both regarding their interactions with clients and regarding their self-identity as providers of public social services. The precise content of these changes depends on the specific national context, but everywhere the transformation processes are far-reaching, implying (in many countries at least) a shift from an administrative, bureaucratic and rule-oriented culture towards a result-oriented, dynamic, innovative and sometimes competitive culture; from a culture of institutional compartmentalisation towards a culture of cooperation, service integration and networking; from a culture focused on providing people with benefits towards a culture focused on labour market integration; from a culture of awarding rights to a culture of influencing, supervising and controlling individual behaviour; from a culture of 'people sustaining' to a culture of 'people transforming'. Early experiences with the New Deals in the UK showed, for example, that frontline workers tended to keep concentrating on income-related issues rather than focusing on work opportunities – and this is not a typically UK experience (also see the Italian case). All countries have by now reached the conclusion that institutional reforms are unavoidable, but many of them seem to underestimate the proportions and consequences of these reforms, which is one of the reasons why reforms often take place in rapid succession.

Fourth, managers and professionals are often confronted and have to cope with contradictory or ambiguous policy directives, regulations, and so on. For example, professionals are expected to sanction 'unwilling' clients, but at the same time to build relations of trust in order to gain reliable information from clients and to motivate them. In the UK, 'tough' elements of individualised activation are downplayed in practice in order to increase the effectiveness of activation. Personal advisers frequently experience tensions between activating people and sanctioning them in the case of non-compliance, and sometimes disassociate themselves from sanctioning in order to be able to build relations of trust and cooperation with their clients. In the Czech Republic, the activation approaches promoted by politicians and policy makers are not necessarily considered to be the most effective ones by frontline workers. Practical experience with activation pilots made clear that activation processes that match activation offers and individual preferences and invest in quality and intensity are more successful than those that follow regular and formal procedures. As Chapter Ten described, this led to a shift in individualised activation from an emphasis on employability to interventions incorporating elements of a capability approach. Finnish social workers sometimes consider sanctions as counter-productive, or decide to threaten with, rather than actually apply, sanctions. Thus, professional pragmatism – considerations of professional workers of what works and what does not work in activation – may result in more room for clients to express their motives, opinions and wishes than officially intended.

Fifth, the availability of resources is another implementation condition confronting all countries without any exception. Individualised activation services require an intensification of contacts between agencies and the individual unemployed. Especially in times or (in cases where resources are distributed inadequately [Italy] or institutional regulations disadvantage high unemployment areas [Czech Republic]) regions of high unemployment, the availability of staff is often problematic, which reduces the caseloads social workers can handle. Several countries (such as Germany) have reduced caseloads, but then ran into trouble financing the extra costs this involves. Consequently, service providers are forced to make strategic decisions: either to reduce the intensity of guidance of their clients, or to be more selective in involving people in activation, which often means that 'more difficult-to-handle cases' are excluded. In the Czech Republic, a lack of resources contributed to activation practices that are more motivation oriented and based on voluntary participation than official policy prescribed. At the same time, it promoted the exclusion from activation of more vulnerable groups. What is more, it resulted in servicing a target group that considerably deviated from the target group at which activation was originally directed: the 'artificial' unemployed. The qualifications and skills of social workers are another crucial resource in realising and implementing individual approaches. The preceding chapters mentioned several examples: skills and qualifications to assess the needs of unemployed people, to coach and support them and to deal with complex problems; insight into available social services; and so on. Other issues of importance in this context are the possibilities to enter into and realise meaningful forms of cooperation, and the availability of specialised services, for example for the most vulnerable groups, and of opportunities for participation in activation programmes. Last, but not least, the availability of jobs and job opportunities is, of course, a vital resource for successful activation. This is often neglected in dominantly supply-oriented activation policies, but it will evidently affect the work of, and selections made by, case managers.

Finally, an important implementation condition that should be mentioned concerns the management and steering of service delivery and the primary process. Against the background of public sector reforms and inspired by New Public Management, steering towards results, performance, effectiveness, quality, client satisfaction, and so on have become increasingly important. Choices and decisions made in this respect have a significant impact on the implementation of individual approaches, and often reflect the saying: 'What is measured gets done' (Noordhoek and Saner, 2005, p 42). For example, Chapter Three reported on situations where the introduction of performance targets strengthened creaming processes, which excluded the most vulnerable groups from programme participation, clearly reflecting tensions between economic efficiency and social equity. In Germany, the introduction of a payment that the FEA has to pay to the federal government for every unemployed person moving from *Arbeitslosengeld I* to *Arbeitslosengeld II*, aimed at creating an incentive for the Federal Employment Agency to invest in activation, had a similar effect of focusing activation on those relatively easy to employ. An article on the provision of activation services in the Netherlands (Van Berkel and Van der Aa, 2005) showed that steering towards job placement figures creates a situation in which service providers focus on realising job placements rather than on paying attention to the situation or wishes of the unemployed individual. Something similar may happen when steering focuses on the numbers of activation trajectories service providers have to realise: this will force service providers to prioritise quantity over quality and may stimulate the production of standardised rather than tailor-made services.

All in all, the case studies clearly show that the role of the professional in providing social services in general and individualised activation specifically is a vital one. The ways in which the professional is expected to cope, is able to cope and actually copes with the potential tensions and contradictions between their own self-identity and self-perception, the needs, wishes and circumstances of clients, management directives and the broader policy context has a significant impact on what individualised service provision looks like.

Future research

To conclude this volume, we would like to mention some issues for further research in activation in general and individualised service provision specifically. Particularly, we would like to advocate research that focuses on micro-processes of service delivery and on the institutional context in which delivery takes place, as this area is relatively under-investigated, at least in the EU.

First, we believe that the actual process of service delivery and the concrete interactions between frontline workers and clients require more attention in social policy research (see Chapter Four). The individualisation of service provision and the shifting institutional context in which it takes place (decentralisation, the involvement of private agencies in service delivery, contractualisation) significantly increase room for discretion at the service delivery level. At the same time, we know relatively little about:

- what happens in the face-to-face interactions of personal advisers and clients;
- how clients try to influence these interactions in order that it leads to desirable results from their perspective;
- how, and on what basis, personal advisers make decisions regarding activation interventions, and how these decisions are influenced by factors such as the wishes and needs of clients; the professional identity of frontline workers; their attitudes towards social policy, governance and organisational reforms; modes of steering they are subjected to; the availability of resources; and so on.

Only when we pay attention to the process of service provision itself can we begin to identify the precise nature and consequences of individualised service provision.

Second, and related to the former, research into the various (informal and institutionalised) ways in which clients try, or are allowed, to exercise voice and choice in their activation process could shed more light on the effects of (various forms of) user voice and user choice, on the advantages and disadvantages that are attributed to them, on the supposedly 'perverse' effects of user voice and choice in activation, on the conditions under which clients can be in charge of their activation 'in an adequate way' (see Chapter Two), and so on. It is evident that the effects of user voice and choice on the effectiveness and successfulness of activation will be an important issue in this context. However, as is pointed out in the literature on contractualism (Sol and Westerveld, 2005), user voice and choice can also be evaluated from other perspectives: for example, the functioning of service markets; the promotion of more democratic forms of social interventions; or, when it comes to redistributing power between service providers and their professionals on the one hand and clients on the other, issues of social justice.

Third, comparative research of individualised service provision could be useful. On the one hand, this could involve international comparative research: different welfare states – and, very likely, different welfare state *regimes* – not only provide different contexts for individualised service provision, but also adopt different approaches in individualising services. Thus, internationally comparative research may provide insight into how specific conditions encourage or prevent the implementation of differentiated forms of individualised service provision. On the other hand, comparative research could focus on how individualised service provision is being introduced in various social service areas. Although this was not the aim of this volume, there are indications (also see Chapter Five) that the social service area and the nature of social services matter when it comes to questions such as what 'individualisation discourse' is dominant, or to what degree and in what ways are user voice and choice developed in a specific domain of social services. Comparative research of various social services could clarify whether and how the nature of social services, the social construction of users of social services, the governance of social services, and so on 'mould' the concrete manifestations of the individualised provision of specific services.

References

Bruttel, O. (2005) 'New private delivery arrangements in Germany: an initial evaluation using new institutional economics', in E. Sol and M. Westerveld (eds) *Contractualism in employment services*, The Hague: Kluwer, pp 209-31.

Du Gay, P. (ed) (2005) *The values of bureaucracy*, Oxford: Oxford University Press.

Freedland, M. and King, D. (2005) 'Client contractualism between the Employment Service and jobseekers in the United Kingdom', in E. Sol and M. Westerveld (eds) *Contractualism in employment services*, The Hague: Kluwer, pp 119-39.

Gilbert, N. (2002) *Transformation of the welfare state: The silent surrender of public responsibility*, Oxford: Oxford University Press.

Hoggett, P. (2005) 'A service to the public: the containment of ethical and moral conflicts by public buraucracies', in P. du Gay (ed) *The values of bureaucracy*, Oxford: Oxford University Press, pp 165-91.

Le Grand, J. (1991) 'Quasi-markets and social policy', *The Economic Journal*, vol 101, no 408, pp 1256-67.

Moreno, L. (2003) 'Europeanisation, mesogovernments and 'safety nets'', *European Journal of Political Research*, vol 42, no 2, pp 271-85.

Noordhoek, P. and Saner, R. (2005) 'Beyond New Public Management: answering the claims of both politics and society', *Public Organization Review*, vol 5, no 1, pp 35-53.

Sol, E. and Westerveld, M. (eds) (2005) *Contractualism in employment services: A new form of welfare state governance*, The Hague: Kluwer.

Van Berkel, R. (2006) 'The decentralisation of social assistance in the Netherlands', *International Journal of Sociology and Social Policy*, vol 26, no 1/2, pp 20-32.

Van Berkel, R. and Van der Aa, P. (2005) 'The marketisation of activation services: a modern panacea? Some lessons from the Dutch experience', *Journal of European Social Policy*, vol 15, no 4, pp 329-43.

Wright, S. (2006) 'The administration of transformation: a case study of implementing welfare reform in the UK', in P. Henman and M. Fenger (eds) *Administering welfare reform: International transformations in welfare governance*, Bristol: The Policy Press, pp 161-83.

Zeitlin, J. and Trubek, D. M. (eds) (2003) *Governing work and welfare in a new economy: European and American experiments*, Oxford: Oxford University Press.

Index